From Socialism to Capitalism

From Socialism to Capitalism

Eight Essays

János Kornai

Central European University Press
Budapest – New York

© 2008 by János Kornai

Published in 2008 by

Central European University Press
An imprint of the
Central European University Share Company
Nádor utca 11, H-1051 Budapest, Hungary
Tel: +36-1-327-3138 or 327-3000
Fax: +36-1-327-3183
E-mail: ceupress@ceu.hu
Website: www.ceupress.com

400 West 59th Street, New York NY 10019, USA
Tel: +1-212-547-6932
Fax: +1-646-557-2416
E-mail: mgreenwald@sorosny.org

All rights reserved. No part of this publication may be reproduced,
stored in a retrieval system, or transmitted,
in any form or by any means, without the permission
of the Publisher.

Cover design and layout by Péter Tóth

ISBN 978-963-9776-16-6 cloth
ISBN 978-963-386-001-4 paperback

Library of Congress Cataloging-in-Publication Data

Kornai, János.
From socialism to capitalism: eight essays / János Kornai.
p. cm.
Includes bibliographical references and index.
ISBN 978-9639776166 (cloth: alk. paper)
1. Capitalism. 2. Communism--History. 3. Democratization. I. Title.

HB501.K584 2008
320.9171'7--dc22

2008001200

Contents

List of Tables and Figures VII
Preface IX

1 The Coherence of the Classical System
Introduction 1
The Main Line of Causality 2
The Affinity among Elements of the System 8
The Prototype and the National Variations 11
The Soviet Effect 16
Verification 19
The Viability of the Classical System 21

2 The Inner Contradictions of Reform Socialism
Introduction 25
Transformation without a Strategy 27
The Evolution of a Private Sector 29
The Persistence of Bureaucracy 34
Alternative Forms of Social Organization 38
The Weakness of "Third Forms" 40
Normative Implications 43

3 Market Socialism? Socialist Market Economy?
Introduction 47
Interpretation of the Term "Market" 48
Interpretation 1: Marx's Concept 49
Interpretation 2: The Walrasian Concept 51
Interpretation 3: The Leninist Concept 53
Interpretation 4: The Social Democratic Concept 55
Interpretation 5: What are the Current Chinese and
                Vietnamese Interpretations of "Socialism"? 57

4 The Speed of Transformation
Introduction 61
Ownership Reform and Development of the Private Sector 64

Macroeconomic Stability 75
Conclusion 79

5 The Great Transformation of Central Eastern Europe: Success and Disappointment
Introduction 81
In the Context of World History 83
From the Perspective of Everyday Life 105
The Tasks of the Economists' Profession 120

6 What Does "Change of System" Mean?
Introduction 123
Positive Versus Normative Approach 124
A Positive Approach to the Change of System 125
A Positive Approach to Changing the Political Structure 132
The Reception of Capitalism and Democracy—A Normative Approach   135
"Replacing the Elite" and "Dispensing Justice"—A Normative Approach 137
Concluding Remarks 146
Appendix: The Transformation of China 147

7 What Can Countries Embarking on Post-Socialist Transformation Learn from the Experiences So Far?
Introduction 151
Starting Points 153
Some Lessons 161
Concluding Remarks 177
Appendix 180

8 The System Paradigm
Introduction 183
A System Paradigm, Not a Transformational Paradigm 185
A Brief Intellectual History 186
The Main Attributes of the System Paradigm 190
Post-Socialist Transformation: The Great Challenge ... 193
Some Other Puzzles 198
Failures of Prediction 201
Appendix: On the Segregation of the Social Sciences 205

Previous Publications of the Studies in this Volume 209
References 211
Name Index 225
Subject Index 229

List of Tables and Figures

Figure 1.1 The main line of causality 3
Figure 2.1 Strong and weak linkages 38
Table 5.1 Growth rates in socialism and capitalism 86
Table 5.2 Growth before and after 1989,
 and after transformational recession 87
Table 5.3 Average growth rates for the years 1995–2003 88
Table 5.4 Electoral dismissals 91
Table 5.5 Comparison of characteristics 94
Table 5.6 Distribution of income: Gini coefficient 106
Table 5.7 Consumption inequality 107
Table 5.8 Total employment (1989 = 100) 108
Table 5.9 Unemployment rates (Percentage of labor force) 108
Table 5.10 Crime rates (1989 = 100) 109
Table 5.11 Confidence in Parliament and other institutions 110
Table 5.12 Life satisfaction over time 111
Table 5.13 Life-time satisfaction: Distribution of responses 112
Table 5.14 Attitudes to regime: Old, new, and future 114
Table 5.15 A historical comparison with Austria 116
Table 5.16 Convergence times to Western Europe 116
Table 5.17 Endorsement of undemocratic alternatives 117
Table 6.1 The share of the private sector in GDP 130
Table 6.2 Values for the EBRD index of transition
 to the market economy 132
Table 6.3 Employment features of the Hungarian elite
 after the change of system (1993), proportions already
 holding such positions in 1988 141
Table 6.4 The proportion of former Communist-party members
 among the economic elite 142

LIST OF TABLES AND FIGURES

Table 6.5 Proportions of former Communist-party members among the elites 142
Table 6.6 Proportions of private and state sectors in China 149
Table 6.7 Proportions of transactions conducted at market prices in China 149
Table 7.1 Survey of countries that counted as "socialist countries" in 1987 180–82
Table 8.1 The citation structure 207
Table 8.2 Distribution of citations assignable to a specific discipline, percent 207

Preface

The political climate in Hungary as I was working on this volume in the fall of 2006 and spring of 2007 was tense and sometimes potentially explosive. What kind of system do we live under? You call this capitalism? Is this what democracy is like? Questions like these were being bandied about in heated harangues on the streets, while I faced just the same questions, sitting at my computer rereading these studies, written between 1990 and 2007.

I have to confess immediately, in these introductory lines, that I was assailed by doubts on some occasions. What is the point, with the passions, provocations, and unmannerly tenor prevailing outside, of attempting, as far as possible, a cool and sensible comparison of socialism and capitalism, or dictatorship and democracy, or interpretation of the change of system? Is there still sense in adopting a dispassionate, professional style? Is there still sense in theory, when attending to it seems less important to people than the least of the problems they face in practice?

These inner doubts were overcome, and eventually, the obstinacy and self-discipline of a researcher reasserted themselves time and again. The greater the blind passions and power struggles became, the more important it seemed to have some who would keep their distance from the political arena and attempt to reach a deeper understanding and explanation of the world around us, on a plane of scholarly theory. After all, this is a passion as well, albeit different in nature from the one prompting the political antagonists. Sometimes I too found it grotesque, as I glanced from my work to a silenced television screen, where blazing overturned trash cans could be seen on the fine avenue of Budapest's Andrássy út last March 15, for instance, while I was engaged in tracking down infelicities in an academic study. But finally I think that this book too may contribute to consolidating the situation in this country. Luckily, some people in the political and the intellectual spheres appreciate clarification, cool analysis, and intellectually backed argument, and they are the ones for whom I designed this book.

Collected here are eight previously published studies—the earliest from 1990 and the latest from the spring of 2007. These were not my entire output in those 17 years. So let me begin by explaining the criteria for selecting them for this volume.

The yardstick was not to select writings with the most bearing on present-day Hungary. If that had been the criterion, the book would have had to have included an article or two on health-care reform or problems of macro stabilization.

The pieces in this volume are connected by *various common main themes*. The most important one is the community of the main subject-matter, well expressed in the title of the Hungarian edition: socialism, capitalism, democracy, change of system. These four expressions cover four phenomena of great and comprehensive importance. Each piece in the book deals with these and the connections between them.

The studies have not been arranged in the chronological order of publication. The arch determining the order was created by history. The starting point is the "classical" socialist system before the reforms (Study 1). That is followed by discussion of reforms that remained within the frames of the socialist system (Studies 2–3). Then comes consideration of the change of system (Studies 4–7).

One of the *Leitmotif*s of the volume is the "capitalism/socialism" pair of opposites. Capitalism obviously has a history of several hundred years, while the regime labelled here, the socialist system, applied only for a few decades. But it must be said that this pair of opposites was central to the history of the twentieth century. First and foremost this antagonism put its stamp on political thinking, on the foreign policy and military preparedness of every country, and on some appallingly destructive armed conflicts. All these had great secondary influence on each country's economic development and the standard of living and disposition of its inhabitants. The memory of the tensions, which seemed so gigantic and threatened to lead to conflict that we feared would threaten humanity's very survival, may fade after a decade or two. Then it will be up to historians to decide whether we, who witnessed and suffered in that period, were exaggerating the significance of those opposites. But we lived in the twentieth, not the twenty-second century, and to *us* it was a problem of immeasurable importance.

Several people warned me after the Hungarian edition appeared that the title of the book bore too strong a resemblance to that of Schumpeter's classic *Capitalism, Socialism and Democracy* (1942). The studies included here certainly refer back in several places to Schumpeter's work, which had a great influence on my thinking. But this volume cannot be seen as a summary of my reactions to the Schumpeter work and so it seems expedient to choose another title for the English edition. The one chosen expresses that my main subject is the change of system, the road from socialism to capitalism.[1]

None of the studies is confined to one country—not to Hungary or to any other. Each tries to embrace the problems common to greater units than that. However, the greater unit comprehended is not the same in each study. One may deal with the capitalist or socialist system in general, another with all the post-socialist countries, and a third with the Central East European region. But all extend the analysis beyond the borders of one country.

This book contains studies of a *theoretical* nature. No consensus has been reached among philosophers of science and exponents of various disciplines about what is meant by theory. Remaining within my own field, many economists confine the honorable term "theory" to work that applies a mathematical apparatus. Those who apply this criterion and find not a single equation in this book will obviously deny it the rank of a theoretical work. For my part, I agree with those who do not regard the methodology applied in research and reflected in the written study as the decisive criterion for determining whether or not to grade it as "theory." I would not like to enter here into any high-flown arguments in the field of philosophy of science, just to make my view known as comprehensibly as possible. Theoretical work can be recognized by the high degree of *generalization* to which it aspires. It is capable of abstracting from many individual features, details, and shades of an object examined, and focusing on the attributes of the object which are most important and most general in the context of

---

[1] The same title was born by an earlier study of mine, published in 1998 (Kornai 1998). That study has not been included in this volume because the ideas in it appear in a fuller and more detailed form in other studies that are republished here. I am grateful to Lord Skidelsky for allowing me to reuse the title.

the question under examination. Defining the word theory in this way, I have gathered in this book the studies of mine that sought to contribute to the theory of the great systems, the political and administrative form, and the change of system.

Although I try to answer the questions I have put, I find the *questions* themselves more important than the answers. The answers are questionable. The least I would like to achieve is to arouse curiosity in readers about the puzzles that concern me. What is socialism? What is capitalism? What is democracy? How can it be determined whether certain institutions functioning in a particular country at a particular time show close resemblance to those in other countries? What do the supporters and opponents of a system say about it—and how does rhetoric and ideology relate to reality? What operative characteristics of a country can be considered system-specific and what can be found under any system? I could continue to give examples, but those may suffice to show the kind of question that concerns me here and I hope may interest readers as well.

So far I have tried to describe from the *content* side (theme, object of examination, "puzzle" to be solved) what the eight studies have in common, but I have also impinged at several points on the other common feature, the *approach* (methodology) characteristic of them all. Only one of the studies is concerned with the actual methodology, the approach to the problems, and the basis in the philosophy of science. This has been placed at the end of the book for good reason. I do not want to begin by explaining to readers what approach I mean to take. Let them first see for themselves how the author works with his own tools. Let them discover that this stock of tools is usable. And when they have been convinced by seeing them at work, so to speak, I then offer an insight into the kind of methodology employed in the previous seven studies. I did things in the same order when I was teaching comparative economics at university or delivering a lecture series on the post-socialist transformation. I found it served its purpose well. If I had begun with the methodological basis, there would have been stronger opposition to such an unusual approach. At the end of the course, students already had in their heads what they had heard in previous lectures, and the concluding line of argument about methodology and philosophy of science had explanatory force. I would like to think that Study 8 in this book can give similar aid to those with the patience to read the previous seven.

Let me mention briefly a few features of the approach taken in this book. One is a "system outlook," or as Study 8 calls it, the "system paradigm." There are no micro analyses or partial examinations to be found in the volume. When I was working on these studies, I always sought to understand the whole, not parts torn out of it. What concerned me was how the parts made up the whole, how they were assembled into a system. A second feature running through the volume is a strict distinction between the positive and the normative approaches. A third is the broad application of comparison as a means of analysis.

These are not methodological innovations of mine. Luckily, I am not alone in the scientific world in taking this approach. But I have to add that such use of them is not trivial or self-explanatory. I would like my readers to contrast for themselves the methodology and outlook applied in this book with what they find in other works, and think over the question of how they differ and how they resemble each other in studying the great systems and great transformations.

Here let me mention another common feature of the studies in this book: they each extend beyond the bounds of my own field of economics; they each show an *interdisciplinary* outlook. The Appendix to Study 8 contains the findings of a survey that show how rare this outlook is: economists scarcely ever cite the works of political scientists, sociologists, historians, or social psychologists, and the same applies to exponents of the other social sciences. The study included entire years of the journals covered, regardless of the specific subjects of the articles. I would like now to describe my experiences with the main subjects covered in this volume. While I was working on Studies 6 and 7, to do with the change of system, I took up numerous works written by historians or political scientists. I found it astonishing that these never mentioned works of economists that were relevant to an understanding of the change of system: relevant in that their intellectual influence helped to erode or destroy the old order, or because they made a contribution to analysis of the change of system itself. The fact that the work had been written by an economist seemed sufficient reason for a political scientist or a historian to ignore it. I would be delighted if this little volume, whose author sees himself not just as an economist, but as an exponent of "social science" in a synthetic sense, could for once break out of the tight ghetto of its discipline.

Although the eight studies have much in common, this remains after all a collection of studies, not a monograph. It would be good to present readers with a monograph whose content corresponded with the vast field delineated by the Hungarian and English titles of this book. I did not undertake to write such a comprehensive account. And that being the case, I ask readers not to expect it, least of all the *completeness* that they could demand justifiably of a monograph. Socialism, capitalism, democracy, change of system—these embrace a multitude of extremely weighty and complex questions, of which only a fragment can be discussed in this little volume.

Without making a virtue of the limitations of a collection of studies, I have to say that the genre does have an advantage as well. Its pages can be turned by readers who may not wish to imbibe the whole volume. Some may only be interested in the one study or another. It is often the case that researchers taking up the communications of others are not interested in the entirety of the author's ideas, only in material or the literary background connected with their own subject. In that case, it is a relief not to have to wade through a long book, to be able to seek the information in writings of study length. Much the same applies to professors setting or recommending literature for their students. It is easier to accommodate a paper or a chapter of a volume in a syllabus than a monograph. I began to pay heed to these considerations in editing this volume, by making sure that each study stood on its own feet and was comprehensible when read separately from the rest of the book. It is more of an extra to find some cross-references within the book, pointing to the connections between the studies.

Thorough study of the volume will come more easily to those who have read my book *The Socialist System* (1992b). In fact I have included two extracts from it as the first study here, while the others follow directly from that comprehensive work, in content and in methodology. However, familiarity with the 1992 book is by no means a condition for understanding the studies in this volume.

I would like to point out that the text of each study appears as it was originally published, unchanged apart from some small inaccuracies and stylistic infelicities. I was pleased to find as I edited the studies that there was no need to change the content. I can still stand by every line of them today.

However, there are one or two specific issues on which my views changed. Where that had happened, I felt obligated to return to the problem in a later publication and state openly how my views in the previous piece had altered. Readers of this volume will find such a partial change in my position exemplified in Study 4, written in 2004, where I present some questions of stabilization and creation of equilibrium differently from the way I put them in my book *The Road to a Free Economy* (1990). I see no problem in people altering their position, having learned from subsequent information, experience, or literature. There is no virtue in intellectual obstinacy or strict insistence on one's opinion. But let the author have the intellectual honesty to inform readers of the change. I for one am averse to the far-from-rare practice of imperceptibly abandoning the initial principles of one's thinking so that readers will fail to notice.

Anybody can check that *The Socialist System*, which I wrote at the end of the 1980s, and the studies in this volume, of which the latest appeared in a journal in the spring of 2007, reflect the same world view, the same set of values, the same intellectual approach, and the same methodology. I would be satisfied if readers felt they could find their bearings in my views and my methods of research and analysis.

In some cases I have made additions to the earlier writings. I did not want to smuggle these into the original texts, and so subsequent insertions, technical in nature (e.g. cross-references within the volume) or substantive, have been placed in square brackets to distinguish them.

I would like to express thanks to all those who have helped me. As with my earlier books, the first to thank is my wife Zsuzsa Dániel. She was the first attentive, critical, and encouraging reader of the manuscript, and I owe it mainly to her that I could work under calm conditions.

Katalin N. Szabó has been my closest associate for many years. She understands not just from half a sentence, but almost before I have spoken just how she can be of assistance to me.

I have had the lucky privilege for many years of having young research assistants to help me in gathering information, unearthing and assessing literature, and editing studies. My colleague in this respect when my book *The Socialist System* appeared (including the part that forms Study 1 of this volume) was Mária Kovács. She was succeeded chronologically by Ágnes Benedict, János Varga, Zdenek Kudrna, Noémi Péter, and Eszter Nagy. I would not like to specify here what appreciation is due to each beyond saying that all of them assisted me conscientiously and gave me much valuable advice. I could always rely on them to be available for whatever the research required.

Many professional and personal links connect me to Central European University, an important bastion of independent spirit, openness and up-to-date scholarship. I am glad that it was Central European Press, the publishing house of this institution, that undertook the publication of my volume.

Brian McLean has been translating my works for some 25 years now. It is thanks to him that my writings can be read in English as if they were the work of an eloquent native speaker rather than translations. It was he who translated most of the studies in this book, and he did the thankless work of language editing for the remaining ones, a task that he performed with exceptional attention to detail.

I am grateful to Anna Patkós, who undertook the editing of the eight studies for consistence and coherence at the time of the preparation of the Hungarian version, for again keeping in hand the difficult work of editing the English language version, which she did attentively and conscientiously. I would also like to thank all those who took part in the preparation of the book for their committed work, in particular, Thomas Cooper, Katalin Csepi, Noémi Kovács, László Tóth, and László Szimonisz.

I express my gratitude to Central European University Press for publishing my book, and to István Bart, Linda Kunos and their colleagues for their editorial support.

The intellectual environment in which these writings were prepared was inspiring; I owe thanks to Collegium Budapest, the Department of Economics at Harvard University (Cambridge, U.S.A.), and the Helsinki-based WIDER international research institute for the help they have given in the completion of my work.

Budapest, October 2007

János Kornai

1
The Coherence of the Classical System*

Introduction

My book titled *The Socialist System* distinguishes three prototypes of the system:
  1. the revolutionary-transitional system (the transition from capitalism to socialism);
  2. the classical system (or classical socialism);
  3. the reform system (or reform socialism).

These are three prototypes or models. At no time in the history of any specific country has its system corresponded exactly to any of these three prototypes. Even so, these models are not descriptions of ideal, Utopian socialism. They set out to provide abstract generalizations of historical realizations of socialism.

Even though it may be quite easy to date the duration of a particular prototype in a particular country to a specific period in history, no one could argue that the system remained unaltered throughout that period. The main attributes of the classical system were apparent in the social-political-economic system of the Soviet Union from the

---

*[Study 1 of this volume consists of parts of Chapter 15 of my book *The Socialist System* (1992b). However, some explanation is necessary for readers to follow Study 1 without having read the book, and so I have inserted some paragraphs from Chapter 2 of the book on pages 19–21.

Chapter 15 of *The Socialist System* makes several references to other chapters of the book. These strands have been cut by extracting the chapter from the context of the book. Such cross-references in the original chapter have either been deleted or replaced by short explanatory texts.]

time when Stalin consolidated his power until his death (for the sake of argument, the twenty-five years from 1928 to 1953), but the system was different at the beginning, when these characteristics were developing and solidifying, and somewhat different again at the end.

The prototype sets out to reflect an intertemporal average. Compiling the conceptual edifice of the prototypes serves the purpose of capturing several decades of history and the conditions prevailing in the individual countries in a condensed form. Neither in subsequent explanations of the events nor in actual prediction of the future can a comprehension of the prototypes be a substitute for concrete historical examination. Nevertheless, these models may prove to be useful conceptual tools in both descriptive and predictive research.

This study provides a summary of the main features of classical socialism. It sets out to identify the main connections among the constituent elements and the regularities in the partial processes of the classical system.

The word *theory* is variously defined by the various schools of philosophy of science and practicing scientists. I subscribe to the view that an edifice of ideas can be deemed a theory if it illuminates and explains the main relationships within an existing, observable, and constant group of phenomena. In that sense this study's task is to outline a few general statements within the subject-area of a positive theory of the classical socialist system.

To that definition of the task I must add right away that the exposition is not intended to yield a universal, comprehensive theory explaining simultaneously all the aspects of the classical system that call for illumination. It is quite compatible with other, complementary theoretical approaches that can play a likewise important part in explaining other aspects of this complex group of phenomena.

The Main Line of Causality

Even though there are mutual influences in several directions between the various phenomena, there is a clearly perceptible main line of causal connections. The main line of causality is represented in diagram form in *Figure 1.1*. The figure purposely ignores the reactions, that is, the reverse effects of all kinds that exist in real life, since it sets out expressly to highlight the main direction.

THE COHERENCE OF THE CLASSICAL SYSTEM

The key to explaining the classical socialist system is an understanding of the political structure. The starting point is the undivided political power of the ruling party, the interpenetration of the party and the state, and the suppression of all forces that depart from or oppose the party's policy. So the classical system, if one looks at its essential marks, is a one-party system (even if one or two socialist countries have other parties that exist nominally and play a formal part in a coalition).

Figure 1.1 The main line of causality

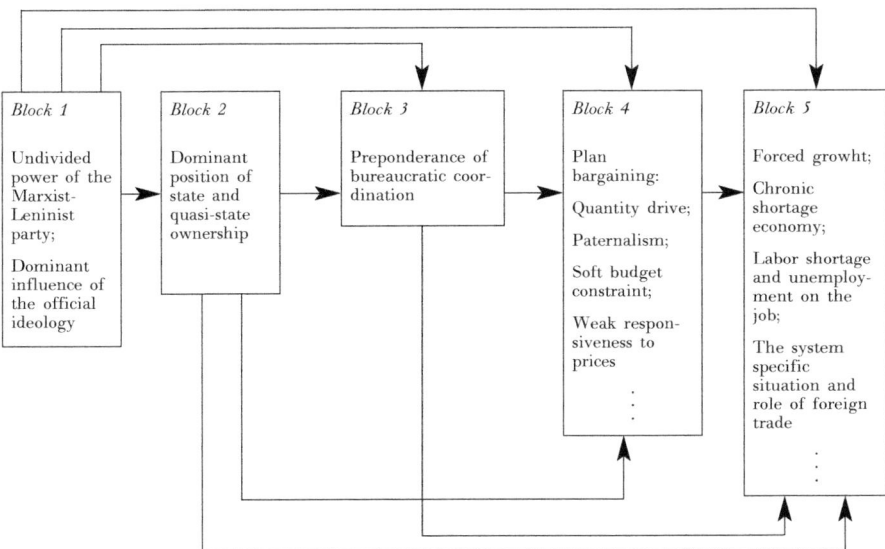

Note: The figure shows the main line of causality from left to right. The arrows point out how each group of phenomena is influenced not only by the previous group of phenomena (i.e., merely the group one layer deeper), but by all the deeper factors directly or indirectly. For instance, one of the groups of phenomena in the last block—the development and reproduction of chronic shortage—is not simply explained by such phenomena as the soft budget constraint or the weak responsiveness to prices; among the explanatory factors that act directly is the preponderance of state ownership and bureaucratic coordination.

The three points at the bottom of the blocks on the right hand side are intended to denote that the blocks contain only examples, not a full list. Only the most important phenomena have been highlighted, although there are numerous other ones, which could be placed in the same block.

STUDY 1

Not all one-party systems lead to the formation of a classical socialist system. For that to happen it is essential for the party exercising power to be imbued with the official ideology of the socialist system. Common parlance permits the term "Marxist-Leninist party," but the official ideology overlaps only in part with the ideas of Marx and Lenin. Much (but not all) has been taken over from them, and all kinds of additions have been made to their ideas.

The prime factor that brings the other system-specific phenomena about is the undivided power of the Communist party prepossessed by its specific ideology. The party's organizational existence and its ideology can only be distinguished on the plane of theoretical analysis: they form an entity, like body and soul. So on the left-hand side of *Figure 1.1* they form Block 1, the first link in the causal chain.

Under the classical system there is either a preponderance of state ownership (including quasi-state, cooperative ownership) or a situation in which at least the key positions, the commanding heights of the economy, are under state ownership. On the figure, this phenomenon is treated as the second factor in the causal chain (Block 2).

Placing the role of property in second place is an arguable position. Some people rate it on a par with the political structure, and there is a view that the preponderance of state ownership is the chief criterion of a socialist economy.[1] The question is not wholly speculative, for it can be analyzed in the light of historical experience. If the Communist party gains undivided power in an economically backward country like China or Vietnam, it sooner or later begins a policy of nationalization and pursues it stubbornly. How fast the pursuit is and how often the process comes to a halt and starts again depend on the socioeconomic circumstances, the difficulties of organization, and the patience or impatience of the party. There are countries where even the barber shops and the village general stores are nationalized quite quickly, while elsewhere the system coexists for a while with the bourgeoisie. But all patience and coexistence of this kind is considered temporary by those in power, who can hardly wait for the nationalization to

---

[1] There is a frequent tendency in the debates in this area to confuse a positive (descriptive, explanatory) approach with a normative one. [For more details on this see Study 6 of this volume on page 124. The question of which factors play a role that is primary, secondary, tertiary, and so on in producing socialist countries' main characteristics already belongs to the province of positive, causal analysis, rather than normative.

advance. Once banking, industry, and transportation have been nationalized, the authorities sooner or later set about eliminating private ownership in agriculture. The party openly proclaimed the objective of nationalization even before it came to power. Once in power, it is doing no more than putting its political program into practice.

It is not the property form—state ownership—that erects the political structure of classical socialism over itself. Quite the reverse: the given political structure brings about the property form it deems desirable. Although in this case the ideology plays a marked role in forming society, it is not the sole explanation for the direction of influence. The indivisibility of power and the concomitant totalitarianism are incompatible with the autonomy that private ownership entails. This kind of rule demands heavy curtailment of individual sovereignty. The further elimination of private ownership is taken, the more consistently can full subjection be imposed.

The three groups of phenomena discussed so far—the political structure and ideology typical of the classical socialist system, and the property form—combine to account for the next cell on *Figure 1.1*, Block 3, the system-specific constellation of coordination mechanisms. Here bureaucratic coordination takes the main part, and all other mechanisms play supporting roles at most or wither away. This is one of the corner-stones of our line of argument. The features of the system cannot be derived from the fact that it is not a market economy, or still less from the fact that the prices are irrational, and so on. Once the political structure, official ideology, and dominant role of state ownership are provided, they produce the preponderance of the mechanism of bureaucratic control.

The actual forms of bureaucratic coordination vary from country to country and period to period. Fulfillment of one plan instruction is rewarded here and another there. Here ministries are merged and there they are split up. Meanwhile, officials in the apparatus and professional economists have lively debates on the advantages and drawbacks of one form or another. But certain essential factors remain unchanged: elimination of free enterprise and autonomous actors on the market, and of the competition among them; centralization of decision making and information; hierarchical dependence and the dominance of vertical relations over horizontal ones.

That brings us to the next cell, Block 4 of the figure. To it belong the interest and motivation of the actors in the classical system, their consequent behavior, and the main features of the relations among them.² Some phenomena that may be placed here are listed in label form, without aiming at a complete list: plan bargaining, the quantity drive, the paternalistic behavior of superiors, the soft budget constraint, the weak responsiveness to prices, and so on. Whichever one is taken, it can be explained separately in terms of underlying factors, the nature of power, the official ideology, and the preponderance of state ownership and bureaucratic coordination.

The next cell, Block 5, contains a list of a few typical lasting economic phenomena. The figure includes only the most important: forced growth, labor shortage and unemployment on the job, the chronic shortage economy, and the system-specific role of foreign trade. The main features of these phenomena can be traced back to the explanatory factors qualified as deeper by the earlier logic. It is not because there is shortage that a huge and almighty bureaucracy develops; it is not because the aim is to force growth that the plans are made taut; it is not because import hunger appears that there is an import-permit system; and so on. Although reactions of this kind exist (and they are dealt with in detail in the next section), the main direction of causality is the contrary: the phenomena cited develop because a specific political structure and ideology have gained sway, as a result of which specific property forms have developed, which has led to the preponderance of bureaucratic coordination and the typical behavior patterns of the participants.

This line of argument contains elements that a researcher raised on Marxist political economy and philosophy can accept without much difficulty, while other elements in it differ radically from the ideas entrenched in the researcher's mind. He or she will be familiar with the approach reflected in the attempt to classify phenomena as "deeper" or "more superficial" and the desire to find the main directions of influence within the web of mutual effects.³ It will be familiar and

---

² Some writers have described the approach that I customarily take in my works as "behaviorist." However, this is not an accurate description. Though much can be explained by the participants' behavior, the behavior itself needs causal analysis. This is reflected in the structure of *Figure 1.1*: the behavioral features can be found in the "middle zone" of the causal chain, midway between the underlying explanatory factors and the directly perceptible economic phenomena.

³ This is one of the ways in which the Marxist researcher differs from the analytical economist living in a world of neoclassical models, who draws conclusions in his or her model from assumptions placed side by side, although there may be "deeper" and "more superficial" premises among the assumptions.

acceptable to attempt to explain a social group's behavior in terms of its self-interest and social situation, rather than contenting oneself with citing the preferences of individuals. Equally akin to Marxist tradition is the way the logical analysis (what is the main direction of causality?) combines with the historical approach (in what characteristic order in time did the main events occur?).

The same economist raised on Marxist political economy may be perplexed to find that the line of argument described here does not follow the usual pattern of discussing a relationship of "base and superstructure." Whatever meaning one attaches to the concept of "base," one cannot state that the base has determined its own superstructure. The historical point of departure, as was first in the case with the Soviet Union and later with almost all the other countries subject to Communist rule, is a poor and backward country. It still has few large factories, and its production and the concentration of capital are low. It is certainly not the case that the forces of production are already being impeded in their development by the capitalist production relations, or that they can only develop once those relations have been destroyed. It is certainly not the case that one only has to drive the capitalists out for a well-organized, concentrated production system ripe for central planning to fall on the plate of the socialist planners. These countries are still in a state that Marx and Engels described in the *Communist Manifesto* (Marx and Engels [1848] 1969), one in which they also say that capitalism is capable of giving enormous impetus to the development of the forces of production.

The historical development course of classical socialism is quite different from the pattern presented in the handbooks on the Marxist philosophy of history. The revolution shatters the old superstructure and artificially erects a new one, or, more precisely, it produces the seed of a new superstructure which then pushes out almost of its own accord. The new superstructure crushes the base that is alien to it and rearranges it entirely. It nationalizes and collectivizes; it steadily eliminates private property and squeezes the market into a smaller and smaller space. The bureaucratic apparatus of economic control springs up and spreads in all directions. As this process goes on, as the property relations, coordination mechanism, and economic processes alter according to the new system, these changes react continually on the political forms and bring a transformation of the ideology in their train.

STUDY 1

The Affinity among Elements of the System

The discussion of the main line of causality in the last section contains repeated references to the fact that the effect reacts on the cause: numerous interactions occur among the elements of the system. Let us recall some as illustrations:

– Once state ownership and the soft budget constraint have produced the investment hunger, the import hunger, the hoarding tendency, and wage-drift, it becomes necessary to use the administrative tools of investment and import permits, material quotas, rationing and allocation systems, and wage funds. Once such tools are being used, it no longer suffices to encourage economic discipline with praise and material rewards. It must be imposed with punishments, and firm measures must be taken against "speculators" and "wage-swindlers." This all has an effect on the political climate and the official ideology. (Blocks 4 and 5 react on Blocks 3 and 1.)

– Bureaucratic control of state-sector wages, which combats the upward pressure on wages even when there is a labor shortage, is incompatible with the higher incomes obtained outside the state sector on the free market. This and other factors tend to encourage as full an elimination of the private sector as possible. (Blocks 3, 4, and 5 react on Block 2.)

– Once the economy has embarked on forced growth, the ideas to explain the necessity and advantages of this type of growth need incorporating in the official ideology. (Block 5 reacts on Block 1.)

– If the managers of production fail to develop a strong intrinsic interest in gaining foreign, hard-currency markets, due to the chronic domestic sellers' market and several other factors, a mechanism and incentive system forcing them to produce for capitalist export purposes must be created. (Block 5 reacts on Block 3.)

As the classical system consolidates, its elements develop a coherence. The various behavioral forms, conventions, and norms rub off on one another. To apply a chemical analogy, the phenomena exhibit affinity: they attract and require each other. The monolithic structure of power, petrified ideological doctrines, almost total domination of state ownership, direct bureaucratic control, forced growth, shortage, and distrustful withdrawal from most of the world (to mention just the main groups of phenomena) all belong together and strengthen each other. This is no loose set of separate parts; the sum of the parts makes up an integral whole. In that sense as well there is justification in considering this formation as a *system*.

A peculiar "natural selection" comes to apply: new institutions, regulations, customs, and moral and legal norms that are easily reconciled with the nature of the system survive and take root; those alien to it are discarded.[4] Let us take a single example. No one planned in advance, before the first socialist system came into being, that personnel affairs—i.e., appointment, transfer, and dismissal—would be strictly centralized. There is no trace in a prior blueprint for socialism of the idea of establishing for the purpose a hierarchical apparatus in which the personnel decisions in every unit at every level would depend on the relevant party organization, on police institutions that keep track of people's political attitudes, on a superior personnel administrator, or on the official state, economic, or mass-movement leader in the field concerned. This very powerful institutional system with its precise forms of career control emerged step by step through trial and error, feeling its way with repeated reorganizations. It first became a permanent part of the system in the Soviet Union, and then developed in each socialist country in a more or less similar form. As a result, no other social system has such close control over individual careers as socialism, with its uniform, centrally controlled apparatus of personnel management. It illustrates that specific forms and institutions grow *organically* within the system.

Tendencies that have arisen and developed show a strong inclination to consummation. Direct bureaucratic control, for example, gains predominance, prescribing economic tasks in instructions. But once prescription of a firm's main assignments, in aggregate indices, has begun, there is no stopping here. Circumvention is too easy: the main assignment is fulfilled, but the details and secondary tasks are neglected. Logically, the next step is to assign each task in more detail, and if that does not suffice, the subordinate's hands must be tied with an even more minute breakdown into even tinier parts. If the net of totalitarian power and its instrument, bureaucratic control, has too large a mesh, many actions can escape from it. The answer is a net with a smaller mesh that cannot be slipped through. The system's internal logic propels bureaucratic power toward "perfectionism."

---

[4] The idea of natural selection among institutions appears in the works of J. A. Schumpeter and F. A. Hayek. For a more detailed explanation, see the article by Alchian (1950).

The examples of positive selection, integration into the system, are followed by an illustration of the opposite process: rejection by the system. Private ownership and private enterprise are foreign to classical socialism, and in the long term it cannot tolerate them. The centralized, nationalized order of this society is disturbed not only by large-scale capital but the existence of small-scale peasant ownership. Central power, sooner or later, depending on its tolerance threshold, sets about eliminating it. The Soviet Union waited more than a decade before launching mass collectivization. In Vietnam it was only a couple of years after the military victory, before much progress had been made on repairing the economic damage caused by the war, when the authorities embarked on eliminating the private farming and produce-trading sector and nationalizing and collectivizing its activities, with catastrophic economic results. The Ethiopian government launched in the midst of a devastating famine a socialist reorganization of agriculture that uprooted the rural population and resettled it on a collectivized basis. Going beyond examples, it should be stressed that property is not the only sphere of phenomena in which the classical system is unable to cohabit lastingly with institutions, customs, attitudes, and norms alien to it. The mature classical system cannot tolerate contrary political opinions, self-governing institutions, and organizations independent of the political institutions organized from above; cultures and world views other than the official ones; or free-market exchange between autonomous economic entities. All these phenomena, though they may recur time after time, are confined into an ever narrowing area. Individual behavior is deeply imbued with conformism: spontaneous use of the ideas and working abilities deriving from a spirit of enterprise is virtually ruled out, as are independent critical opinions and rebellion against the superior organizations.[5]

To sum up the lesson common to these examples of integration and rejection: a natural selection of institutions and behavior patterns takes place, and ultimately enormously strengthens and greatly consolidates the inner coherence of the system.

---

[5] The lines above emphasize a tendency against which countertendencies also apply. Even at a time of extreme totalitarian power, a measure of narrow individual autonomy survives in many spheres of life, though confined to a very constricted area. The spirit of enterprise remains latently present (and occasionally breaks out in a distorted form). Some people, if few of them, dare to oppose the repression. All these features suddenly strengthen when the social environment offers more favorable chances for them to develop.

Marx and Lenin expected the victorious socialist revolution to be followed by a transitional period in which the remnant of capitalism would still leave their impression on society. "What we have to deal with here is a communist society, not as it has *developed* on its own foundations, but, on the contrary, as it *emerges* from capitalist society; which is thus in every respect, economically, morally and intellectually, still stamped with the birthmarks of the old society from whose womb it emerges," Marx says of socialism (Marx [1875] 1970, p. 18.) According to this view, later incorporated into the official ideology of classical socialism, the existence of the remnants of capitalism causes the difficulties in the transitional period, and once they have been done away with, all the communist system's beneficial features can develop unhindered. Experience, however, seems to deny that the tendencies and internal contradictions have survived as a legacy of the capitalist system. On the contrary, the classical socialist system's characteristics *sui generis* have brought them into being.

The Prototype and the National Variations

It does not follow from this line of argument that some kind of ultimate determinism or fatalism applies in history. There are two issues worth considering in this respect. The first is the departure along a specific historical path, and the second the broader or narrower determination of the path itself.

Beginning with the first issue, it depends on a conjunction of a great many circumstances whether or not a society sets out on the path toward classical socialism. As mentioned in the last section, the Communist party must gain undivided possession of political power for the process to get under way. This historical configuration bears the "genetic program" that transmits the main characteristics of the system to every cell within it.[6]

---

[6] The analogy was inspired by the modern genetic theory of biology that inherited traits are transmitted by a particular substance, DNA, whose molecule has the special ability to control its own reproduction. It can transfer the inherited traits to further molecules formed under its control. The inherited genetic program is coded in the specific DNA chemical "language," and the code then reproduced in every single cell of the organism. Under the command of the program hidden in the DNA, all the biochemical, anatomical, physiological, and to some extent behavioral characteristics of the biological organism are determined during its development. The consistency of the DNA in the living world is species-specific. See J.D. Watson's famous book (Watson 1968). For the short account above, the author used a university biology textbook (Campbell 1987).

This is the seed of the new society from which the whole organism grows.

The approach outlined here contradicts the frequently expressed view that each elementary particle of the classical system is imposed artificially on the fabric of society, which resists it from first to last. According to this superficial notion, it is a case of nothing more than a merciless dictator and his slavish hirelings imposing their rule on the people by intimidation and violence. If that were so, this external layer would easily be shed by the body of society; but it is not a question of that at all. Throughout there is certainly resistance, sometimes weaker and sometimes stronger, which the possessors of power break by force, but the new structure proliferates with an elemental force, propagating itself and penetrating into every social relationship.[7] Once the start of the process is imposed upon the society, it goes on in a spontaneous manner, proceeding, to use Marx's phrase, as a "natural growth process," indigenously (*naturwüchsig*). If another "genetic program" applies in some country at that particular historical turning point, the result will differ despite the similarity of the starting point. Consider North and South Korea, which were in the same economic position after the Second World War. The South resembled the North not only in its point of departure but even in certain features of its political and administrative structure applying in the postwar period: it was ruled by a relentless dictatorship that brooked no opposition; the bureaucracy of the state played a big part in running the economy, intervening in decisions on foreign trade, investment, and the extension of credit; and so on. Yet the difference is fundamentally significant: the official ideology in South Korea differed utterly from North Korea's; the possessors of undivided political power, far from intending to eliminate private property, cooperated with it and sought to assist its prosperity. Although a big part was played by bureaucratic coordination, there was no mention of abolishing the market, which operated with great vitality. As time went by, North Korea finally came to display all the classical system's essential features, while South Korea, after decades of suffering and sacrifices, developed a political

---

[7] The Hungarian poet Gyula Illyés describes this with moving force in his poem *A Sentence on Tyranny:* "Prisoner and jailer, you are both; ... Thus the slave forges with care/The fetters the himself must wear; ... Where seek tyranny? Think again:/Everyone is a link in the chain;/Of tyranny's stench you are not free:/You yourself are tyranny ..." (Illyés 1950, 1999, pp. 70–76), first publication in 1956.

and economic system that increasingly resembles Japan's path of development and differs ever more sharply from North Korea's. Similar statements could be based on comparing Taiwan with mainland China or West Germany with East Germany.

Let us turn to the second issue raised at the beginning of the section: how widely or narrowly is the path determined? If in some country the power of the Communist party is consolidated and society departs on the path of historical development with its own "genetic program," according to the theory outlined in the book, certain main features are sure to develop. No one will be in any doubt later that such a country belongs to the family of socialist systems. At the beginning of the path it might have been uncertain what Czechoslovakia in the early years after 1945 or Cuba in the first years of Fidel Castro's rule might turn into, but by now it is indisputable that the systems that came into being are closely akin to the Soviet Union of Lenin and Stalin and to the China of Mao.

Whereas light has been shed on the main common features, it must be recalled here that this does not amount to perfect identity. Each socialist country has numerous individual characteristics. This too is suggested by the earlier biological-genetic analogy: not even the monozygotic twin offspring of the same parents are perfectly identical. To return to the subject, several factors affect the specific structure of a society and the economy within it: geographical and natural conditions, the economic and cultural legacy from the previous regime, the political line taken by the new possessors of power, the personal traits of the supreme leader, the behavior of foreign countries toward the country concerned, world political events, and so on. So it would be quite wrong to imagine that given the "genetic program," the accession of the Communist party to power, all has been determined and history will "take its course." The strength of application and the specific constellation of the tendencies will vary appreciably from country to country and from period to period. There is repression in every country at every stage in the classical system, but in one it applies on a mass scale in a particularly merciless way, while in another country or period it can be felt to be relatively mild. There is a command economy everywhere, but in one place it operates pedantically, with painstaking concern for the smallest detail, while in another it works sloppily and unreliably. Everywhere and always there is a shortage economy, but while the food shortage is unbearable in one country, the accustomed degree of shortage is quite tolerable in another.

This analysis describes the *inclinations* of the system. An inclination may prevail or it may be restrainable to some extent. A measure of choice affects the actual combination of mutually compensatory tendencies that arises. To take an example, the classical system is inclined toward forced growth. The more the leadership forces growth, the greater the problems in supplying the public and the graver the repression used to stifle the consequent discontent. If a more moderate leadership chooses to restrain the expansion drive and investment hunger (which happens in certain countries at certain times), it can afford to loosen the constraints on political and intellectual activity a little. So there is "play," some freedom to maneuver, although it is limited.

Understanding and accepting a theoretical model, a prototype of classical socialism does not act as a substitute for concrete historical analysis of individual countries. That task remains for other works. My aim here is merely to clarify where the constant constraints on choice in decision making lie or, more precisely, which constraints derive form the "genetic program," the basic, common features of this family of systems.

Some observers and critics of the socialist economy tend to ask why a better information and incentive system is not introduced under socialism. They think society can be perceived as the realization of a gigantic "principal-agent" model.[8] If the principal's purpose is known, an incentive scheme that best serves the objectives can be devised, and immediately the system will operate better. Willy-nilly, this line of argument implies that the principal has been rather stupid not to have lit before upon the information and incentive system that suits him best.

The approach in this analysis is not to start by deciding what the leadership's "objectives" are, not least because the objectives are difficult to observe. They are not necessarily reflected faithfully in public resolutions and political speeches, since these form parts of the offi-

---

[8] The author has encountered this approach mainly among Western theoretical economists without a close acquaintance with socialism but interested in its problems. A similar notion is not infrequently seen in the thinking of staff at the International Monetary Fund, World Bank, and other international agencies. Raised in the West, they suddenly engage in studying the problems of a socialist country, and even in preparing for practical decisions. For a long time a similar concept appeared among the mathematical economists in the Soviet Union: they sought to elaborate proposals for an "optimal economic system" for the official leadership of the day. For a description of this school, see, for instance, books by Ellman (1973) and Sutela (1984).

cial ideology. The only way of establishing the "true" purpose of leaders is to observe their actual deeds, in which their intentions (and any forced modifications of their original intentions) are incarnated. Moreover, there is no community of purpose anyway, due to the multitude of conflicts within the sphere of the leadership.

All those controlling the classical socialist system, from the tip to the base of the bureaucratic pyramid, are not stupid at all. They are quite capable of asserting their interests and objectives. The system evolved in the way it did precisely because this is the structure that can perform the functions expected of it. It is naïve to imagine that the main features of the system can be altered by applying a few ideas for reorganization.

The attention in another kind of critical approach is concentrated on the extreme examples. This course is taken by confirmed opponents of socialism who think they can present their message most effectively by drawing attention to the worst enormities, the unbridled mass terror, or the most conspicuous instances of waste. The same approach is taken by some confirmed adherents of socialism, who are glad to talk about the ultimate negative examples because they hope that the problems can be solved by curbing the "extremes" and "excesses." I try a different approach, focusing attention on what is general, typical, and normal in the system; in other words, on the average, the expected value of the random fluctuations. I do so in the hope that although this approach has less influence on the feelings of the reader, it may place the drawing of the conclusions on a sounder footing.

During the debates around the reforms and "de-Stalinization," one issue raised not infrequently is this: could the Stalin terror have been avoided? Was it worth paying the price signified by the victims of Stalin's rule that the socialist system might survive? Although the intellectual and moral content of these questions is fully understandable, it is not my intention to answer them here. The theoretical model being described is one that does not necessarily imply the extremisms of Stalin's rule, although it does not exclude them. The issue presented during the analysis of this prototype is as follows: Given the power structure, ideology, and property relations typical of classical socialism, what are the main features of the structure and operation of society that appear, at least as a tendency or inclination? Is the existence of this "genetic program," that is, the specific power structure and ideology, a sufficient and necessary condition for the inclinations and tendencies mentioned to arise? I consider this to be a stricter, not a more lenient, set of questions to put than the one at the beginning of the paragraph about the necessity or avoidability of the "extremisms."

The Soviet Effect

What effect on the structure and main attributes of the classical system has been exercised by the historical accident that the Communist party first took power in former tsarist Russia? What kind of system would the socialist system have become if its development on a worldwide scale had started out from a different country?

Those posing these questions tend to point out how deeply the characteristics associated with Lenin's and Stalin's Soviet Union are rooted in Russia's past. The KGB continues the practice of the tsarist secret police; the rigid and soulless apparatus is the heir to the bureaucracy of the old Russian governors and *chinovnik*s; the bleakness of a *kolkhoz* village and the passiveness of a *kolkhoz* peasant recall the way of life of the *muzhik*s under the old regime. They customarily project the application of this line of argument beyond the Soviet borders as well. Socialism would have developed otherwise in other countries too if backwardness and a semi-Asian lack of civilization had not been branded upon it at the historical point of departure.

History cannot be reversed. There is no way of conducting an experiment in which the autocracy of the Communist country develops in some other country first and the new system in that other country exercises the global effect that the Soviet Union had in the actual course of history. To that extent one cannot give an answer with complete certainty to the question put at the beginning of the section. Nonetheless, the line of thinking in this analysis does suggest a few hypotheses.

1. One can certainly consider it an accident that the circumstances in which the Communist party could seize power should have arisen in Russia first. But the fact that nearly *all* countries where the socialist revolution triumphed largely by internal efforts were backward and poor must be rated a recurrent regularity. The regime preceding socialism governed by brutal means; there were notably sharp inequalities in society. The specifically Russian antecedents may have played some part in developing the general features of the socialist system,

but the antecedents equally characteristic of all the countries, seem to be far more important. Apart from one or two exceptions, in not one of those countries had genuine parliamentary democracy developed; in not one of them had mature capitalism been attained; in not one of them had the market become the dominant coordination mechanism. All these countries were "late arrivers."[9] These common antecedents certainly had an effect on the political structure (total elimination of democratic institutions), the development of the pattern of forced growth for the sake of eliminating backwardness, the radicalism of the redistribution of income, and a good many other characteristics of the system. This is the type of society prone to accept the "genetic program" that creates the socialist system.[10]

2. The Soviet example played an important part in all countries in shaping specific elements of classical socialism (its official ideology, institutions, and norms of behavior).

In part the Soviet Union enforced this, by various methods. Great pressure was exerted on all the Eastern European countries under Soviet military occupation by the very presence of the Soviet troops. If the population tried to oppose the system, as happened, for instance, in 1953 in East Berlin, 1956 in Budapest, and 1968 in Prague, the resistance was crushed by the military might of the Soviet Army. Moreover, awareness of the threat of Soviet military intervention had the desired effect in the other countries as well.

Apart from direct intervention, another very influential factor was the tie that the Communist parties felt with the Soviet Union and its Communist party. The Moscow center imposed its will on the Communists of other countries with fire and sword in the early decades of the world Communist movement. Unconditional acceptance of every Soviet institution and action was the prime condition before a party could claim to be Communist. When the Communists took power in other countries, leaders who had returned from exile in the Soviet

---

[9] See Gerschenkron (1962). Szűcs (1983) provides deep historical analysis of the belated development of Eastern Europe.

[10] Another reason why this is worth underlining is that the crisis in the socialist world and the break made by many countries with the socialist system does not end that inclination once and for all. The leading Communists of Eastern Europe, the Soviet Union, and China are branded as traitors by Latin American guerilas fighting to the death against the outrageous injustices of their own social systems. They trust they will gain power, and then they will be the ones who create true socialism.

Union and continued to be controlled from the Moscow center played a big part in them; they unhesitatingly transplanted Soviet practice into their own countries. The presence of Soviet advisers exercised a great influence, and so did the fact that many politicians, army officers, and economic experts in the other socialist countries had completed their studies in the Soviet Union.

The compulsion was augmented and made more effective by voluntary zeal. The Communists who came to power after a long and often heroic struggle looked on the Soviet Union as the paragon of human progress. They were sincerely convinced that the more faithfully they copied the Soviet model, the sooner they would attain the socialism they ardently desired.

All this explains how the countries of classical socialism can be seen to have followed the Soviet example, not only in essential attributes but often in minor external details ranging from the design of the national crest and the uniforms of their soldiers to the managerial structure of their firms.

3. Strong though the Soviet effect was, an even stronger influence seems to have been exerted by the inherent logic of the classical system. The section "The Affinity among Elements of the System" described the process of natural selection among institutions and operative mechanisms that ultimately welds the system into a coherent whole. Once the genetic program mentioned earlier starts to work (as the combined resultant of the Soviet effect and internal forces), the coherent features of the system develop and bring each other into being. It is not the following of the example of the Soviet shortage economy that produces the East German or Mongolian shortage economy, but the inherent nature of the system. The counsel of Soviet security advisers is not the main factor behind the emergence in every country of the secret police, which builds up its network of informers and stamps out the least signs of resistance. This police apparatus arises out of the inherent needs of the system, which cannot survive without intimidation, repression, and limitations on civil liberties. The following conclusions can be drawn. One of the explanatory factors behind the differences among the national variants of the system is the relative strength or weakness of the Soviet influence. But what shaped the prototype itself was not the Soviet impact but a combination of far more profound effects, namely, the causal chain outlined in the section "The Main Line of Causality."

Verification

The previous sections contain a number of propositions:

1. The classical socialist system is distinguished from other system-families by several basic attributes; these are the system-specific features.

2. Specific causal relationships obtain between the groups of system-specific phenomena: there is a specific main direction of causality within the complex of mutual effects.

3. Certain conditions are necessary and sufficient for the system to emerge and consolidate. The seed of this "genetic program" is a particular political structure and related ideology: the undivided power of the Communist party and the prevalence of an official ideology whose cardinal precepts include the establishment of hegemony, and then dominance for public ownership.

4. This "genetic program" fashions society in its own image; it creates a coherent system whose various elements connect, and assume and reinforce each other.

On the one hand, this theory has a deductive character. The initial, basic assumptions and the intermediate conclusions act as the premises for the later analyses. So the internal consistency of the thought process can be checked: Does the analysis include no mutually contradictory assumptions? Have no logically faulty steps been made?

On the other hand, the theory has an empirical nature, resting ultimately on observation of the practice of classical socialism. So the relationship between the theory and historical reality deserves special attention.

It was stressed throughout the expositions that they outline a theoretical model compatible with the "dispersion" of actual historical realities around the theory. So the theory is not falsified if the situation in one particular country or other is not identical to the one described by the model, or the events there differ somewhat from the course assumed in the model. But that poses a question: Is the book dealing with a theory at all, or just with the definition of a category, "classical socialism," which can neither be verified nor falsified?

In this respect I accept the criteria of the positivist theory of science (see Popper 1959), in particular the criterion that a theory must be falsifiable. The wording of the definitions and the line of argument must not render the statements tautological, that is, exclude *a priori* the possibility of discovering the falsity of the statements in some way.

STUDY 1

In the context of this book, the theory needs confronting with historical experience observed in many countries over a long period. It is not possible (or necessary) to prove or refute the theory with a mathematical-logical model. At most a few of the theory's partial conclusions can be tested econometrically, using mathematical-statistical analysis of economic statistics.[11] The most important propositions must undergo less subtle but weightier historical tests.

The most important testing ground is the process of reform taking place in socialism. Returning to *Figure 1.1*, Block 1 contains the "genetic program," the power structure and ideology. In many countries the reform proceeds as an attempt to alter Blocks 2, 3, and 4 while keeping essential features of Block 1 unchanged. The main characteristics of the power structure are retained, yet profound alterations in the system are awaited. Major indirect evidence of the theoretical statements just outlined is provided by the constraints, inconsistencies, and failures of the reform process and the tendencies to regress toward the classical system—the repeated restorations. If the whole system is capable, however, of developing new features in Blocks 2, 3, and 4, sharply different from the classical ones, and if it is also capable of surviving and growing in this modified form without a fundamental change ensuing in Block 1, the theory is weakened, or possibly falsified altogether.[12]

This analysis suggests a revolutionary theory. The socialist system is not capable of a renewal that could free it of its dysfunctional features while retaining the sole rule of the Communist party and the dominance of the state sector. To use the terminology of *Figure 1.1*,

---

[11] Should a statistical examination falsify one partial conclusion or another, one would have to examine the extent to which the phenomenon now known and described more accurately was compatible with the original premises of the thought process leading to the partial conclusions. If need be, those too must be altered. So in that sense statistical examination of a partial phenomenon is an important means of supporting or refuting the more general theoretical premises.

This procedure is well known in some natural sciences. It is impossible to test the validity of certain fundamental theories directly by experiments. But then there are some less basic propositions, which are derived by logical reasoning from the fundamental theory, and which are empirically testable. If the test would prove the truth of the derived proposition, it would mean also a strong indirect empirical support of the fundamental theory.

[12] [The interpretation of the Chinese and the Vietnamese reforms are of key importance in this respect. Here Block 1 has apparently remained unaltered, while the other blocks have undergone profound changes. We will return to this issue in Study 3 (pp. 57–60) and Study 6 (pp. 147–50) of this volume.]

THE COHERENCE OF THE CLASSICAL SYSTEM

a profound, lasting and from the economic point of view effective transformation of Blocks 3, 4, and 5 requires a radical change in Blocks 1 and 2—the political structure and property relations.

The author is convinced that experience did not refute the propositions summed up in points 1–4 up to now. The remainder of this volume examines the process by which several countries move away from the classical form of the socialist system and reforms and revolutions take place. These analyses support the theoretical propositions made above with further observations, although the ultimate verification or falsification of them can only be done by the future course of history and the scientific analysis that processes it.

The Viability of the Classical System

Can the classical system survive permanently? The answer depends on the time-scale applied, on how one defines the word "permanently."

The dominance of the classical system has terminated in most socialist countries. The period has ended, because the process of reform has started or a still more profound change of system has taken place. There are only two countries where the classical system still prevails: North Korea and Cuba. All one can say about them is that so far, up to the time of writing the book *The Socialist System*, the classical system has operated in them for three or four decades.[13] I have no desire to offer a guess as to what the future will bring for these two countries when the general position in the world around them is that all the other socialist countries, including the two great powers, the Soviet Union and China, have gone beyond the classical system.

But even if one refrains from a direct prediction about these two countries, one can certainly say that on the scale of centuries on which world history is measured, the classical system is transitory. It proves

---

[13] [I wrote these lines in 1991. A total of 15 years have passed ever since and the classical socialist system still functions in both North Korea and Cuba. This is an important verification of one major statement of the theory summarized in the above analysis and presented in details in my book *The Socialist System*. A socialist system is able to prevail as long as it maintains coherence and—above all—the repressive features of the political structure. Once it loosens up, citizens' lives become far more tolerable; it will, however, launch an erosion of the system that will ultimately lead to its collapse.]

relatively short-lived compared with the socio-economic formations that have managed to survive for centuries.

But alongside the scale of centuries for measuring world history there is a need to use other, shorter time-scales as well. The periods of decades from the emergence until the end of classical socialism cover the entire adult lives of generations. Taking a medium-term view, the classical system is viable. It can perform the basic functions of controlling social activities vital for survival. It organizes production and supply to the public of the goods and services they need to survive. It ensures in its own way the discipline required for the coordination of activities and for human coexistence. It founds a legal and moral system in which people can find their bearings. What is more, the system enjoys the support of a certain part of society that feels such support is to its advantage. The system's elements cohere with each other. Under certain conditions it is capable not only of reproducing an existing standard but of expansion, growth, and qualitative development. It can gather a large military force, allowing armed defense in case of attack. Though the system is replete with contradiction and inner conflict, for a long time this does not threaten its existence as such.

The previous paragraph makes no value judgment. It is, in fact, possible to compile a "school report" on a system; in other words, one can rate its performance in relation to various intrinsic values. It has emerged that classical socialism fails to display superiority over the capitalist system in materializing certain values, for example equality and solidarity. What is more, for several other fundamental values, like welfare, efficiency, and liberty, the socialist system falls far short of the attainments of developed, modern capitalism operating under democratic political forms. This, however, is an assessment supplementary to the positive analysis, made exogenously, i.e. outside the system. How the general public judges the system endogenously, i.e. from within, is quite another matter. Some members are biased in favor of the existing system because they share in power and benefit from it, and subscribe to the system's official ideology. Others are disaffected, but they cannot assess the performance of the system properly because they have not way of comparing it with other systems. Yet others hold strongly condemnatory opinions but have no chance of expressing them. If the discontent increases, those in power can ensure the survival of the system by stepping up repression.

This leads back to the question discussed before. The classical system can survive while the discontent remains suppressed. Measuring its viability on a scale of decades, not centuries, the classical system looks tenacious and durable.

But one must add that the survival of the system is hard to ensure. Certain inherent contradictions are exacerbated. Not only is the socialist system behind in many areas in its competition with capitalism, but the lag increases. This all provides a motive behind the efforts to change the classical system, which brings us to new subjects: the erosion and crisis of classical socialism, the reform, and the revolution.

2
The Inner Contradictions of Reform Socialism*

Introduction

Let me begin my remarks by defining the concept of "reform socialism." I ascribe it to the socialist regimes that differ from the Stalinist model of classical socialism in several important respects, made some steps toward liberalization in the political sphere, somewhat decentralized the control of their state-owned sector, and allowed somewhat larger scope for the private sector. These changes warrant the attribute "reform." At the same time, these countries still maintained the fundamental attributes of a socialist system: the Communist party did not share power with any other political force, the state-owned sector still played a dominant role in the economy, and the main coordinator of economic activities was the centralized bureaucracy, even though coordination was effected with the aid of less rigid instruments. Yugoslavia qualified as a reform socialist system four decades ago and still belongs to that type of system. Reform socialism has been operating in China for a decade and a half and in the Soviet Union for eight or eight years.

Disregarding the early efforts in 1953–5, Hungary became a reform socialist country in the 1960s. But now the breakneck changes

---

* [An earlier version of the study was presented at the Round-Table Conference on "Market Forces in Planned Economies" organized jointly by the International Economic Association and the USSR Academy of Sciences in Moscow, March 28–30, 1989. I would like to express my thanks to Mária Kovács, Carla Krüger, Shailendra Raj Mehta, and Judit Szabó for their devoted help in the research behind this study and in editing the final text of the publications.]

of the last few months mean it is displaying the signs of a real *change of system*, principally in the political sphere.[1] The political structure is undergoing a transformation that will lead to the Communist party losing its monopoly of power. To that extent, the change is of a *revolutionary* nature. I would no longer place today's Hungary among the "reform socialist" countries, but I would place yesterday's Hungary among them, and that "yesterday" lasted two or three decades.

Poland had hardly moved from classical, pre-reform socialism into the reform socialist group of systems before it was moving on again. As in Hungary, there is a profound change of system taking place. As this article was taking final shape, transformations had also begun in the GDR and Bulgaria. There is no way to predict whether the changes will cease at the stage termed reform socialism in this article (i.e., the undivided power of the Communist party and the dominance of the state sector will remain), or whether this stage will soon be superseded.

The study deals exclusively with the "reform socialist system," seeking to present some of its characteristics. Its aim is a *positive* analysis, not a normative position. It tries to decide, if a country is at this historical stage, what features will mark its property relations and coordination mechanisms. So it has nothing to say about (1) whether the country remains at this stage; or (2) if not, how it can emerge from this stage and what it should do during the change of system. I expressed my views on these matters in a recent work of mine *(The Road to a Free Economy* 1990). I will not repeat in this study the normative ideas and economic policy recommendations expressed there, but instead shed light on some matters to do with the background of experience. The starting point for the Hungarian change of system is provided by the economic relations inherited from reform socialism. These leave their mark on the state and private sectors and on the state and business apparatus. The recommendations for change must be based on reconsidering the features of the inheritance, and this piece is intended to make a contribution to that.

The study does not discuss the specific events in one reform socialist country or another, but aims for a high degree of *generalization*. Attention is focused primarily on what the various reform socialist countries have in common. In that sense it is theoretical in nature. Nonetheless, readers should be cautious. The sample is very small:

---

1 [To enable the reader to correctly understand the word "now" I have to emphasize that this study was written in 1988–9.]

there are few countries where reform socialism pertains or has pertained, and in some the period of observation has been short. I cannot undertake to provide a mature positive theory adequately verifiable on the basis of experience. But even under these conditions, it is useful to make some positive theoretical guesses that emphasize some essential common features in reform socialism.

Since the object of the analysis is to offer a few general observations, I will not attempt here to support the conjectures with data and empirical evidence.[2] In other words, the emphasis is less on purely factual description and more on outlining a *specific approach* to the analysis of these well-known facts.

The issues to be discussed in the study have many political ramifications. Decisions concerning ownership and coordination mechanisms are, of course, strongly linked to the questions concerning power, political institutions and ideology. Apart from a few sort hints, the study does not elaborate on the political aspects of the topics.[3]

Transformation without a Strategy

Looking at the history of the reform socialist countries, it is found without exception that the actual period of reform was preceded by the circulation of reform blueprints or programs. In many cases, these blueprints were prepared by scholars. As a matter of fact, the first example of such an academic program for reform within socialism goes back as far as Oscar Lange's famous proposal for market socialism and the debate to which his ideas gave rise in the 1930s (Lange 1936–1937). Some blueprints were also prepared by the leaderships, that is to say by party and government officials, in Yugoslavia, Hungary, China, the Soviet Union, and other countries. Finally, there have been instances of programs published illegally or semi-legally by dissident politicians, for instance, by authors close to the unofficial trade union Solidarity in Poland, and by opposition intellectuals in Hungary and in the Soviet Union.

---

[2] There is a voluminous literature on the description and analysis of reform processes in the various socialist countries. To mention only a few examples: Burkett (1989) on Yugoslavia; Kornai (1986b) and Antal et al. (1987) on Hungary; Perkins (1988) on China; Afanas'ev (ed.) (1988), Hewett (1988), Schroeder (1987), and Shmelev (1987) on the Soviet Union.

[3] My book *The Socialist System* (1992b) examines in detail the relations between the political structure, the ideology, the ownership types, and the coordination mechanisms.

While all these reform proposals became interesting historical documents, and some had a measure of influence on the course of events, the reality in the reforming countries has never corresponded to any of the blueprints. In fact, not even the officially publicized intentions of party and government were usually realized consistently. The departures from the original program were sometimes so great that they bore no resemblance to the initial guidelines. Of course, history has witnessed many other cases of a gap between intent and outcome: the French Revolution came to reflect few of the ideas that the Encyclopedists like Rousseau had been discussing in their works, and the Soviet Union in the 1930s turned out to be a country quite different from the one Marx or the 1917 revolutionaries had envisaged.

It is ironic to note, nevertheless, that major transformations in centrally planned economies occur without being based on a central plan. There is a Chinese adage that talks of "crossing the river by touching the stones." The reform processes in socialist economies have conformed exactly to this: whole societies have set out across deep water without accurate knowledge of their final destination, by a process of moving from one stone to another. Because of this lack of strategy, the reality of reform in socialist countries has been marked by historical compromise, by backward as well as forward movements, euphoria and optimism alternating with disillusionment and frustration. It is also founded frequently that changes cannot be maintained, despite great efforts to do so. People often learn the limits of potential reform by running, so to speak, up against a stone wall. In any case, the limits of a society's ability to transform cannot be gauged accurately until the transforming process has begun.

Under such circumstances, it becomes extremely important to recognize what evolved *spontaneously* in the reform process. Marx used the German term *naturwüchsig* (naturally grown) to characterize spontaneous historical processes: phenomena that appear not by government behest or under administrative pressure, but by the free will of certain social groups.

The study of "naturally grown" changes is all the more important because individual freedom of choice typically increased as a result of reform, though certain restrictions were imposed by unchangeable taboos. Nevertheless, spontaneous changes reflect to some extent voluntary decisions and revealed preferences of various social groups.

This is exactly the approach that distinguishes this study from many others. Most work on reform deals with normative issues, and even in the realm of positive analysis, the discussion concerns the intentions and actions of the leadership and the apparatus. This study seeks to point to another, no less important aspect: what occurs spontaneously, not on the orders or despite the orders of leading groups.

The Evolution of a Private Sector

The first area to focus on is the evolution of a private sector. Let us recall briefly the period in which the first reform proposals were drawn up. When, for example, the author began to participate in the East European thinking on reform in 1954, 1955, and 1956, all the scholars taking part in the debate were concerned almost exclusively with questions of reform as applied to the state-owned sector.[4]

Discussions turned on the issues of how to give more autonomy and stronger profit-based incentives to state-owned firms, of how to decentralize economic administration, while at the same time maintaining state ownership in all but the most marginal sectors of the economy. These were the views of radical reformers in those days.

Taking a thirty-year leap in history, it turns out that, quite in accordance with the previous section of this study, history has taken quite a different course from the one outlined in the blueprints of academic economists. In the author's view, the emergence of a significant private sector in all socialist economies where reforms had time to develop, and especially in Hungary, Poland, and China, was the most important result of economic reform.

The most important inroad by private activity in socialist economies occurs through private farming. This exists in a variety of forms. Land may be reprivatized *de facto* (as, for example, under the Chinese "family responsibility system") or private farming may never have been abolished and survive all kinds of political changes (as, for example, in Yugoslavia or in Poland). In Hungary, the role of the

---

[4] See for example, the following sample of the earliest papers advocating decentralization-based reform in Eastern Europe: Kidric (papers from the 1950s in the 1985 volume) for Yugoslavia, Péter (1954a and b, 1956) and Kornai (1959) for Hungary, Brus (1972) for Poland, Liberman (1972) for the Soviet Union, and Sun Yefang (1982) for China.

household plot and of private farming also increased in the wake of the reform. In addition, there typically exists some kind of family subcontracting within the agricultural cooperative.

Apart from these private and semi-private agricultural businesses, there is legal, tax-paying private activity in various other sectors. A significant private sector has emerged in various branches of the services, transport, and construction; and to a lesser extent in manufacturing.[5] There appear various forms of income derived from private property, for example, renting out private homes in cities or privately owned second homes in resort areas.

In addition to the formal private sector, various types of informal "moonlighting" often appear; these unlicensed and perhaps illegal, yet tolerated activities proliferate in the services, commerce, transport, and construction.[6] Reform economies also experienced a significant increase in elaborate *do-it-yourself* activities.

In some countries and some sectors, such as housing and agriculture, even property owned by the state or some other social organization may be sold or leased to individuals.[7] But in practice, the larger part of the private-sector growth resulted from entrepreneurial initiative, based sometimes on private savings, but sometimes almost exclusively on individual labor input.

It must be stressed that the government typically does not have to convince its citizens to enter the private sector through a propaganda campaign. Usually, once certain prohibitions on private activity are lifted, the private sector begins to grow spontaneously, with individual enterprises sprouting up like mushrooms in a forest after rain. The explosion of private activity is all the more remarkable as it often follows a period of brutal repression of any form of private venture. As soon as the repression ends, the private sector immediately begins to expand in reform socialist countries in a genuinely spontaneous manner. People do

---

[5] Private business partnerships, owned and operated by groups of people belong to the private sector, along with businesses owned and operated by individuals or families. Such partnerships are called "cooperative" in the Soviet Union, although everybody knows they are in fact private business partnerships.

[6] On the formal and informal private sector, see Grossman (1977), Gábor (1985), Davis (1988), Pomorski (1988), and Dallago (1989).

[7] Sales of state property to private citizens and foreign investors have become common in Poland and Hungary. This is a tangible sign that the two countries are exceeding the bounds of "reform socialism" and entering on a "change of system."

not have to be cajoled or coerced into choosing this life.[8] In fact, they are immediately attracted by the higher earnings, the more direct link between effort and reward, and the greater autonomy and freedom the private sector offers. The third reason in particular—the prospect of greater autonomy in private activity—should not be underestimated.

Private activities generate relatively high income because they can meet demand left unsatisfied by the state-owned sector. A craftsman or the owner of a corner grocery store or a small restaurant is typically in the middle income bracket in a private enterprise-based capitalist economy. But in the environment of a chronic shortage economy, such activities catapult people into the highest income group, not because they were particularly smart or greedy, but because the service they provide is scarce. The price they receive for their output is just the *market clearing price* in the small segment of the economy where a genuine market operates. They can be grateful to the state-owned sector and to the fiscal and monetary systems that create supply and demand conditions leading to free market prices significantly higher than the official prices in the state-owned sector.

The dimensions of this growth in private economic activity are even more remarkable if one thinks that private business has to adjust to a hostile environment in a half-heartedly reforming socialist economy. Despite some improvements, the daily life of private businesses is still marked by a multitude of bureaucratic interventions and restrictions. The private sector has limited access to supplies of materials and almost none to credit or foreign exchange, so that these are often acquired in illegal or semi-legal ways.

A further sign of hostility is jealousy of people observing the widening income differentials. This envy of individuals who suddenly come to earn more than others occurs under all systems, but it is likely to be all the more divisive in a society where people have been brought up to consider equality a major social desideratum. Finally, further difficulties are caused by the absence of legal institutions to provide consistent protection for private property and enforce private contracts, as well as the absence of political movements and associa-

---

[8] The Soviet Union, especially the Soviet agricultural sector, may be an exception. The memory of the terror that accompanied mass collectivization and the "liquidation of the kulaks" is so deeply imprinted on the collective conscience that it has been passed from generation to generation. Many people still shy away from starting individual farming or any other kind of private business.

tions devoted to articulating private-sector interests. And that leads on to the ideological aspects of the issue.

Is it justifiable to assume that this small-scale private activity under reform socialism leads inevitably to capitalism? For instance, if there were now in a meeting called in the Soviet Union to decide on the pragmatic question of how many licenses to issue to private taxi owners, would it be pertinent to argue that private cabs are not genuine capitalist ventures and that Soviet socialism will not be endangered if a few more are allowed on the streets? Nevertheless, if the aim is to be objective, the question cannot be dismissed lightly.

Using now the terminology of Marxian political economy, the overwhelming part of private sector activity in a socialist economy can be classed as small commodity production. Roughly speaking, the decisive distinction between small commodity production and genuine capitalism in the Marxian sense is that the former uses only the labor input of an individual, possibly with that of family members, whereas the latter uses hired labor regularly and so becomes exploitative, as it seeks to extract surplus value from employees. In this context, the ideology and practice of socialist countries has been much influenced by Lenin's oft-quoted dictum: "Small production engenders capitalism and the bourgeoisie continuously, daily, hourly, spontaneously, and on a mass scale" (Lenin [1920] 1964–1972c, p. 8). Lenin, in the author's opinion, was absolutely right. If a society allows for the existence of a large number of small commodity producers, and if it permits them to accumulate capital and grow over time, a genuine group of capitalists will emerge sooner or later. To appreciate this, readers may imagine for a moment what would happen if private producers had the same access to credit and to all kinds of inputs necessary for production as the state-owned enterprises in a socialist economy, and if they were to be treated equally under the tax and subsidy systems. Without a doubt, the more successful private businesses would begin to accumulate and grow. So the negative answer to the question as to whether small commodity production breeds capitalism in pragmatic discussions of particular cases is predicated on the assumption that the government will not allow private business to grow beyond a certain critical threshold. In other words, the growth of the private sector in a socialist economy is not simply hampered by the excessive red tape of a ubiquitous and omnipotent bureaucracy. The sustained growth of private businesses also runs counter to the ideological premises of the system, and will therefore be held in check by a ruling party and government unwilling to tolerate a significant capitalist sector.

There are various ways of imposing constraints on the private sector's ability to grow. Sometimes, these constraints simply take the form of legal restrictions (for example, a ceiling on the number of people a legal private firm may employ, or on the amount of capital that may be invested in it.) Obstacles to growth may also be incorporated in the tax system. The extent of taxation of a particular activity at a given time may vary substantially, so providing the authorities with an additional tool for keeping the private sector under control. For example, private craftsmen and private traders may be able to identify the exact level of taxation up to which they are able to sustain their private venture, and beyond which they will have to abandon it and return to work in the state-owned sector. Of course, these critical thresholds may vary from sector to sector, from period to period, and from business to business. But it is important to note that they exist and they impose institutional limits on the survival of a private firm. The most powerful upper limit on accumulation is uncertainty and the fear of future nationalization and confiscation. Memories of past repression are vivid and individuals may be scared that that they and their children may one day be stigmatized as "bourgeois" or "kulak."

Thus economies of scale cannot be enjoyed, due to the limitations on capital accumulation. It may be socially more reasonable in a given political and ideological climate to squander profits rather than put them to productive use. Historical accounts of capitalist economies commonly mention the thrift of the founders of family businesses, who try to bequeath their wealth to future generations. In the picture painted in Thomas Mann's novel *Buddenbrooks*, extravagance appears only in the second and subsequent generations of a capitalist family line. By contrast, waste in family businesses in socialist countries often begins on the first day of their existence, as it is quite uncertain whether ventures will survive even as long as their founders.

Myopic behavior is also encouraged by the social environment of the private sector. Private firms are typically indifferent to building up a solid clientele, because their owners feel they may not even be in business in a year's time. In an extreme case, the overall environment of a sellers' market may prompt private firms to be downright dishonest with customers and reap the largest possible one-off profit. Since consumers are used to queues and shortages in the state-owned sector, it is generally easy for private firms to keep their customers, though their employees may be hardly more forthcoming or polite than their counterparts in the state-owned sector, if there is one. Instead of raising overall standards of service of sellers under state ownership in the direction of those of a buyers' market, the standards of new small private ventures drop to those of sellers in a chronic shortage economy.

Private ventures have to adapt to the use of bribery, too, in acquiring necessary inputs. Cheating is needed not only to acquire inputs, but to defend the business against the state. Many individuals joining the private sector are not entrepreneurs, but adventurers. Such is the natural process of selection under the given conditions.

These circumstances set the trap for the social position of the private sector. Daily experience supplies arguments for "anti-capitalist" demagoguery and popular slogans against profiteering, greediness, and cheating.[9] Such propaganda fuels further restrictions and interventions which lead to further deterioration: to capitalism at its worst.

The resulting vicious cycle is reminiscent of a marriage between an anti-Semite and a Jew or a racist and a black. As the marriage goes on, husband and wife irritate each other and may even hate each other, but they know they must cohabit out of strong common economic interest. The reform socialist system needs the active contribution of a private sector; otherwise it cannot supply its citizens with goods. Socialism has apparently arrived at a stage in history when it is unable to survive in its pure, strictly non-capitalist fashion and must coexist with its self-acknowledged arch-enemy, not only worldwide but within its own borders as well.

The Persistence of Bureaucracy

The state-owned sector remains the dominant sector of the economy in Eastern Europe, in the Soviet Union, and in China as well, though not to the same extent.[10]

---

[9] It's ironic that some politicians and journalists in reform socialist countries, (sometimes even in "new left" circles within oppositionist groups) argue against high prices and profiteering on *moral* grounds. It is not recognized that it is inconsistent to declare the desirability of a market and at the same time deny the legitimacy of a price generated by that same market mechanism.

[10] [The original version of the article, published in 1990, continued with the sentence, "As China

The central idea behind the original reform blueprints was to abolish the command economy, that is, eliminate mandatory output targets and input quotas. At present, Yugoslavia and Hungary are the only countries to implement this more or less consistently. It has been done only partially in the two biggest socialist countries, China and the Soviet Union.[11]

The initial expectation of the reformers was that once the administrative system had been abolished, the momentary vacuum would then be filled by the market mechanism. In other words, bureaucratic commands would be instantaneously replaced by market signals. The assumption underlying this position was that of a simple complementarity between the two mechanisms of coordination, bureaucratic and market.[12] This expectation, shared by this author in 1955-6, has turned out to be naive. What actually happens is that the vacuum left by eliminating administrative commands, and thus *direct* bureaucratic coordination, is filled not by the market, but by other, *indirect* tools of bureaucratic coordination.[13]

The role of the market, which was not completely eliminated even under the classical socialist system of planning, has of course increased in the wake of reform. But the role of the bureaucracy has continued to be pervasive and is asserted in many different ways.[14] To summarize, the role of the bureaucracy remains paramount in selection and promotion of managers, and in decision-making power over the entry and the

---

proceeds on the road to industrialization, however, the role of state-owned enterprises is likely to increase." This prediction has not come true. The relative weight of state enterprise in China has fallen, not risen. This phenomenon is considered in Studies 3 and 7 of this volume.]

[11] [While the Soviet Union broke up at the beginning of the 1990s and a change of system began in Russia and the other successor states, one of the great achievements of the "reform socialist" stage in China has been to restrict substantially or eliminate the planning-command mechanism in various segments of the state sector.]

[12] The term bureaucratic coordination, here as in other works of the author, is used in a value-free sense, without any of the negative connotations it bears as in many East European writings and speeches. It refers to certain types of controlling and coordinating activities. The main characteristics of the mechanism include multi-level hierarchical organization of control, dependence of subordinate on superior, and the mandatory or even coercive character of the superior's instructions.

[13] The notions of direct and indirect control were first applied by Kálmán Szabó, Tamás Nagy, and László Antal.

[14] In the spirit of note 12, a word of explanation is needed about the term *bureaucracy*. This notion is also used in a value-free way, without any negative connotations. It denotes the hierarchical apparatus in control of all social and economic affairs and includes not only government officials and managers, but functionaries of the party and the mass organizations as well.

exit of firms. While the bureaucracy has reduced or completely relinquished direct administrative control over the quantities of output and input by state-owned firms, it can still control them by informal interventions, through formal state orders and informal requests, and through administrative price setting and extremely strong financial dependence of the firm on its superior organs. So the state-owned firm is strongly dependent on the various branches of the bureaucracy, the ministries in charge of production, foreign trade authorities, the price control office, financial bodies, the police, and so on. There is also frequent intervention in enterprise affairs by party organizations. A change has occurred in the form, but not the intensity of dependence.

This description of the private sector has employed the terms spontaneous or naturally grown. Here it should be emphasized that persistence of the bureaucracy is a spontaneous and natural outgrowth of the socialist economy as well.[15] The Central Committee or Politburo does not have to decide to maintain as much of the bureaucracy as possible during the reform process. On the contrary, the bureaucracy may grow *despite* sincere attempts to reduce it and dramatic campaigns to get rid of it, such as the one during the Cultural Revolution in China. The current Soviet campaign of *perestroika* (restructuring) again sets out to reduce the size of the bureaucracy, but experience so far does not warrant much confidence in the chance of checking the natural growth of the bureaucracy, even if drastic methods are employed. There is parthenogenesis of bureaucracy in the sense that if it is eliminated in one place and one form, it reappears in another place and another form.

This continual regeneration of bureaucratic control is explained by many factors. One is, of course, the material advantage associated with bureaucratic positions: financial benefits, privileges, and access to goods and services in short supply. Even more important is the lure of power. Here we arrive at a highly political issue again. The relative shares of the role played by bureaucratic and market coordination is not simply a matter of finding the most efficient division of labor between two neutral forms of control. The bureaucracy rules the socialist economy. Allowing genuine functioning of the market entails

---

[15] As before, the term *natural* is not used here in the sense of American advertising, as a synonym for words like good, wholesome, and non-artificial. It is used to denote a phenomenon that reproduces without government support and sometimes despite policies designed to oppose it, simply as a consequence of the social situation.

voluntary surrender of an important part of its realm.

The main consequences of this are constraints on the reformability of the state-owned sector imposed by the systemic tendency of regeneration of the bureaucracy. The point may be clearer if the question of the constituency for reform is considered. For greater state tolerance for private economic activity, this constituency is large and well-defined. It consists of all the citizens of a socialist country who chose to, or at least would like to have the option to work in the private sector, as entrepreneurs or employees.

But nobody is an unqualified winner by decentralization of the state-owned sector. Everyone involved in the sector gains as well as loses by genuine decentralization. Members of the bureaucratic apparatus may gain some autonomy from superiors, but simultaneously lose power over subordinates. A reduction in paternalism and concomitant hardening of the budget constraint entails advantages and disadvantages to managers and to workers in state-owned firms.[16] They are winners and losers at the same time for they gain in autonomy, but lose in support. While it is typically true that people disapprove of, or are at best indifferent to the support of others, they usually like to be supported themselves. In a capitalist economy, this ambivalent feeling towards protection is best reflected in the complex attitude towards free trade: evaluated favorably when it allows a company to market its own products in foreign markets with only minimal tariffs, but less eagerly welcomed when it brings foreign competitors into the domestic market. In a socialist economy, not only managers, but every individual working in the state-owned sector has these ambivalent feelings about the soft budget constraint, paternalism, support and protection.

While high taxes were disliked, subsidies, even if the firm is not receiving them at the time, may come in handy in the future, and so cannot be opposed quite so strongly. Similar ambivalence appearance over shortage, which inconveniences buyers, but suits sellers.

It turns out that neither bureaucrats nor managers, nor indeed workers are enthusiastic exponents of competition or of marketization of the state-owned sector. At most, some enlightened government officials and intellectuals may come to the conclusion that hardening of

---

[16] For the terms "soft" and "hard budget constraint", see Kornai (1980, 1986b). [There is a comprehensive account of more recent theory about hardness and softness of the budget constraint in Kornai, Maskin, and Roland (2003).]

the budget constraint and a decrease in paternalism is needed to improve the performance of the economy. As for the masses, there are no strikes or street protests in favor of increasing economic efficiency at the expense of state protection. There exists no grassroots movement for decentralizing the state-owned sector. On the one hand, there is a strong inducement to maintain bureaucratic positions, and on the other, no clear constituency against maintaining them. So the final result is permanent reproduction of bureaucratic coordination.

Alternative Forms of Social Organization

After this discussion of the private and state-owned sectors, and the roles of bureaucracy and the market in a prototype reform socialist economy, let us now approach the theme of this study from a somewhat more general point of view. Consider *Figure 2.1*.

Figure 2.1. Strong and weak linkages

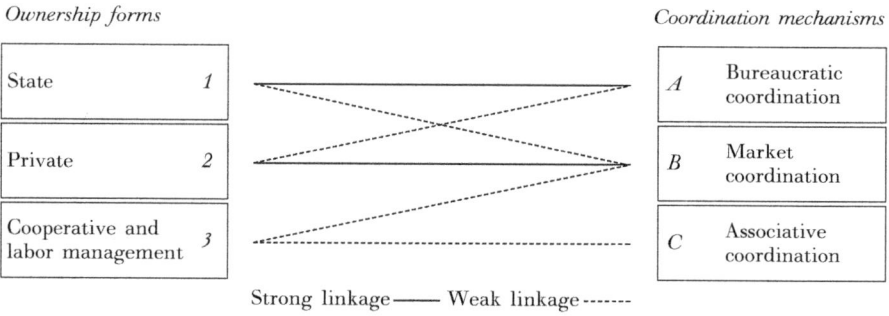

When referring to state ownership *1*, we have in mind the classical case of bureaucratic centralized state ownership; *2* is private ownership, while *A* and *B* refer respectively to bureaucratic and market coordination.

Two *strong* linkages exist between ownership form and coordination mechanism. So it is common to encounter classical, pre-reform socialist economies that combine state ownership with bureaucratic control and classical capitalist economies that combine private ownership with market control. These two simple cases might be looked upon as historical benchmark models. It seems quite natural that when economic units based on private ownership operate in the market, as sellers and as buyers, they should be motivated by the incentives of financial gain and highly responsive to costs and prices. Similarly, economic units under state control are operated by the bureaucracy, using bureaucratic instruments.

By contrast, the private sector in reform socialist economies, while mainly controlled by the market, is also subject to bureaucratic control, as symbolized by the dotted line from 2 to A. Yet this attempt to impose bureaucratic control on private activities does not and cannot work smoothly, due to the basic incongruity of this pair.

In addition, there exist other, generally also inconsistent attempts to coordinate the state-owned sector via market coordination (the dotted line from 1 to B). This idea was, of course, at the center of the blueprint for market socialism. But it turned out not to be possible to decrease the dominant influence of the bureaucracy. The influence of the market on coordination of state-owned firms is full of frictions, as has been seen in the earlier section of this study. Despite the efforts of reformers to strengthen the linkage of 1 to B, there is an inclination to restore that of 1 to A: bureaucratic coordination penetrates and pushes out the influence of the market. To sum up: the linkages between the latter two pairs—those between 1 and B, and between 2 and A—can be classed as *weak*.

The notion of *strong* and *weak* linkages do not imply a value judgement or indicate any preference on the part of the author. These are descriptive categories. In accordance with the general philosophy of the study, a linkage between an ownership form and a type of coordination is strong if it emerges spontaneously and prevails in spite of resistance and countermeasures. It is based on a natural affinity and cohesion between certain types of ownership and certain types of coordination mechanism, respectively. The adjective *weak* refers to linkages that are to some extent artificial and not sufficiently robust to withstand the impact of a strong linkage. Weak linkages are pushed aside by strong time and again, whether intellectual and political leaders like it or not.[17]

---

[17] There are many other combinations of 1, 2, A, and B worth considering. For example, if the private sector of an economy is strong and stable, and the linkage of 2 to B is the dominant one; a certain segment of the economy can be successfully subjected to the linkage of 1 to B. In other words, in a basically private market economy, the state-owned sector can adjust to the rules of the market

STUDY 2

The Weakness of "Third Forms"

Is there a "third way"? First let us turn to the issue of ownership. In row *3*, where *Figure 2.1* refers to cooperatives and labor management, it is necessary to emphasize the non-private and also non-bureaucratic character of social ownership, such as that found in genuine workers' management.[18] The idea of cooperative socialism has long been part of social thinking. As for coordination of type *C*, the term "associative mechanism" is the collective name of a set of potential mechanisms. It is possibly easiest to define the set in negative way, as any mechanism of coordination avoiding the use of bureaucratic and market coordination; a mechanism based on self-governance, free association, reciprocity, altruism, or mutual voluntary adjustment. The literature on socialism is rich in proposals for basing socialist society on cooperative ownership and non-market, non-bureaucratic associative coordination. In referring to this tradition of thought, Marx coined the somewhat derogatory term "Utopian Socialism." Early representatives of this line included Proudhon, Fourier (to some extent), Owen, and others.

The literature does not always couple *3*, co-operative, self-governed ownership and *C*, associative coordination. Some authors emphasize *3*, others *C*, while in some cases, the two are considered together. Ideas of this kind came up frequently in reform discussions in socialist countries.[19] The whole Yugoslav experience constitutes an attempt, albeit a highly imperfect one, to move in the direction of this third way to socialism, away from exclusive reliance on state or private ownership and on bureaucracy or the market. The Chinese Cultural Revolution may be looked upon as another attempt to smash the bureaucracy and proceed to a non-bureaucratic type of socialism, without introducing market ele-

---

[18] In accordance with the definitions used in this study, private business partnerships in the Soviet Union cannot be regarded as genuine cooperatives. They belong to form *2* and not to form *3*.

[19] Of course, cooperative ownership can be linked not only to coordination mechanisms of type *C*, but to the market mechanism as well. For example, Yugoslavia experimented with coupling ownership form *3* (labor management) with coordination mechanisms *B* and *C* (market and "associative" coordination). Large segments of the economy were coordinated in the unusual way by the market mechanism. At the same time, so-called "social compacts" were arranged to establish direct contracts between representatives of producers and of consumers; they were expected voluntarily to make mutual adjustments. While official policy alternated in the emphasis given to mechanisms *B* and *C*, in fact bureaucratic coordination mechanism *A* prevailed all the time, and was in a latent fashion the dominant force.

ments. But neither of these two great historical experiments leads to conclusive results.[20] In both cases the transformation was forced on society by the political leadership, and although the initiative from the top initially had enthusiastic support from at least some of the population, it was subsequently institutionalized and forced through, without any deviation from the central party line being tolerated. So the fact that something resembling ownership form *3* was and still is the dominant form in Yugoslavia or that the rhetoric of Mao's Cultural Revolution reasserted principles similar to coordination mechanism *C* does not allow any conclusions to be reached on the true strength of these forms.

Let us apply instead the criterion proposed previously—whether cooperative ownership and associative coordination grow *spontaneously and naturally* during the reform process of socialist systems. This question is meaningful because establishment of genuine voluntary cooperatives, voluntary adjustments, and other forms of associative coordination are not prohibited in these countries. Small cooperatives are far better tolerated by the system than are private economic activities. Altruism and non-commercialized reciprocity are legal under any system, of course.

However, it can be seen that while *3* and *C* exist, and existed even at the peak of bureaucratic centralization, these forms have not experienced spectacular growth since the command system was abolished. When other forms beside centralized state ownership were permitted, only private ownership gained rapidly ground. While elimination of direct bureaucratic control left a momentary vacuum, this has been filled mainly by indirect bureaucratic control and by some form of market coordination. Cooperative ownership and associative coordination have played an auxiliary role at most.[21]

---

[20] [With today's eyes, based on the available information about the motives and destructive consequences of the Chinese Cultural Revolution launched by Mao, this assessment may seem too mild. It is doubtful how sincerely the instigators of the sequence of events, Mao and his immediate circle, believed in their own rhetoric against party bureaucracy, even if the misguided masses were deceived, especially the young people so enthusiastic about Mao. Ultimately, the final result was not just an experiment that went wrong, but the deaths, torture, degradation, and loss of livelihood of very many people, not to mention to the huge losses it caused in the economy.]

[21] Ownership form *3* and coordination mechanism *C* are associated in many writings with certain political ideas such as administrative decentralization of government activities, the increased role of local governments, participatory democracy and self-governance, corporative ideas of various sorts and so on. Again, the discussion of these aspects is beyond the limits of the present study.

It is time to sum up the general conclusions made about the strengths or weaknesses of the forms of social organization. While ownership forms *1* and *2* are robust, *3* has few followers. Similarly, coordination forms *A* and *B* are widely applied, but *C* operates only in a rather restricted area. In contrast to the strong linkages between *1* and *A*, and between *2* and *B*, all other potential linkages from *1*, *2*, and *3* on the ownership side to *A*, *B*, and *C* on the coordination mechanism side are weak. (*Figure 2.1* shows only four of the potential weak linkages using dotted lines. There are others, of course.) The validity of conjectures about the strengths or weaknesses of certain ownership forms, coordination mechanisms, and linkages between ownership and coordination mechanism is an *empirical* matter. As indicated in the Introduction, this study does not provide empirical evidence. All that needs to be added here is that the validity of the conjectures being made is *testable*. They can be accepted, modified, or rejected by inference from empirical studies reported in available literature or to be conducted in the future. In any case, the issue of the validity of empirically testable conjectures has to be strictly separated from the normative issue: political and moral preferences among the set of alternative forms of ownership and coordination mechanisms.

It has to be admitted that the observations about the weakness of third forms are drawn from a small sample of historical episodes observed over a relatively brief period. Researchers in perhaps twenty or thirty years may observe this tendency terminating and history taking an alternative route. History is always unpredictable. But as long as no contrary evidence is provided by experience, it is worth bearing in mind these observations about the strength or weakness of alternative ownership forms and coordination mechanisms.

It is fully understandable for various social groups and intellectual currents to advocate greater scope for third forms. Such efforts may have beneficial effects so long as those advocating them do not nourish false hopes or strive for the domination of non-state and non-private ownership, with non-bureaucratic and non-marketized coordination. It would be intellectually dishonest to conceal the evidence about the weakness of third forms and the observation that these forms can play at most an auxiliary role beside the forms that are truly robust.

Normative Implications

No search for third forms of ownership and/or coordination mechanism can circumvent the really tough choices. So what really needs to be decided is the relative importance of the two robust forms of ownership: state and private. Closely allied to this is the choice over the relative shares of the two robust coordination mechanisms: bureaucratic and market.

Here a *caveat* is required. Discussions of ideas for reform often put a *normative twist* on the critical propositions generated by the positive analysis of an existing socialist system, with the following logical structure: "If you say that the phenomenon A has harmful effects, then it implies a value judgment and a perspective suggestion as well: the elimination of phenomenon A eliminates the harmful effects. Therefore phenomenon A should be eliminated." This train of thought is logically false and also dangerous. Even if one can expect that phenomenon A has harmful effects, it does *not* follow from that proposition that (1) elimination of phenomenon A is at all feasible under the given conditions; or (2) that eliminating phenomenon A is a sufficient condition for eliminating the harmful consequences.

Now let us return to the ideas elaborated in this study. The author would like to avoid normative twists to his positive analysis. The positive statements to the effect that both state and private ownership are robust forms, and that each has a strong linkage to either bureaucratic or market coordination does *not* imply a clear normative economic policy proposal about these forms. The positive statements do not bring with them the proposal that society must give up state ownership and shift to private ownership. They do not imply the opposite either: elimination of private property and exclusive validity for state ownership. Nor is the study suggesting that we faced an either/or type of binary choice between mutually exclusive forms: either state ownership with bureaucratic coordination, or private ownership with market coordination. But instead of these *non sequitur*s, the ideas presented in the study, do entail the following:

1. State and private ownership can coexist within the same society. In the reform socialist political, social and ideological environment, this is an uneasy symbiosis, burdened by many grave dysfunctional features.

2. The decision on the actual proportions of state and private ownership and the associated decision on the combination of bureau-

cratic and market coordination both depend on the *ultimate value judgments* of the individual, movement or party participating in the choice. The relation to state and to private ownership is not strictly economic. It is not based only on considerations of efficiency. It is deeply influenced by political belief, world view, ethical postulates, and sentimental ties and antipathies as well.

This study does not comment on these value judgments, nor on the political and ethical criteria underlying the choices among them. I have expressed my views on these matters, based on my own system of values, in my recent work *The Road to a Free Economy* (Kornai 1990), mentioned in the Introduction. There I stress my conviction that rapid development and a rapid increase in the share of the private sector are expedient. But I repeat that the approach there is of a different kind (likewise justified and important). This study is intended to remain within the bounds of *positive* (descriptive, interpretive) analysis, and is therefore confined to *conditional predictions* based on theoretical conjectures about the strengths and weaknesses of various possible linkages between ownership and coordination mechanisms.

This study merely warns: let us have no illusions or false expectations. Let logical consequences be expressed. Once one opts for a large share for state ownership, one gets a "package deal," and the package inevitably contains a big dose of bureaucratic coordination. Another warning is also needed: if one really wants a larger share for market coordination, one must *ipso facto* accept a larger and ever increasing share for private ownership and individual activity. The desired coordination mechanism (market, say) does not arrive without significant backing from the appropriate ownership form (private ownership). Likewise, the desired ownership form (public, say) is not obtained without its associated form of coordination (bureaucratic). Such is the *Realpolitik* of reform of the socialist system and of socio-economic transformation of it. Market socialism is a pipedream. The usual slogans demanding state ownership with market forces entail a misunderstanding or engender naïve, false expectations that are certainly disproved by the bitter track record of experimentation with semi-reforms. It might even be said that some economists and policymakers have used this catch-phrase as a tool of mass manipulation, or to put that less pejoratively, as an educational instrument. ("After a long period in which it has been alleged that $2 \times 2 = 8$, it is reasonable to allege initially that $2 \times 2 = 6$. Declaring immediately that $2 \times 2 = 4$

causes too much of a shock.") But then, must every socialist country tread the painful path of gradual disenchantment? Is it really hopeless to expect that latecomers to the reform process, such as China, the Soviet Union, or maybe in the future East Germany or Bulgaria, can learn from the disappointments of such countries as Yugoslavia or Hungary, which have gone before them?

3. Those who sincerely seek a larger role for the market must allow more room for formal and informal private activities, for free entry and exit, for competition, for individual entrepreneurship, and for private property. Only radical expansion of the private sector can create favorable conditions for marketization of the whole economy. Movement in that direction—towards expanding the private sector—is the most important yardstick of economic reform. Without such movement, reforming slogans pay only lip service to decentralization and market coordination. I do not think the change of system that Hungary is undergoing has made reconsideration of the questions explored here redundant. There are very strong illusions being held by many influential people, especially about "market socialism" by economic leaders and economic researchers. Many hope it will prove possible to transform the state-owned enterprise into a truly market-oriented organization. In my view, Gáspár Miklós Tamás was right in saying that this is one of the "third-road" views (Tamás 1989). I am convinced that the practical economic-policy tasks of the change of system and the economic transition to the new system can be performed only by those willing to face the failures of "reform socialism" and the deeper explanation for those failures. One factor in that deeper explanation is to reconsider what property forms and coordination mechanisms prove compatible and attractive to one another, and which have an underlying incompatibility between them.

3
Market Socialism?
Socialist Market Economy?*

Introduction

The linking of the two terms socialism and market has a long history. Various combinations and ties between them have emerged in long-lasting, sometimes rather heated debates, in academic circles and in the political sphere, including "market socialism" and "socialist market economy," to mention but two frequent ones.[1]

To look at recent experience in China and Vietnam and the study of their actual history may help in a reconsideration of the relationship between socialism and the market. An opposite approach may also prove useful. Recalling past political and academic debates may contribute to a better understanding of the realities of contemporary history. Analysts are at risk of getting lost in minor details. Confronting today's experience with intense, century-old debates will help to place Chinese and Vietnamese development in a wider historical context.

The debates so far have always been blurred by conceptual confusion. This study attempts to apply some conceptual clarification to them.

---

* [The author gratefully acknowledges the valuable assistance of Yingyi Qian and Ágnes Schönner.]
[1] [The terminology ("market socialism")—as it is going to be dealt with in this study—has originally been used by academic economists, while the expression "socialist market economy" is characteristic of the language of the official Chinese ideology.]

STUDY 3

Interpretation of the Term "Market"

The interpretation of the concept of *market* is not too difficult. There is more or less a consensus. The market is a mechanism for coordinating human activities. It is a social arrangement for integration of society.[2]

The market is not the only mechanism of coordination and integration. Let me mention just one alternative, the feasible and powerful one of bureaucratic coordination, as an example of special relevance in the context of Chinese and Vietnamese experience. It served as the main coordinator in these two countries for decades. Bureaucratic and market coordination display many important differences, in degree of centralization or decentralization, in the nature of information flows, and in the incentives associated with the coordination type. Market and bureaucratic coordination are only two, albeit especially relevant types; history has generated other coordination mechanisms as well. As time goes by, societies choose between alternative coordination mechanisms—deliberately or spontaneously. Reform in China and Vietnam includes, among other changes, a shift away from the predominance of bureaucratic coordination toward predominance of market coordination.

While there is wide consensus on the meaning of the term market, there are great difficulties with the concept of "socialism." Several interpretations coexist, in what is not simply hairsplitting linguistic disagreement. On the surface the controversy seems to be about the interpretation of a single word, but in fact the conceptual debate is heavily loaded with political values, with the struggle to realize alternative visions of a "good society," and with sharp divisions on the strategy for creating the new order. It is not about words, but about political rhetoric and ideologies.[3]

---

[2] Most textbooks and dictionaries of economics offer a concise characterization of the concept of "market," and also various classifications of markets. See, for example, Mankiw (2004), or Samuelson and Nordhaus (2004). I am using here, and in later parts of the paper, the conceptual framework of my book *The Socialist System* (1992b).

[3] [There was a large number of Chinese and Vietnamese economists and other social scientists present at the 2004 conference in Hong Kong at which the previous version of this paper was presented. I therefore saw it as important in that venue to make the following observation, which I quote: "I understand that some of my colleagues have pay heed to tactical considerations, cannot be entirely outspoken, and may see it as more expedient to avoid clearly circumscribed definitions. My personal situation is easier. So I can allow myself to lay aside 'diplomatic' considerations and address the real problems."]

I will discuss five interpretations of the term "socialism." There are many more, but most of the others can be treated as blends or combinations of these five, pure interpretations, or as intermediate, temporal, or transitional stages between them.

Interpretation 1: Marx's Concept

Let us start with Karl Marx. He was not the first to use the term "socialism." Official courses in Marxism as practiced in the countries under the rule of a Communist party liked to use the somewhat pejorative label "Utopian socialists" for such towering figures in intellectual and political history as Saint-Simon, Owen and Fourier, and to contrast their ideas with the "scientific socialism" that allegedly began with Marx.

Certainly Marx opens a new chapter in the history of socialist ideas, and his teachings have had and still has tremendous influence on political thought and action. So it seems proper to focus first on his contribution.

Marx was not eager to give a detailed description of a future socialist system. He even made sarcastic comments about German professors who drew up minutely detailed blueprints of a desired socialist order. He restricted himself to dropping a few hints here and there. His thoughts on socialism can partly be constructed by a negative approach: what features of capitalism did he furiously reject?

Political structure. Marx had no clear design for the political regime of socialism. There are only fragmentary references in his works from which to build up the organization behind his thoughts on the subject. Marx certainly did not appreciate "bourgeois democracy." He was keen to ridicule the emptiness of liberal political ideas. There are oft-quoted lines where he advocated dictatorship of the proletariat, needed on the way to the full-fledged communist system.

He also had some naïve, semi-Anarchist ideas about the political situation that would pertain at the stage of "communism." Since every need would be met, the necessity for any kind of force or repression would cease automatically. The state would spontaneously shrink and eventually wither away; only the rational self-governance of the community would remain.

Marx certainly did not advocate any brutal, repressive, totalitarian Leninist-Stalinist-Maoist state. Nevertheless, dictatorship was not incompatible with Marx, at least as applied to an indefinite period of transition to communism.[4]

Ownership. Marx's thoughts are the following: under the capitalist system, productive assets are owned and managed by the capitalists. The capitalist class exploits the proletariat because it consists, not of mercilessly cruel people, but of the legal owners of capital. So the world has to be changed—it is time to expropriate the expropriators. It emerges from this train of thought that Marx and Engels were opting for public ownership. "The proletariat will use its political supremacy to wrest, by degrees, all capital from the bourgeoisie, to centralize all instruments of production in the hands of the State, i.e. of the proletariat organized as the ruling class..." (Marx and Engels, *Communist Manifesto* [1848] 1969). But they did not specify the route to complete centralization of all means of production in the state's hands or the institutional framework of public ownership.

In any case, Marx had a strong position on the ownership issue. In the *Communist Manifesto,* he expressed high appreciation of the progressive role played by early capitalism in cleansing society from the remnants of feudalism. But that period was over and capitalists had become a hindrance to progress. He made no fine distinctions between capitalists great and small. He simply wanted capitalism to give way to a new, more productive system.

Coordination mechanism. The three huge volumes of *Capital* are devoted to the study of the market economy. Marx's scholarly interest is focused on understanding of how the market works. His summary verdict is in stark contrast to that of his admired predecessor in classical economics, Adam Smith. Smith had great respect for the

---

[4] Marx and Engels already wrote in the *Communist Manifesto* that the proletariat would assume "political supremacy" after the victorious revolution. Later, Engels formulated the Marxist position in this way: "...the necessity of the political action of the proletariat and of the dictatorship of the proletariat as the transitional stage to the abolition of classes and with them of the state..." (Engels [1872] 1976, p. 370). Lenin quoted the words of Marx and Engels with great emphasis in his famous book *State and Revolution* ([1917] 1964–1972a), which laid the groundwork for constructing the Leninist theory on the state and dictatorship. He wanted to demonstrate a theoretical continuity between the ideas of Marx and Engels and his own thoughts on the issues of creating dictatorship and rejecting.

incredible achievement of the "invisible hand." Millions of uncoordinated, decentralized decision-makers finally come up with a balanced state of the economy. Marx was not impressed by that. On the contrary, he regarded the market as a spectacular manifestation of anarchy. He did not study the problem of efficiency carefully, but arrived almost by instinct at the conclusion that the operation of the market led to waste.

Again his thoughts on coordination mechanism, similarly to those on the political regime of socialism, can be reconstructed mainly by a negative approach. Coordination mechanism under socialism has to be exactly the opposite of the mechanism at work under capitalism. If that is irrational—coordination under socialism will be rational. It will be a conscious and reasonable allocation of production forces, or of labor, or of time spent on labor. Marx, as usual, did not offer a blueprint for central planning, but his idea of rational allocation is compatible with central planning and incompatible with the market.

The market—as the chief coordinator of a future socialist system—is a sharply anti-Marxist idea. It is completely alien not only to the words of Marx, but more importantly still, to the spirit of Marx's distinction between capitalism and socialism.

Ideology. Marx was among the first social scientists who recognized the importance of ideology. But he did not claim to be a prophet himself. He would probably have been embarrassed to see what various political groups were doing a hundred years later under the banner of Marxism. He tried to understand the ideologies of capitalism, but he did not suggest a new ideology for socialism.

Interpretation 2: The Walrasian Concept

This interpretation emerged in the quiet groves of Academe. The pioneer of the so-called "theory of socialism" was the Italian economist Enrico Barone, a disciple of Pareto. Although his early works met with some response in the economic profession, the real breakthrough came with a seminal paper on the theory of socialism by Oscar Lange, the Polish economist (Lange 1936–1937). There were quite a few other economists who subsequently elaborated on Lange's ideas, above all Abba Lerner, in his influential *Economics of Control*

(1946). For the sake of conciseness, let me concentrate solely on Lange's theory.

Lange's model of socialism fits tightly into the theoretical framework of Walrasian economics. In fact, it is a special application of the General Equilibrium Theory pioneered by Leon Walras and reaching its later climax in the works of Arrow, Debreu, and other contemporary theorists. There is no need to outline the whole train of thought here, as we are exclusively concerned to interpret the term "socialism."

In the realm of the Lange model, "socialism" means public ownership—and nothing else. That is the necessary and sufficient condition for calling a system "socialist." Reading the Lange paper carefully again, one finds no word of power, the structure of the political regime, or ideology. Only ownership matters.

However, Lange does not clarify the exact place of public ownership in the total composition of ownership structure. Is the publicly owned sector just part of the whole economy? Is it the dominant part, or are all assets owned by the public? The Lange paper contains the following tacit alternative assumptions: all the productive assets of the economy are in public ownership or the dominant part of them. Or it may be assumed that the publicly owned sector can be perfectly isolated from the rest of the economy.

Here then is the final reduction: Lange's "market socialism" is a vision of an economy based on public ownership and coordinated by the market. "Socialism" and the market—these two institutional-cum-structural arrangements—are deemed compatible.

The Lange model stirred up a great storm, suffering two great waves of vehement attack. The first refutation came in a brilliant essay by Friedrich von Hayek (1935a), based on the argument that such a vast quantity of information and knowledge cannot be collected, stored and utilized in a centralized way. It is indispensable to have decentralized incentives for gathering and applying knowledge. That is assured by the market and private property, which automatically combine incentives and information.

The second wave emerged in the context of reforming the Soviet and Eastern European socialist economies. The Hayekian incentive and information argument was corroborated by empirical evidence. My own work, inspired by the reform experience, contributed additional arguments for refuting the Lange theory. It seems to be highly improbable that a strong cost-minimizing or profit-maximizing incentive, taken as granted in the world of Lange's theory, can be generated in a public firm under a soft budget constraint regime. (The Lange theory assumes there is no difficulty with bringing such strong incentives to bear.)

It is impossible to couple an arbitrarily chosen ownership structure and a likewise arbitrarily chosen set of coordination mechanisms. There is close affinity between certain ownership forms and certain coordination mechanisms. (See Study 2 for more detailed arguments.) Decentralized market and private ownership belong together.

A further important counter-argument comes from the political and ideological sphere. The smooth functioning of the market depends on the "climate." It requires a market-friendly environment. If the politicians ruling a country are sworn enemies of genuine decentralization, the market will be banned to the black and grey area of the economy and cannot become its fundamental coordinator and integrator.[5]

Some kind of ideas of market socialism have cropped up here and there since the collapse of communist rule, along with other naïve ideas of a "third way." These proposals, however, have been energetically rejected.

Let us now move away from academic debates and look at political history. The socialist movement was split about the time of the First World War by a traumatic chasm between two political movements, two programs and two ideologies. These not only divided, but began to combat each other, in some places and in some periods with sad or even tragic consequences.

Interpretation 3: The Leninist Concept

Communist parties began to emerge around the time of the First World War, under the leadership of Lenin. I do not intend to trace here the history of the Communist parties, starting from before they took power, and ending when they lost power in the Soviet Union and Eastern Europe. Let me focus only on the time when the power of the Communist party had been consolidated, but erosion of their rule had

---

[5] For a broad overview of the contemporary debate on "market socialism," see Bardhan and Roemer (eds.) (1993). My own critical remarks are summarized in Kornai (1992b).

not yet started. That is what I call the period of "classical socialism." The best example is Stalin's rule for the several decades after he eliminated his enemies and completed the "expropriation of the expropriators," i.e. finished nationalization and collectivization, but before the process of "de-Stalinization" began after the tyrant's death. We could, of course, find historical realizations of the same type of system in other countries as well. Here is a summary of its characteristics.

Political structure. Democracy is despised and rejected in the rhetoric of the Leninist-Stalinist parties. They proudly announce that they exercise dictatorship of the proletariat. The truth is that this consists of unshared power of the Communist party, i.e. a regime in which the party has complete political monopoly. All competitors are not only excluded, but brutally prosecuted and oppressed.

Ownership. A fundamental feature of the system is public ownership of practically all the productive assets. Confiscation of private property, nationalization and collectivization form a core element of the political program before taking power, and remain so after power is assumed. The program is implemented consistently and with cruel force. Some pockets of private property remain, but the size of them is almost irrelevant compared with dominance of public property.

The Leninist position on private property is confrontational. Even minor remnants of it are viewed with animosity and suspicion. "Small commodity production engenders capitalism and bourgeoisie, continuously, daily, hourly, spontaneously, and on a mass scale" (Lenin [1920] 1964–1972c, p. 24).

Coordination. The overwhelming role of the market is replaced by predominance of central management. The usual name given to this form of coordination is "central planning." A more adequate characterization is bureaucratic coordination, central control, and a system of enforcing instructions: a "command economy."

Market coordination cannot be expunged completely. It plays a certain role, partly legally tolerated within narrow bounds, partly illegally in the various forms of the "black" or "gray" economy.

Ideology. Marxism (later Marxism-Leninism, and still later Marxism-Leninism-Stalinism or Marxism-Leninism-Maoism.) is treated as sacrosanct. Although it cannot retain a perfect monopoly over the minds of all people, it retains a monopoly in education, all legal publications, the media, etc. The official ideology rejects all thoughts friendly to capitalism, private ownership, or the market.

According to the official ideology of the regime, the exclusive legitimate user of the term "socialism" is its own system. The Marxist-Leninist-Stalinist-Maoist position on socialism is utterly incompatible with any significant role for the market.

Interpretation 4: The Social Democratic Concept

Here we discuss the first hundred or more years of social democracy, up to the 1980s and leave out of the scope of conceptual clarification the later changes in social democratic thought. The model countries to keep in mind are Sweden, other Scandinavian countries, and at a later historical stage West Germany and other countries in Western Europe. The movement of social democracy in countries and periods to be studied in the following adheres to a set of principles. They accept and implement these principles when they assume power, but respect them also before winning or after losing an election.

Political structure. Being a social democrat means unconditional acceptance of the idea of parliamentary democracy. Exactly here is the deep dividing line between the two great currents of the twentieth century. Communists want "socialism" by all means. "If you are able to get to power by election, fine. But if not, take power by revolution, by violence, by imposing the will of the party on the people." Social democrats want their own kind of "socialism" if, and only if the majority of people is ready to support their program by voting for their party.

Once a Communist party is in power, it does not surrender that power, even if it becomes clear that it does not have the support of the majority. It is not ready to test that support in competitive elections. A social democratic party, on the other hand, is ready to surrender its power if election results demonstrate that it has lost its majority support.

The chasm between Leninists and social democrats started with heated debates about tyranny and political competition, the role of parliament, and elections. That, to this day remains the crucial, decisive criterion for distinguishing Interpretation 3 from Interpretation 4.

Ownership. Social democracy does not reject private ownership out of hand. Old-style social democrats always rejected crude means of confiscation. But in some countries (e.g., Britain), they were inclined to assign a significant role to nationalization. As doubts about the efficiency of nationalized industries were shed by worldwide experience (including their disappointing performance in the Soviet Union and the East European countries), the social democrats gradually gave up their plans for nationalization and accepted the predominance of private ownership. Still, they are ready to maintain a larger segment of the education and medical care sector in public (typically municipal) ownership.

Coordination. Social democrats unhesitatingly rely on the market as the chief coordinator of economic activities. But they do not support unfettered free competition. On the contrary, they would insist on using the power of the state for income redistribution. The great accomplishment of their political influence is creation of the modern welfare state, with all its well-known attributes: progressive taxation, free or heavily subsidized education and health care, an extended system of state pensions, unemployment insurance, financial support for the very poor, and so on. Whatever the current fiscal problems caused by expansion of the welfare state, social democrats try to preserve what they feel is the main achievement of their political struggle in Parliament as an opposition party, or after electoral victories, in government.

These remarks on ownership and coordination lead to the conclusion that social democrats do not want to create a new socialist system, fundamentally different from capitalism. What they want is a profound reform of the existing capitalist system. In other words, they would like to see a variation of the capitalist system, closer to their own political and ethical ideals. That includes:

– Extensive redistribution, for greater equity, fairness and justice.

– Establishment, maintenance and development of the institutions of a modern welfare state (a national health service, free education, pensions for all citizens, etc.)

Modern social democracy seeks new ways to overcome the deep fiscal troubles partly associated with the commitments of the welfare state toward citizens. The problems are mounting under the pressures of demographic changes, new conditions on the labor market created by new information and communication technology, and competitive forces of globalization.⁶ But certain elements of the traditional social-democratic approach to redistribution and welfare commitments are still maintained.

Ideology. The set of ideas, values and objectives espoused by social democrats is linked closely to the "welfare state" and the democratic political process. It is a hundred years since a debate arose between Lenin, founding father of the communist stream of the socialist movement, and Kautsky, a highly respected theoretician and party leader of what would become later the social democratic stream.⁷ Both sides in the controversy still referred at that time to Marx as the common theoretical source and highest authority. As time passed, social democrats distanced themselves increasingly from Marx. Ideological links with Marxism were completely cut off after World War II, as a new chapter in the movement's history opened with the 1959 program accepted at the party meeting of German social democrats in Bad Godesberg. European social democracy had publicly abandoned Marxism and dropped nationalization as an essential ingredient of its program. Sooner or later, all social democratic parties would follow the German example (Hodge 1993, Przeworski 1985).⁸

Let us now turn to the problem of China and Vietnam!

Interpretation 5: What are the Current Chinese and Vietnamese Interpretations of "Socialism"?

The subtitle takes a question form because it is raised here but no answer is given. If there is an answer, it is unclear whether it is identical in China and in Vietnam. But let us lay aside any difference in

---

⁶ Exploring the feasibility of a "Third Way" is certainly one of the attempts to modernize the traditional objectives of the social democrats and adjust them to present worldwide economic conditions. (See Giddens 2000.)

⁷ The climax of the debate was a confrontation between the German socialist leader Karl Kautsky, advocating the social democrats' position, and Lenin, who attacked him bitterly in his famous pamphlets *State and Revolution* ([1917] 1964–1972a) and *The Proletarian Revolution and the Renegade Kautsky* ([1918] 1964–1972b).

⁸ There is a certain kinship between the traditional social democratic interpretation of socialism and the ideas of "Christian Socialism," and the related concept of a "Social Market Economy," a term conceived in postwar West Germany. At the same time, there is a strong demarcation line concerning the accompanying ideology. (Christianity versus a strictly secular approach to political and ethical issues.) The discussion of this important political and intellectual current goes beyond the limits of this paper.

the understanding of the notion "socialism" between these two countries. For even if there is such, it is still legitimate to ask the question in respect to both.

While I do not undertake to reply, I can offer a few negative observations. The study so far has outlined four interpretations of the term "socialism." What is going on in China and in Vietnam, currently and in the foreseeable future, does not fit any of these.

In Interpretation 1, Marx was an outspoken opponent of private property and expressed deep distrust in the market. China and Vietnam have allowed the private sector to grow fast, so that it produces the major part of their GDP and its share is increasing by the day, while that of the public sector is shrinking. The dominant role in coordination is played by the market mechanism. If Marx's interpretation is allowed, neither China nor Vietnam is a socialist system anymore.

Turning to Interpretation 2, China and Vietnam cannot be seen as historical realizations of Oscar Lange's theoretical construct of "market socialism." The productive assets in Lange's abstract world are in public ownership. He put great intellectual effort into proving the market can fulfill its coordination role in the *absence* of private ownership. In the real world of China and Vietnam, the market has become the chief coordinator. That may be a welcome change, but the profound changes in the ownership structure mean the present state of affairs has nothing to do with that earlier intellectual vision of "market socialism."

As for Interpretation 3, China and Vietnam have kept an extremely important attribute of the Leninist type of "socialism": the political structure has remained basically unchanged. The Communist party still holds its political monopoly and the party-state has unrestricted totalitarian power. There is no legally permitted political competition between parties or ideologies; any opposition, dissident or truly independent, is repressed.

However, the ownership structure has undergone fundamental changes, in which the state-owned sector has given up its leading role. The role of bureaucratic coordination and central management has been drastically reduced and largely replaced by the market. The result is far from a classical socialist system, and fairly close to a typical capitalist system.

Moreover the official ideology has undergone drastic changes. The Communist party has shed its traditional opposition to private property and market and become friendly to them, moving from a vehemently anti-capitalist view of the world to one that favors capitalist values and principles. Today's Communist parties in China and Vietnam are parties friendly to capitalism, although this is disguised by Marxist-Leninist slogans and faithful references to the thoughts of Chairmen Mao and Ho Chi Minh.

When it comes to Interpretation 4, the two main attributes of true social democracy are lacking. First, dictatorship and single-party rule are retained and the idea of competitive elections is angrily rejected.

An old-style communist regime would make serious efforts to build up at least some elements of a welfare state in the education, health care and pension sectors, for all citizens, or for some services, at least for employees of public enterprises. The former governments were, of course, limited in doing so by low levels of production and development, so that the efforts made could not lead to a modern, well-funded welfare state and in some cases went beyond the bounds of affordability, producing a premature welfare state. That situation is now over. The state has begun to withdraw from welfare services, in pursuit of a better fiscal balance and the greater efficiency and competitiveness of the private sector. The degree of redistribution is diminishing, inequality is dramatically increasing, and the gap between rich and poor is growing. China and Vietnam are not moving (in relative terms, in the pattern of income distribution and social services) toward the social democratic, Scandinavian model, but toward an early 19th century Manchester model, or that of some strikingly unequal Latin American societies.

Four definite *no*'s add up to an emphatically negative: The system in China and Vietnam can emphatically not be called "socialism" according to the criteria of the four interpretations described.[9]

This is a *factual* observation without any *normative* implications. I do not class the label "socialism" as a badge of honor. I am not the advocate of Leninist socialism. I do not discuss the issue whether China or Vietnam "deserve" to be called socialist countries, or whether they departed from the only true way of Leninism. Similarly, I am no advocate of social democracy, and do not blame countries for failing to follow the social democratic pattern of parliamentary democracy and a welfare state.

[9] [For more details see the Appendix of Study 6 (pp. 147–50).]

STUDY 3

"Socialism" is no registered trademark. Nobody has a right to put forward a mandatory, exclusive definition as the only legitimate one. If the Chinese or Vietnamese leadership should insist on calling their regime "socialist," no one can deny them the right to do so. Of course, it remains an intriguing question for scholars specializing in ideology, symbol, ritual, and political rhetoric, what motive lies behind that insistence. These leaders took the risk of departing from the Leninist route and did not join the social democratic route either, but decided to follow a new path with actions. So why are they so conservative or stubborn about retaining the old *words* and labels? Scholars of ideology may have an answer. They may observe that words do matter. In politics (and perhaps in private life), it may often be much easier to alter practical actions than to admit to being a renegade to one's earlier beliefs and values. Conversions such as Paul's on the road to Damascus, with open admission of the change of faith and acceptance of the consequences, are rare, very rare exceptions in political history.

Intellectuals who make their living by written or spoken word are keen to clarify their concepts. But life must go on amidst conceptual confusion. I have tried in this study to offer some conceptual clarification. Whatever the result, discussion of the Chinese and Vietnamese reforms and their true nature must continue, even if it is impossible to decide what to call the system now prevalent in those two countries. The most important task is to understand not the rhetoric, but the true nature of the changes in these two countries.

4
The Speed of Transformation*

Introduction

Ten years have passed since the publication of my book *The Road to a Free Economy: Shifting from a Socialist System—the Example of Hungary* (referred to hereafter as *Road*.) It was the first book in the international literature to put forward comprehensive proposals for the post-socialist transition. This study sets out to assess the book as the author sees it ten years later.[1] Is this not an extremely self-centered undertaking? An advertisement for an old book nobody is buying these days? No, there are good ethical and intellectual reasons for reassessing the book, and I hope the motivation will become clear in the course of the discussion.

The customary indices of success in the academic world, such as the number of citations, are attempts to measure the impact that a work has had on its author's colleagues. Here I can be satisfied. Several hundred references have been made to the book, including, of

---

* [I delivered the present paper as a Keynote Address to the Annual Bank Conference on Development Economics convened by the World Bank in Washington on April 20, 2000. I delivered an earlier version of this paper in Stockholm, as the Keynote Address to the Nobel Symposium held on September 11, 1999, marking the tenth anniversary of the beginning of the post-socialist transition. I am indebted to Stanislaw Gomulka, Karel Kouba, Kazimir Poznanski, Mihály Laki, and Peter Murrell for their stimulating comments and suggestions. I am grateful to Mária Barát, Ágnes Benedict, Andrea Despot, Cecília Hornok, and Julianna Parti for their efficient research assistance, and to Brian McLean for his excellent translation.]

[1] I deal mainly with *Road* (1990), but there were a few other public lectures and publications at the beginning of the post-socialist transition that gave me a chance to clarify my views. The Tinbergen Lecture (1992a), delivered in 1991, concerned privatization. The Myrdal Lecture (1993b), which I gave in 1992, was about hardening the budget constraint. I have included these in this retrospective evaluation.

61

course, ones by scholars who disagree with what I say. Authors are gratified also if their work turns out to be controversial.

But with the work discussed here, this is not a sufficient criterion of success. The book offered policy recommendations, which means that a much more serious question has to be put. What was its impact on the outside world? I am not like a meteorologist, who makes a forecast, but the weather develops of its own accord. When I launched my book, I could expect it to have at least a modest impact on public opinion and political decision-makers, and ultimately, therefore, to influence the course of events.

History is not simply shaped by blind forces. It is influenced by conscious people who bear responsibility for their actions. The main historical responsibility falls on political decision-makers, but in addition, it falls secondarily on advisers from the academic world. They too are accountable for what they say.[2]

Heated debate broke out at the beginning of the 1990s on what strategy to adopt for the transition. I will return to that debate, but let me emphasize in advance, not in a combative form. I will contrast my views with those of others, but without pointing a finger at anyone. There is a Hungarian proverb: "If it's not your shirt, don't put it on."[3] Perhaps this approach may help to prevent the debate from becoming personal and direct attention to the problems themselves.

---

[2] The word "adviser" in a narrower sense means people whom a government, a state or an international organization, a political party or a movement has officially called upon and invited to advise it. Many economists in the countries of the region and outside them, undertook to do this at the beginning of the post-socialist transition. For my part, I turned down all invitations of that kind.

However, there is a broader, literal meaning to the word "adviser": people who not only do positive research, but make policy recommendations as well, without anyone commissioning them to do so. As the author of *Road* (1990), I can count myself an adviser in the broader sense. When I was a young man, just before the 1956 Revolution, I belonged to a working group that made recommendations for reforms. After the defeat of the revolution (and here I quote from the postscript to *Road*), "Thirty-three years have gone by in which I have never once undertaken to draw up another comprehensive economic policy proposal." I concentrated my energies on positive research. My role did not change radically until the first free elections were announced, at which point I realized that "if some proposals have formed in my mind, this is the moment when I must present them."

[3] As I do not name those with whom I was in dispute, I feel it would be inappropriate likewise to list those with whom I was on the same side. I take responsibility for omitting from this study the usual full list of references.

Excellent summaries of the debates at that time are provided in Roland (2000), especially Chapters 4 and 10.

The emphasis in this study is on self-evaluation. I will do all I can to avoid self-justification at any cost, and self-congratulation. I will aim to be self-critical. On the other hand, customary modesty will not deter me from subsequent endorsement of my earlier views, if I feel it is legitimate to do so.

How can it be established, after the event, whether the message of the book was right or wrong? It is not enough simply to compare it with the facts. It could be unfortunate if the actual course of events coincided with my advice and it was mistaken. Alternatively, it could be fortunate if subsequent events did not coincide with my advice and it was mistaken.

Whatever approach is taken to judging the recommendations after the event, the task is really to assess the events themselves, the actual course of history. That cannot be done without making value judgments. I will refrain from stating in advance the system of values by which I view the events. These will be revealed step by step. Ultimately, the judge is my own conscience.

The book was written originally for a Hungarian public.[4] It appeared in altogether 16 languages, with minor alterations. The foreword to the foreign-language editions contained a warning that the recommendations could not be applied mechanically to other countries. Although I considered that many aspects of them had universal validity, they needed adapting to each country's conditions. So it seems expedient to concentrate in this study mainly on Hungarian experience, augmenting it occasionally with references to Polish, Czech, and Russian developments.

A full and detailed account would have to cover all the 15–20 issues discussed in the book. With hindsight, I see that I was right on many of them, but wrong on quite a few. I hope I will have a chance to make a more detailed assessment one day, but I will confine myself in this study to just two of the issues.

The first is ownership reform. According to my present beliefs, my recommendations at that time were fundamentally correct. The second is macroeconomic stabilization. Here my report card is mixed. My present view is that my position at that time was partly right and partly wrong.

---

[4] The Hungarian edition appeared in 1989, before the country's first free elections to Parliament.

STUDY 4

Ownership Reform and Development of the Private Sector

R*oad* took issue with the basic concept of "market socialism." It rejected the idea that the dominance of state ownership could be retained if it were connected with market coordination. My position on this caused irritation to advocates of market socialism. It incurred the wrath of many reform economists in Eastern Europe and many old-style social democrats in the West.

The book reflected its author's credo in supporting an economic system in which private ownership would be dominant. In this respect, the views in the book did not differ from many proposals originating from the West. However, this broad agreement leaves open some important questions. What is the best road to such a system? Once the transition is over, what will the ownership structure of the economy be like? Which of many possible variants of capitalism based on private ownership is the one to aim for?

Many ideas arose. This study sets out two pure strategies in compact form. Most of the detailed, practical proposals came close to one or other of these strategies, and the debates centered on confrontation between them.

Strategy A Retrospectively, I would call this the *strategy of organic development.* It has five main characteristics.

1. The most important task is to create favorable conditions for "bottom-up" development of the private sector. The main impetus behind the growth of the private sector is mass *de novo* entry. This development has to be assisted by several means:

– The legal barriers to free entry have to be broken down.

– Private ownership has to be guaranteed security. Institutions have to be founded that enforce the fulfillment of private contracts.

– "Affirmative action" applied with the requisite caution is needed to promote development of the private sector, for instance in tax and credit policy.

2. Most of the companies hitherto in state ownership will have to be privatized. The basic technique for doing so is sale. The state assets have to be sold mainly to outsiders, giving preference to those who not only offer a fair price, but in addition make a commitment to invest in the company.

A genuine price must still be paid if the buyer is an insider. Insider privatization cannot be allowed to degenerate into a concealed form of free distribution.

3. As implied in No. 2, any give-away distribution of state property must be avoided.

4. Preference must be given to sales schemes that produce an ownership structure with the following features:

The company has a dominant owner. This may be a business person or a group of owners, or a privately owned company that already has a history of private ownership. The last may be domestically owned or foreign-owned. A particularly desirable type of owner is a strategic investor prepared to back the company with a significant injection of new capital.

Where the form of a joint stock company is chosen, there is no need to avoid a situation in which part of the shares become dispersed. However, it is desirable for every company, including joint stock companies, where possible, to have a few core owners in the sense just outlined.

5. The budget constraint on companies has to be hardened. This is the key to ensuring the financial discipline essential to operating a market economy. A set of new laws will have to be passed, including bankruptcy law, accounting law and banking law. Following the legislative phase, all these laws should be consistently enforced. The "trinity" of privatization, liberalization and stabilization will not suffice for a successful transition. Hardening the budget constraint has equal importance with these.

State-owned companies that are making chronic losses do not need to be privatized at all costs or sustained artificially for too long. As the budget constraint hardens, it performs a process of natural selection among them. Those that are profitable can be sold, sooner or later. Those that are unsaleable, because they have zero or a negative value, must have insolvency proceedings taken against them, and not be given away. Privatization through bankruptcy and liquidation is one of the main techniques used for changing ownership.

The private sector's proportion in total production will grow on the one hand because new private businesses are appearing, and on the other because the state sector is shrinking. The second process takes place in two ways: state-owned companies may be sold to private owners, or they may go bankrupt and exit.

STUDY 4

Strategy B This I would call retrospectively the *strategy of accelerated privatization*. It can be described in terms of three characteristics.

1. The most important task is to eliminate state ownership as fast as possible.

2. The main technique for privatization is some form of give-away, for instance a voucher scheme, whereby the property rights in state-owned companies to be privatized are distributed free and equally among the country's citizens.

This approach may be linked with toleration or even encouragement for takeovers by managers. In many cases, this turns out to be a fake management buyout, as the managers pay a very low price, which is almost tantamount to receiving the property rights in the company free of charge.

3. There is no need to show any dispreference for dispersed ownership. In fact, it may actually be preferred. What needs to be emphasized is that all citizens will share in the property rights of the formerly state-owned companies, so that "people's capitalism" develops.

Here there are only three characteristics, not five, as with *Strategy A*. As for the two attributes not mentioned:

Advocates of *Strategy B* also approved of "bottom-up" private enterprise developing, but they did not give it emphasis in their proposals, whereas it was placed in the forefront of ownership reform by advocates of *Strategy A*.

If the supporters of *Strategy B* had been asked at the time, they would have approved of hardening the budget constraint in principle. Nevertheless they did not press in their writings for the retention of a soft budget constraint, but the requirement of a hard budget constraint became lost in their proposals, and not by chance. They expected that privatization would harden the budget constraint automatically. I will return to this in the context of the Czech and Russian experiences.

The most important difference between the two types of strategy lies not in the items in each set of characteristics, but in which items receive the greatest emphasis. Where should political attention, legislative and administrative capacity, intellectual interest and research activity be focused? There is a strong difference between the two strategies in this respect. *Strategy A* emphasizes healthy growth of the new private sector, while *B* underlines rapid liquidation of the state sector.

Road and other writings of mine that appeared about the same time outlined and recommended *Strategy A*. I was not alone in doing so; quite a few others put forward similar views. Here and throughout the rest of the study, I confine the survey only to the views taken by the *Western* profession, in the academic world and at the international financial institutions.[5] I would like to underline with high appreciation here the positions taken by Andreff (1992), Bolton and Roland (1992), Brabant (1992), McKinnon (1992), Murrell (1992a, 1992b, and 1992c), Murrell and Wang (1993), and Poznanski (1993). However, it was certainly a small minority among Western academic economists who supported a strategy of organic development of the private sector. The vast majority of the profession accepted and popularized the strategy of rapid privatization, often using quite aggressive arguments to do so.

Ten years after, I am reassured that *Strategy A*, promoting organic growth of the private sector, was the correct position to take. *Strategy B*, a forced rate of privatization, as compared with *Strategy A*, was inferior at best and expressly harmful at worst.[6]

Before making comments on the performances of four countries, a brief statistical comparison is needed to provide some background information. There is a close causal relation between healthy development of the private sector, hardening of the budget constraint, forceful restructuring of production, and the growth of labor productivity. The last of these indicators is more expressive, in the present context, than the figure for per capita GDP, because it sheds a clearer light on the effect of restructuring. The state-socialist system left behind it a legacy of mass unemployment on the job. *Strategy A* is prepared to dispose of this legacy, even if it means taking painful and unpopular measures. *Strategy B* shrinks from doing so. Now the labor productivity in Hungary in 1998 was 36 per cent higher than in 1989, while in Poland it was 29 per cent higher. In the Czech Republic it was

---

[5] Economists working in the post-socialist countries were deeply divided. A highly informative insight into the debate between political parties in Hungary is provided by Laki (2000); that was the political environment in which the first edition of *Road* appeared. However, analysis and *ex post* evaluation of the debate on the strategy of transition *within* the post-socialist region would go beyond the limits of this study.

[6] Dyck (2000, p. 38) shows that most countries with direct sales, and concentrated ownership with openness to outsiders, had growth rates higher than the mean for the post-socialist region. At the same time, countries adopting the voucher scheme with predominantly dispersed ownership had growth rates lower than the mean.

still 6 per cent lower than in the last year of socialism. The situation is especially serious in Russia, where labor productivity in 1998 was still 33 per cent lower than in 1989 (UNECE 1999, pp. 128–31).[7]

Clearly, *Hungary* has followed *Strategy A*.[8] But the Hungarian road should not be idealized by any means. Many abuses occurred, bearing in mind that not only free distribution can be used for unfair businesses, but the various methods of privatization by sale as well. Although none of the great corruption scandals came to a head, experts and the public strongly suspect that abuses were not rare. There were numerous shortcomings in all five listed features: judicial enforcement of private contract left much to be desired; there was not enough support for developing small and medium-sized business ventures; company managers sometimes acquired state-owned assets at unjustifiably low prices; hardening of the budget constraint was not accomplished consistently.

Nonetheless, in terms of all five characteristics described earlier, the Hungarian transition came closest to following a line of organic development in the private sector. The economic achievement is impressive. Hundreds of thousands of new small and medium-sized firms came into being. Tightening of the budget constraint in the first half of the 1990s allowed a process of natural selection to sweep over the corporate sphere. This coincided with a perceptible strengthening of financial discipline. The chains of mutual debt among companies were broken and the standing of private contracts improved. A start was made to consolidating the banking sector. All these developments were a big attraction for foreign capital. The strong inward flow of capital was one of the main factors explaining Hungary's productivity and export performance.

Occasional statements in *Poland* were flirting with the idea of *Strategy B*, but economic policy in practice remained close to *Strategy A*. A high proportion of Polish economists today recognize that the main explanations for Poland's development successes, apart from success-

---

[7] The outstanding embodiment of the success of *strategy A* is, of course, China. Nevertheless, I do not include it in the cross-country comparison. A careful evaluation has to include a comparison of initial conditions and the prevailing political structure, which are vastly different in the post-Soviet and Eastern European regions on the one hand and in China on the other. The task of analyzing that would go far beyond the scope of this study.

[8] It is not possible to say how far *Road* influenced the Hungarian governments that succeeded each other at four-year intervals. Government politicians do not usually make acknowledgments of their intellectual debts. At the time, the book was hotly debated in Hungary, not only in the specialist press, but also in daily papers and on radio and television. Certainly, many leading politicians and their advisers must have read it.

ful macro stabilization, included the mass of new entries, the vigorous "bottom-up" growth of the private sector, and the inflow of foreign capital. (See Dabrowski, Gomulka, and Rostowski 2000.)

The first who sought to apply strategy *B* were the leaders of what became the *Czech Republic*, at the beginning of the 1990s. Václav Klaus, the country's economist prime minister, championed the voucher scheme and argued in the international arena for its adoption.[9]

The program was applied energetically. The question of why it did not yield the results expected by its initiators has been the subject of several subsequent analyses. (See Coffee 1996 and 1998; Ellerman 1998; Nellis 1999; OECD 1998 and 2000.) In the first phase, the assets were dispersed among millions of voucher owners, only to be concentrated again in what are known as investment funds. However, the funds lacked the capital strength to develop the backward companies in their charge or put in real investment. Such an ownership structure failed to encourage strong corporate governance. The restructuring dragged on. The budget constraint remained soft in reality, despite strident, Chicago-style free-enterprise rhetoric directed by the government at the outside world. Whereas privatization by sale engenders natural selection, the transfer of property rights by giveaway distribution conserves the existing structure.

So the performance proved to be disappointing. Strategy *B* seems to have been a significant factor behind the problems, although some serious mistakes in macroeconomic policy also contributed to the way the economy has lagged and relapsed.

Perhaps the saddest example of the failure of strategy *B* is provided by *Russia*. Here every feature of the strategy appeared in an extreme form: a voucher scheme imposed on the country, coupled with mass manipulated transfers of property into the hands of management and privileged bureaucrats. In this environment there occurred a historically unprecedented "ownership reform" in which the property rights of natural resources, especially oil and gas, were expropriated by the "oligarchs."[10]

---

[9] The idea did not originate in the Czech Republic. It had appeared earlier in Poland, in a paper by Lewandowski and Szomburg (1989). Of the Czech program, Klaus wrote in 1992, "Our non-standard voucher privatization proved to be rapid and efficient" (1997, p. 72).

[10] For a profound critical analysis of the micro and macro consequences of Russian privatization, see Black, Kraakman, and Tarasova (2000) and Filatotchev, Wright, and Bleaney (1999). On the barriers to free entry, see Broadman (2000) and Desai and Goldberg (2000).

STUDY 4

All these occurrences are closely connected with survival of the syndrome of the soft budget constraint, in a form that infiltrates and does yet greater damage to every cell in the economy and body politic. Russia has become a "nonpayment society," as a recent study appropriately described it (Pinto et al. 1999). Companies do not pay their suppliers, any more than employers do their employees or debtors their lending banks. This is all tolerated by the executive and the judiciary. In fact, the state sets a bad example by often falling behind with the wages and insurance contributions of state employees and with pensions.

What were the intellectual sources for those who advanced the two strategies? It should be remembered that no one came forward with a strict line of thinking or produced a model that drew conclusions from precisely formulated assumptions. The advocates of both *Strategy A* and *Strategy B* blended knowledge drawn from economics with intuition, or it could also be said, with some vision of how capitalism would develop and consolidate. So my purpose now, having reread the writings of those times, is not to discover which authors are cited in the footnotes. It is more a question of reading between the lines in another way, to work out what ideas inspired the visions. I realize I am treading on uncertain ground and could well put a false construction on things. Nonetheless, I will try to answer the question.

Let me begin with the easier part of the task, the introspection. Which works and intellectual strands influenced me most as I thought about ownership reform at the end of the 1980s?

One source was the work of Hayek, or more precisely his ideas on the development of the market economy and its opposition to "constructivism" (Hayek 1960 and 1989). I felt it was grotesque that our Czech colleagues should refer to Hayek on several occasions while sitting at their desks concocting rules of the game for their voucher scheme and state prescriptions for putting it into practice. For Hayek attached enormous importance to the spontaneity of capitalism, to the way it picks out, by evolutionary means, the viable institutions that are capable of survival.

My other intellectual source was Schumpeter—not the Schumpeter of *Capitalism, Socialism and Democracy* ([1942] 1976), placing naïve hopes in market socialism, but an earlier Schumpeter ([1911] 1968), identifying the entrepreneur as the central figure of capitalism. Schumpeter's market economy is not a sterile, equilibrium-bound, Walrasian world, but one of real rivalry, in which live people set about founding new firms, conquering new markets, and introducing new products. I felt that Eastern Europe, after its numbing dose of bureaucracy, needed thousands and tens of thousands of Schumpeterian entrepreneurs. Closely connected with this is Schumpeter's other, oft-quoted idea of creative destruction. This combines in my current of thinking with hardening of the budget constraint and the painful, but essential process of natural selection by the market that ensues from it. A powerful process of exit and entry is the driving engine for reallocating resources from less productive to more productive firms (Caballero and Hammour 2000, pp. 10–1).

A third source is the image of the beginnings, development and consolidation of capitalism, formed in my mind from a variety of readings. This includes the French "Annales School," the writings of Fernand Braudel and others, which clarify the evolutionary nature of the process, and studies of the commercial laws and financial discipline introduced with a firm hand under early capitalism.[11]

Finally, I was certainly strongly influenced by the study of socialist systems. I did not use the term "institution" in every second paragraph as it recently has become fashionable to do so, but I think I understood what a "system" means, and what the difference is between socialism and capitalism; and I was sufficiently aware that this difference will not disappear just through privatization, stabilization and liberalization.

What intellectual influences could have worked upon the advocates of *Strategy B*, to produce their vision of how to "construct" capitalism at a rapid pace? It is not sufficient to refer in general terms to the influence of "mainstream economics." Even if the adherents of *Strategy B* do not refer to them, I am convinced that they were strongly influenced—consciously or almost unconsciously—by two authors. One (by an irony of fate indeed) was Marx and the other was Coase. I concede that they make strange bedfellows.

Sophisticated Marxists would call what *Strategy B* adopted "vulgar Marxism." I might add that what it took over from Coase is "vulgar Coase-ism" as well.

Vulgar Marxism in this context means a simplified formula: the change of ownership is not just a necessary condition of capitalism,

---

[11] See primarily Braudel's great summarizing work ([1975] 1985).

but a sufficient one. Capitalist property relations form the base that goes on to create its own superstructure: the institutions, political organization, and ideology required to operate the capitalist base.

The real course of history showed earlier and the post-socialist transition confirmed that the relation of base and superstructure is far more complicated than that. The mere existence of capitalist property relations is not a sufficient condition for the consolidation of capitalism. Transformations of the economy and society in their various spheres often proceed in parallel, with many types of interaction occurring. Now one sphere advances and now another, reacting on the first. There is no universal rule governing the sequence in which the interactions occur. If a drastic reform of ownership should happen, in one place, to precede the transformation of political, legal, and cultural institutions, the latter may only follow very slowly and painfully, at grave social cost. So even if it is feasible under certain conditions, it is not certain that having a rapid and drastic ownership reform before the transformation of the auxiliary institutions is the most beneficial sequence.

I would express the simplified formula of "vulgar Coase-ism" like this. It does not matter if the initial allocation of legal entitlements is inefficient. An efficient allocation will ultimately appear.

This statement is imbued with the optimism of Voltaire's Pangloss. I think Coase, if he had taken part in this debate, would have added three warnings to the second sentence of the formula (Coase 1960). An efficient allocation will appear *provided*:

– the exchange is on a perfectly competitive market;
– there are no barriers to recontracting; and
– the recontracting involves no transaction costs, or at least, the costs are very low.

But what is the situation if these conditions fail to apply? In fact, this is the case with the post-socialist transition: there are serious problems with these conditions. The renegotiation and recontracting of the allocation of property rights may be blocked by interest groups with enormous power (as they have been in Russia.) It is no less worth considering that appalling social costs appear in the reallocation period, which is accompanied by suffering and victims.

Let us return to the arguments heard in the debate.

1. The advocates of *Strategy B* were eager to cite *ethical* considerations. Every citizen must be given an equal share of the former property

of the state for reasons of fairness.[12] Experience has proved conclusively that this is a hypocritical argument. The initial allocation remained for a very short period, before it gave way to a high degree of concentration of ownership of the former property of the state. In the case of Russia, it obviously led to the development of an absurd, perverse and extremely unfair and distorted form of oligarchic capitalism.[13]

The sale of state assets, if it takes place at a correct price, does not alter the distribution of wealth or income. The wealth of the state is not reduced; it simply changes form. Revenue from privatization has to be invested usefully, not consumed. Hungary managed to employ its receipts to reduce foreign debt, at least during the big wave of privatization, when much of the energy and telecommunications sectors were sold. The consequent reduction in interest payments and marked improvement in the country's credit rating brought real benefits for all the country's citizens.

2. Great emphasis was placed on the *sociological* aspect in the line of argument pursued by the advocates of organic development. The process of *embourgeoisement* of society, with the development of a property-owning class, is essential to the consolidation of capitalism. It is well known that at a certain stage in the maturity of capitalism, a great role is played by the dispersed ownership of shares, coupled with institutional ownership. However, there can be no running ahead; no attack without strong rear-guard action. The appearance of big institutional investors cannot substitute for radical transformation in the stratification of society.

This argument was confirmed by the first decade of post-socialism. There is a close correlation between the measures of economic success and the restratification of society.

3. The arguments that most appealed to economists concerned *economic efficiency*. This field has demonstrated the superiority of strategy A most convincingly of all. It has been shown that *de novo* private companies are generally more productive than those that remain in state

---

[12] The majority of the Russian public looked on the vouchers with suspicion from the outset and did not expect them to bring an appreciable improvement in their financial position. (See Blasi, Kroumova, and Kruse 1997, pp. 76–7.)

[13] From the ethical viewpoint, I am not claiming that privatization by sale, as opposed to give-away, is necessarily "clean." I mentioned earlier in connection with Hungary that there were presumably several shady transactions. All I seek to do here is to refute the argument that free distribution, by its nature, is "fair."

ownership or those that were formerly in state ownership and privatized during the transition (Konings, Lehmann, and Schaffer 1996; Konings 1997). Experience supports the proposition that diffuse ownership and the preservation of the soft budget constraint is retarding the increase of productivity (Djankov and Murrell 2002). The Schumpeterian spirit of enterprise, sweeping aside inefficient, non-viable companies; new, real owners' strong intent on establishing order; foreign capital glad to make large, modern investments in an environment of financial discipline and observance of contracts—these together boosted the growth of productivity and enhancement of export performance.

4. Finally, there are the *political arguments*. There is no disputing today that the voucher program and postponement of painful restructuring were crucial to the victory of the governing party in the second free Czech elections. That was the single case in the Eastern European region in the last decade in which the same government continued for a second term. By that yardstick, the privatization campaign was a success.[14] By contrast, the coalitions that ruled in the first parliamentary cycle in Hungary and Poland fell at the second general elections. The rival coalitions that took office pursued basically the same strategy *A* as their predecessors. Four years later, after abstaining from using give-away privatization as an election weapon, they suffered defeat in their turn. So *Strategy B* has proved more favorable according to the Machiavellian criterion of retaining power.

The advocates of *Strategy B* everywhere, and especially in Russia, cited repeatedly the argument that if the "window of opportunity" opens for privatization, the opportunity has to be seized and the privatization carried out rapidly. It has to be done while the state bureaucracy is still in a confused, weak state, and unable to resist. While that is still the case, the change in ownership relations has to be made irreversible, lest there never be another chance of doing so.

This argument can be neither confirmed nor denied by purely logical, speculative means. No counterfactual scenario that differs from the actual course of history can be supplied with great assurance. Although it is clear retrospectively that Czech democracy, for instance, was not under any threat of communist restoration or a reappearance of Soviet tanks, it has to be admitted that the matter was not so clear in 1991.

---

[14] On the other hand, the same government fell two years later, in the middle of the parliamentary cycle, not least because of economic-policy mistakes it had made.

Reassessing the events in Russia is especially problematic from this point of view. The following line of argument has been constantly heard. The mass privatization had to be carried out swiftly before the Communist party gained its electoral victory. No kind of privatization could have been pushed through the Duma once the Communist party had become the tone-setter there.

I think there is a faulty, upside-down causal explanation behind this argument. If the privatization had taken another course, without so many glaring abuses and unavailing social losses associated with it, there would not be such strong nostalgia in Russia for the communist system. An ownership reform thrust on society may bring irreversibility. But a more solid foundation for an irreversible advance of capitalism would be provided if a broad bourgeoisie developed, property rights and private contracts applied consistently, democracy were institutionalized, and the market economy enjoyed political support from the majority of voters.

Macroeconomic Stability[15]

When I was preparing this study, I read *Road* again and felt satisfied as I read the chapter on privatization right through. I cannot say the same of the chapter on stabilization. If some miraculous time machine could take me back to that time (with my thoughts as they are today), I would rewrite the chapter before sending it to the press. The chapter dealt with several questions, of which I pick out three here.

The timing. When I wrote the book in 1989, the Hungarian economy was suffering from a series of severe macroeconomic problems, which required strong correction. It was clear that the adjustment

---

[15] [A distinction can be drawn between "system-specific" changes and the "non-system-specific" changes that can occur under any system without affecting that system's primary determining characteristics. Change in ownership relations is a system-specific transformation. It is a basic constituent of a country's change from a socialist to a capitalist system. On the other hand, most elements of macroeconomic stabilization, such as the exchange rate, changes in fiscal parameters, or cuts in budgetary spending, appear also in stabilization and adjustment programs in countries operating under an established capitalist system. To that extent the discussion of macro stabilization in the second half of Study 4 falls outside the subject-matter of this volume—*the change of system*—but the section is included nonetheless because it belongs to the subject-matter of Study 4, the author's self-assessment of earlier work.]

would be painful, and the question arose as to when it should be done. My book recommended doing it straight away, in the next one or two years. That recommendation was repeated not long afterwards in the Czech, Polish and Russian editions of the book and in several other foreign editions. The main argument was that a new chapter of history was being opened. At that precise moment, a freely elected government would have the moral legitimacy to call upon the public to make a sacrifice. It would still be possible to claim that the government was trying to remedy the previous regime's worst omissions (and it might be added, those that could be corrected most swiftly). If there were postponement, people would feel, justifiably or unjustifiably, that the troubles had been caused by the shortcomings in the democratically elected government, not the previous system.

I still think that position is a correct one. A dramatic step of that kind was taken in Poland, with the Balcerowicz program of 1990. In the first section of this study, I criticized the Czech government several times, but I would like here to pay tribute to the Klaus government for the boldness of the drastic measures of adjustment it made to its macro policy in 1991.

As a Hungarian citizen, I sincerely regret that the government of my country rejected that proposal and the opposition at the time did not press for its acceptance either. Their decisions depended on political will, not the objective economic conditions. The leading political forces were afraid to take unpopular action. Adjustment was postponed for several years, through the whole of the first four-year Parliament until eight months into the second. It was eventually taken in 1995, when Hungary came close to financial collapse, in the wake of the Mexican crisis. Considered advice was not sufficient. It took "catastrophe signals" at the frantic, last but one minute before the government could steel itself to take corrective measures to *avert* the crisis.

Most experts agree that this postponed adjustment cost more than it would have done if it had been implemented earlier. No one should be lulled into thinking that such a decision is taken in a purely rational, economic context. There is an ethical and political dilemma posed here. It is a question of the inter-temporal distribution of pain and gain, and concurrently, of acceptance of the political price of unpopular measures.

The predictions. The proposals I made rested on definite forecasts of the macro consequences of the post-socialist transition. My prognosis was wrong. I did not predict the deep recession that followed; I was too optimistic in my expectations of future growth. I have to recognize that many colleagues of mine in Hungary and abroad made predictions that were more realistic.

I can fault myself because I really had available to me the information on which I could have made a better forecast. For instance, I could have read more carefully at least my own book, *The Socialist System* (1992b), which might have initiated in me the following line of thinking:

The socialist system left as a legacy a badly distorted structure of input and output. Correcting this called for creative destruction. However, while destruction is rapid, creation goes much more slowly, so that the balance of the two processes in itself implied there would be deep recession.

The socialist system established a special mechanism for coordinating activities. Although this mechanism operated at a low level of efficiency and went wrong in the end, it did at least operate. With the change of system, the old mechanism broke down, but the new market mechanism could not yet take over all the tasks of coordination. In the study I wrote later on the transformational recession (1993c), I called this situation institutional no-man's land and disruption.[16]

These changes, along with several other factors, led to the region suffering the deepest recession in international economic history. The classic recipes for macroeconomic stabilization had to be altered and augmented before any program of adjustment and transformation could be really successful.

What action at one stroke can achieve. My book recommended that a radical program of action should be taken at one stroke. As I assess that advice retrospectively, I will try to consider both the Hungarian case and the experience in other countries.

Even today, I do not reject the notion of a radical adjustment package, in which several measures are taken simultaneously. A well-compiled package of correctly calibrated measures is capable of restoring the equilibrium in several important dimensions of the macro economy at once, or at least bringing the economic state much closer to a tolerable degree of disequilibrium (for instance, reducing the deficit on the current account or the budget deficit to a sustainable level).

---

[16] Olivier Blanchard (1997), analyzing this phenomenon on a theoretical plane, termed it "disorganization."

What I criticize in that proposal today is its misplaced emphasis. Too much heed went to what could be achieved rapidly by a drastic adjustment package and too little to how to consolidate the effects of quick fix and produce further, lasting improvement.

It is hard to achieve economic equilibrium, but very easy to lose it again. It seemed time and again, in Hungary, Poland, the Czech Republic, and Russia, as if the macro economy was on the right track again. Then came another jolt: deceleration or even absolute deterioration in certain indicators. For growth to be sustainable, there has to be not just one macroeconomic intervention, but a deep, comprehensive program of institutional reforms.

My work dealt adequately with everything connected, directly or indirectly, with the budget constraint, but I cannot acquit myself of a mistake many people made, of not pointing sufficiently to the importance of other reforms. It is easy to improve the budget balance rapidly, at a single stroke, for instance by raising the rates of existing taxes, as mentioned earlier. But a lasting improvement needs radical tax reforms, a broader tax base, the introduction of new taxes, and a consistent system of tax collection. And that is only one side, perhaps the easier side of fiscal reform. The other means reducing state expenditure, which involves reorganizing the state apparatus and the financing of education, health care, and other welfare systems. It is relatively easy to declare that the currency is convertible. It takes much harder work to organize an effective system of international payments, to develop well-oiled connections between the domestic and international banking systems, and to guarantee that international payment agreements will be observed.

It is not the task of this study to analyze in detail which features of the Yegor Gaidar package of 1992 were favorable and which were unfavorable. However, I can say this much: the problem was not that the Gaidar government sought to end the slide towards hyperinflation by taking drastic measures. The trouble (not the only trouble, but the main one) was that no institutional system for consolidating the macro equilibrium was ever built, either before or afterwards.

Macro stabilization is not a battle, but an endless war. Stabilization cannot be gained by a *Blitzkrieg*. Institutional reforms can only be obtained step by step, by a series of larger and smaller blocks of reforms. I see that now. I regret that this idea did not feature in *Road*.

Conclusion

The polemics of the early 1990s concerned the choice between "gradualism" and "shock therapy." In those days, that was one of the favorite topics of classroom discussion on comparative courses. That was what many students had to write about in their exam papers.

In my view, the question was badly put, and so I am not going to try to answer it. The question itself implies a yardstick: *speed*. I am convinced that speed, while important, is *not* the primary measure of success. In those days, many participants in the post-socialist transformation suffered from an obsession with speed.[17] The Czech Republic was warmly congratulated on being the first to complete the privatization of the bulk of the economy. Hungary's private sector was not making an equivalent contribution until two years later and Poland's not until perhaps three years later. But so what? The transformation of society is not a horse race. The main indicator of success is not who passes the winning post first.

Excessive emphasis on speed leads to impatience, aggressiveness and arrogance. "We can do everything we want." It sounds ironic, but the truth is that the expression "mass privatization," used as a synonym for give-away and voucher schemes, is the inverse of the "mass collectivization" familiar from the history of Stalinism. Stalin did not want to spend long bothering with voluntary collectivization. Using brutal, merciless violence, he imposed collective ownership on the peasantry within two or three years. I do not want to exaggerate the comparison. Luckily, no gulags were required and no brutality in the 1990s. The forcing of the change was done by milder means. Nonetheless, there were similarities: the subordination of the ownership reform to political and power purposes, the horror of gradual change, the impatience, and the obsession with speed.[18]

The transition from socialism to capitalism has to be an organic development. It cannot be done otherwise. It is a curious amalgam of

---

[17] Anatoly Chubais, the leading figure in Russian privatization, gave a lecture to the Carnegie Endowment in Washington DC, on May 17, 1999. Let me quote from the report issued by the inviting institution: "Asked about his role as privatization minister from 1992 to 1994, Chubais conceded that his privatization efforts could be characterized as 'Bolshevik-style'—lacking public support and quickly executed.... His strategy was to privatize as quickly as possible, using every minute of the day to privatize: 'I did not speak, I privatized,' Chubais proclaimed."

[18] [For more details on the phenomenon of "speed mania" see Study 7. (pp. 160–1)]

revolution and evolution. It is a trial-and-error process, which retains or liquidates old institutions, and tries out, accepts or rejects new ones. Each element in the process might be very rapid, fairly rapid or slow. Each has its own appropriate speed. Some episodes call for a one-stroke intervention. Many other processes advance by incremental changes.

There are more important criteria than speed. I start from the conviction (not the assumption, but the conviction) that the capitalist system is superior to the socialist system. From that, it follows that the firmer capitalism's foundations are, the better the medium and long-term performance of the system will be. So the emphasis has to be placed on consolidation and stability, and at the same time, on sustainability of growth, not on breaking records with it.

5
The Great Transformation of Central Eastern Europe: Success and Disappointment*

Introduction

The study examines eight particular countries that became members of the European Union in 2004: the Czech Republic, Estonia, Poland, Latvia, Lithuania, Hungary, Slovakia, and Slovenia.[1] I will take the liberty of referring collectively to these countries as Central Eastern Europe or the Central East European region, although of course that is a bit geographically imprecise. As I am writing these lines, the European Union is undergoing trying times, and it is impossible to guess what the future will bring. Whatever influence the eventual fate of the European Union will exert on the eight countries under consideration is a distinct issue from the topic of this study. On the other hand, it may be worthwhile to take a look at this region separately, since the status of each country was subjected to microscopic examination by various EU bodies before their accession. The memberships may be seen as certificates, supposed to attest to the fact that these countries boast democratic political systems and functioning market economies.

After 1990, the Communist party's dictatorship came to an end in ten countries, namely in the Soviet Union and in countries that were in

---

* [The basis of the study was the *Presidential Address* delivered by the author to the 14th World Congress of the International Economics Association on August 29, 2005 in Morocco. I am grateful to Zdenek Kudrna and Noémi Péter, who helped me in my work with careful data collection and useful comments, and to Philippe Aghion, Jean-Paul Fitoussi, Tamar Gendler, Stephan Haggard, Gérard Roland, András Simonovits, and István Gy. Tóth, who commented on earlier versions of the manuscript.]

[1] [Two other post-socialist countries, Bulgaria and Romania, have become EU members since the study was written and first published.]

close military and economic alliance with it, such as Bulgaria, Czechoslovakia, Poland, Hungary, Mongolia, the German Democratic Republic, and Romania, and additionally in the former Yugoslavia and Albania, which already had rather loose ties with the Soviet Union at that time. I would not even dare to attempt to review the entire area in this study, if for no other reason because there are huge differences among them, primarily from the standpoint of their political structures. From this standpoint, the eight countries comprising the subject of my analysis are rather homogenous. So although they share a number of important characteristics with the larger group, the set of countries I am focusing on cannot be viewed as a "representative sample" of that wider class. In delineating the topics of my analysis, I made a deliberate choice: I wanted to focus on the region where reforms had been most consistent and far-reaching. With the eight new member-states, I confine myself solely to discussion of their similarities; I do not deal with description or explication of the considerable differences between them.

Let us jump back in time a couple of decades and recall the mood and expectations of the people living in this region, who opposed the communist system. At that time, they felt it was a hopeless daydream that their countries could become democratic market economies in the foreseeable future. Although this has become a reality today, many are disappointed and bitter.

A number of analyses, both official and scholarly, have been published on this topic. They contain the most relevant statistical data revealing a great deal about the current political and economic situation of each of the countries under consideration, as well as their relative standing. Noteworthy studies have appeared offering causal analyses of the results, difficulties, and problems.[2] I will not attempt to summarize this rich and valuable body of literature, nor is my aim to confirm or refute these prior analyses. Instead, I would like to complement them by focusing on aspects of the transformation that have not yet received sufficient attention.

---

[2] There have been several documents commissioned by the European Union to evaluate the status of the candidate countries. For example, there appeared just before accession a publication entitled the *Comprehensive Monitoring Report* (European Commission, 2003). A good insight into this topic is provided by the annual Transition Reports of the European Bank for Reconstruction and Development (e.g. EBRD 2002).

I would also mention some recent publications by academic authors, often cited by experts: Campos and Coricelli (2002), Csaba (2005), Kolodko (2000), Kornai (2000a), Roland (2000), Stiglitz (1999), and Svejnar (2002).

In the discussion below, I will take special care to separate my *description of the facts* from the *normative judgments* I will make about those facts, and from the system of values that underlies those judgments.

The study is divided into two parts, according to the time horizons in which those value judgments are shaped. The first attempts to examine the transformation in the context of world history, and the second considers it from the angle of a person's present everyday life.

In the Context of World History

First of all, let us look at long historical periods, at historical units of decades or perhaps even centuries. And though the focus will remain on Central Eastern Europe, I will be looking at other regions of the world for purposes of comparison. The methodology of the first section is concisely epitomized by the title of a book by Charles Tilly (1984): *Big Structures, Large Processes, Huge Comparisons*.

The Main Direction of Economic Transformation in Western Civilization

During the last millennium, various capitalist forms of the economy have gained more and more ground in Western civilization.[3] Traces of this had already appeared in Antiquity and formed important building blocks of medieval society from the beginning. The characteristic institutions of capitalism—private property, hired labor, market-type buying and selling, a credit system, and a legal system protecting the sanctity of private property and contracts—evolved in various countries at var-

---

[3] It is not within the scope of this study to offer a definition of the term "Western civilization," enumerate its characteristics or delineate its borders. I use the term merely suggestively. Since it does not belong to the subject of my analysis, I leave open the question of whether the trends outlined in this study have already appeared or will appear in the future outside the region often referred to as that of "Western civilization."

The historical spread of the capitalist economy is primarily emphasized by the various Marxist and neo-Marxist schools (e.g. Brenner 1976 and the literature of the so-called "Brenner Debate"). Other streams of historical science, such as representatives of the French *Annales* school, also recognize the tendency as important. I refer primarily to the works of Fernand Braudel (1972–1973 and 1992) and of Immanuel Wallerstein (1974 and 1979), in which he combined Braudel's ideas with the findings of the neo-Marxist schools.

ious speeds, more quickly in some places, more slowly in others, sometimes accelerating, other times slowing down. Institutional transformation has been inseparably associated with such profound processes as urbanization, industrialization and commercialization. All the above comprise what is known as the capitalist economy.[4]

There is no agreement among historians as to when the Middle Ages ended and when the Modern Age began.[5] Moreover, there is not even agreement on whether any criteria could be provided to separate the end from the beginning, and if so, whether it should be sought in the economic, political, or religious-ideological-intellectual sphere. However, there is fairly wide agreement that the capitalist economy is dominant in what most historians refer to as the Modern Age or modernity. The economy is in a constant state of motion and transformation. This transformation has a characteristic *main direction*, toward expansion of the capitalist economic order, accompanied by deepening of its effects.

The spread of capitalism has been a slow, spontaneous, and evolutionary process. In some cases capitalist and pre-capitalist forms coexist in a long-lasting intertwined fashion. In other cases (in various countries at different points in time), there is rapid acceleration, perhaps followed by stagnation or even reversal. And the causes of acceleration, when it occurs, may be numerous: political revolution, new rules introduced by an innovative great statesman or political group, geographical discoveries (such as the conquest of the New World), or the introduction of great inventions (such as the steam engine, railroads, or the harnessing of electricity).

---

[4] In some of my other writings, for example in *The Socialist System* (1992b), I have attempted to give a more concise definition. I content myself here with a looser description of "capitalism," one which is sufficient to encompass other characterizations and avert conceptual debate. [For my definition of capitalism see Study 6 (pp. 125–7).]

[5] Consider the following representative publications that concern the issue of periodization—in particular, the topic of the beginning and end of the Middle Ages: Bloch [1939] (1989), Le Goff (1982), Pirenne [1933] (1937), and Raeds (2001).

I am grateful to Gábor Klaniczay, who assisted me in gaining insight into the discourse of historians examining this very subject; his article (2001) provides an in-depth overview of the literature written on the subject of transition from the Middle Ages to the Modern Age.

In an interview, Burke (1990), the well-known British historian stated: "Nobody can agree as to when the early modern period begins.... Perhaps we as present-day economists and other scholars of the social sciences are too close to the events and it is for this reason that we could so easily agree on one thing: the fall of the Berlin Wall is viewed as the start of a new period in the region. Or, perhaps there is a greater degree of homogeneity and synchronization present in the events than there was during earlier periods of history."

Before the Communist parties came into power, they were influenced by Marx's theory to endorse the principle that economic history had a main direction. This, however, according to the Marxists, points beyond capitalism. The Communist parties considered it fundamental to create a system that would *supersede* capitalism. They offered explicit criteria for comparing the two systems: growth in labor productivity and its concomitants, notably rates of production and increases in standards of living.

The ensuing monumental attempt at verification, which eventually failed, lasted for over 70 years in the Soviet Union and for about 40 years in Eastern Europe. There were moments in the race between the socialist and capitalist systems when even some adherents of the capitalist system became uncertain. Remember that in the years following the Great Depression of 1929, the most developed countries went into deep recession, while the first Five-Year Plan of the Soviet Union had spectacular results and produced a high growth rate. Remember also how the successful launch of the first Sputnik was taken by many as the dawn of an age of Soviet technical and military superiority! However, if these events are measured on a scale of long decades and the entire period of existence of the socialist system is observed, one thing is definitely proven: capitalism is more productive and more innovative, with a faster growth rate producing a higher increase in the standard of living. *Table 5.1* provides a growth comparison between the socialist and capitalist countries in the last four decades before the collapse. The socialist countries are represented by the Soviet Union and by three of the new EU members (Czechoslovakia, Poland, and Hungary). The capitalist economy is represented by 13 old EU members. The table clearly indicates the growing superiority of the capitalist economy.

Note that in saying this I am certainly not claiming that we have come to the end of history, nor am I suggesting that capitalism will never be superseded at some point in the future. I do not undertake to prophesy. However, it is irrefutable that *existing* (or hitherto existing) socialism has lost the race against *existing* (or hitherto existing) capitalism. This is not a value judgment; it is an observable, statistically accountable fact: the main trend of history until now, in the world of Western civilization, has pointed in the direction of expansion of capitalism.

The painful and bitter series of actions during the creation of the socialist system formed a deviation from the main direction. Now the countries of the Central Eastern European region have turned around. After backing out of their dead end 15 years ago, they are following the main path again completely.

While this is a value-free statement of fact, the closely associated question of whether this is to be considered a *success* can be answered only by offering a value-based judgment. I will return to this later.

Higher productivity and increased growth rates did not begin immediately: the transition to the new economic system started with

Table 5.1   Growth rates in socialism and capitalism

Country	GDP per capita (1990 international dollars)		1990 (1950 = 100)	Average growth rates of GDP per capita (percent)			
	1950	1989		1950s	1960s	1970s	1980s
Czechoslovakia	3,501	8,768	250	3.9	2.9	2.1	1.2
Hungary	2,480	6,903	278	4.0	3.8	2.1	1.0
Poland	2,447	5,684	232	2.4	3.2	3.4	−0.4
USSR	2,841	7,098	250	3.4	3.6	2.2	0.9
Post-Socialist 4	*2,819*	*7,013*	*239*	*3.3*	*3.5*	*2.3*	*0.8*
Austria	3,706	16,369	442	6.3	4.2	3.9	2.0
Belgium	5,462	16,744	307	2.4	4.2	3.3	1.9
Denmark	6,943	18,261	263	2.9	3.8	2.0	1.8
Finland	4,253	16,946	398	3.3	4.4	3.3	3.2
France	5,271	17,730	336	3.7	4.6	3.0	1.7
Greece	1,915	10,086	527	5.0	6.6	4.4	1.3
Ireland	3,453	10,880	315	1.7	4.2	3.2	2.7
Italy	3,502	15,969	456	5.6	5.4	2.9	2.3
Netherlands	5,996	16,695	278	2.8	4.0	2.5	1.3
Portugal	2,086	10,372	497	3.1	6.0	4.5	3.0
Spain	2,189	11,582	529	3.5	7.1	4.2	2.5
Sweden	6,739	17,593	261	2.5	3.8	2.0	1.8
UK	6,939	16,414	237	1.7	2.5	2.2	2.2
EU–13	*4,688*	*15,519*	*337*	*3.2*	*4.3*	*2.9*	*2.1*

Notes: Data for Luxembourg are not available. Data for Germany were excluded, because they were available only for Germany in its 1991 (unified) borders. The 1949 figure was not available for Poland to calculate percentage growth in 1950; the 1950s average growth rate is for the 1951–9 period.
Source: OECD database accompanying Maddison (2003).

Table 5.2
Growth before and after 1989, and after transformational recession

Country	GDP/NMP index (1989 = 100)				Average annual growth rate (percent)	
	1980	1990	1995	2003	1980–1989	1995–2003
Czech Republic	85	99	94	106	1.8	1.5
Estonia	75	92	66	101	3.2	5.5
Hungary	86	97	86	116	1.7	3.8
Latvia	69	103	51	79	4.2	5.6
Lithuania	65	97	56	81	4.9	4.7
Poland	91	88	99	135	1.1	4.0
Slovakia	85	98	84	117	1.8	4.2
Slovenia	99	92	89	120	0.1	3.8
CEE–8	*86*	*94*	*91*	*121*	*1.7*	*3.6*
EU–15	..	*103*	*111*	*132*	..	*2.2*

Notes: Pre-1990 growth rates for CEE–8 are based on the net material product (NMP) used for growth accounting by the socialist countries. The 1980 figure for the Czech and Slovak Republics is for Czechoslovakia.
Sources: Based on UN Economic Commission for Europe (UNECE) (2001, n. 1, 254) and UNECE (1999, n.1, Table A1); updated from UNECE (2005, n.1, 117).

a serious slowdown. But by this time growth has speeded up. The growth rate in the past ten years, in six out of the eight countries has been significantly higher than in the decade before 1990 as *Table 5.2*, shows. During the period between 1995 and 2003, per capita GDP in the region where the eight new members are located, grew at a much higher rate than in other countries of the European Union, as did with labor productivity (GDP per employee) and per capita real consumption. This is shown in *Table 5.3*. The difference is especially impressive in labor productivity, which improved more than four times as fast in the new member-states as it did in the old ones.

Let us be careful with interpreting these figures. At this point in the analysis, the intention is to compare a *system* with another *system*, the *permanent* attributes of one system with the *permanent* attributes of the other. Applying a historical scale, only a very brief period of time has gone by. We do not know how much of the rapid growth can be traced to the new order's utilization of formerly hidden reserves not exploited by the previous inefficient system. The high rate of growth could be partially attributed to the fact that deep recessions are usually

Table 5.3 Average growth rates for the years 1995–2003

Country	Average real GDP per capita growth	Average labor productivity growth (percent)	Average consumption per capita growth
Czech Republic	2.2	2.6	3.0
Estonia	6.6	6.6	7.3
Hungary	4.1	3.2	4.5
Latvia	7.3	8.2	7.6
Lithuania	6.3	6.6	7.1
Poland	4.2	4.8	4.5
Slovakia	3.9	3.6	3.7
Slovenia	3.8	3.3	2.6
CEE–8	*4.0*	*4.2*	*4.3*
Austria	2.0	1.7	1.3
Belgium	1.9	1.3	1.7
Denmark	1.7	1.5	1.0
Finland	3.4	2.3	3.0
France	1.8	1.2	1.8
Germany	1.2	0.9	1.0
Greece	3.6	2.5	2.7
Ireland	6.0	3.6	4.2
Italy	1.3	0.3	1.7
Luxembourg	3.9	3.4	2.6
Netherlands	1.7	0.7	1.8
Portugal	1.8	0.2	2.1
Spain	2.8	−0.2	2.9
Sweden	2.4	2.0	2.1
UK	2.5	1.7	3.2
EU–15	*1.8*	*0.9*	*1.9*

Source: Economist Intelligence Unit: *Country Data*.

followed by rapid recoveries. These obvious, easily mobilized reserves will sooner or later be depleted. It would be misleading to draw final conclusions based on the numbers of a single decade. It will be a long time before the superiority of the new capitalist system can be proven unambiguously and conclusively. However, past experience suggests we can be optimistic about the growth potential of the new system.

The Main Direction of Political Transformation in Western Civilization

The main direction of transformation in Western civilization in the last few centuries has been felt not only in the economic, but also in the political sphere. Alongside almost unlimited monarchical power, also condoned by the churches, could be found limited precursors of democracy, among them the various self-governing organizations and forms of representation available to the urban middle classes, and certain church institutions. In some countries, laws curtailing the absolute power of the monarchy were enacted and the first elements of parliamentarianism—"enlightened" versions of monarchy—appeared. Later, Parliament obtained an ever-increasing range of rights, and the franchise was extended to a growing share of the public. Institutions of modern parliamentary democracy were gradually formed and strengthened. More and more countries have become democracies over the centuries.

Closely tied to the changes in the political structure has been the fact that an ever-increasing percentage of the population has been able to exercise basic human rights, freedom of speech, freedom of association, and the right to participate in the decision-making process. Discrimination based on criteria such as gender, race, and religious affiliation is being progressively eliminated.

A number of remarkable studies have described the "waves" of democratization that occurred in the second half of the twentieth century.[6] The third such wave swept through Southern Europe, Latin America, and Asia from the 1970s through the 1980s. The fourth was the one we have just witnessed, after the collapse of the Soviet and East European communist regimes.[7]

Of course, the specific path of history differs from country to country. Progress towards democracy may come to a standstill or be reversed. But even an earthshaking change like Hitler's rise to power, which led to the destruction of many millions of people and a cataclysm of immeasurable proportions, appears on a historical scale to have been a short-lived diversion from a main direction that eventually wins.

The present topic calls for scrutiny of the way the Communist party gained power. This is inextricably intertwined with the other "deviation" just discussed: how the Communists, in countries where they came to power, switched the economic system off the main track by forcing

---

[6] I would like to emphasize a few works from the rich literature on the subject: Haggard and Kaufman (2005); Huntington (1991); O'Donnell, Schmitter, and Whitehead (1988); and Przeworski (1991).

[7] See, for example, Offe (1996) and McFaul (2002).

their socialist program on society. That was made possible by their seizure of political power and imposition of totalitarian dictatorship.

During the last 15 years, the Central Eastern European region has been successful in backing out of the dead end of the political sphere and returning to the main direction. Although there have been many discussions about the strength of the prevailing democratic order and the extent to which it satisfies various requirements, it should suffice for the present analysis to apply the "minimalist" criteria of democracy. A "democratic minimum" is fulfilled if the government of a country comes to power by competing for the votes of citizens and can be removed from office through a civilized process,[8] in other words, if no palace putsch, military coup, assassination, or revolution is needed to replace the leaders of a country with new ones. Elections held on the basis of political competition, together with the guarantee of other civil rights, create the procedures and mechanisms for officials to be removed and leadership to be transferred to others. This makes sure that tyrannical rule is eliminated. It is true that beyond these minimum criteria, one might require a thriving, consolidated democracy to fulfill various additional criteria, but to those who have recently been freed from the clutches of tyranny, even the democratic minimum means a great deal. The research presented here employs the following test: the process of attaining power meets the democratic minimum if incumbent governments have been replaced at least twice since 1989 as a result of elections. The Central Eastern European region easily passes the numerical threshold set by the test: each of the eight countries has had at least three such elections, where the incumbent government's replacement through a civilized election process gave office to a newly and democratically elected government. As *Table 5.4* illustrates, 30 out of the 38 elections in which political parties contended have resulted in replacement of an incumbent governing political power, party, or coalition.

The two categories of historical changes discussed so far are asymmetrically interconnected. The appearance of a capitalist economic sys-

---

[8] Schumpeter ([1942] 1976) introduced this criterion, which put the procedure of attaining and forfeiting power in the foreground, into the realm of political philosophy. Following Schumpeter's interpretation, I highlighted in my study of post-socialist regime change (Kornai 1998) the replacement of a government as a result of parliamentary election results as a practicable test. Susan Rose-Ackerman in her book (2005) very aptly dubbed the procedural approach a "minimalist" interpretation of democracy. On the interpretation of democracy, see also Dahl (1971), and Schmitter and Karl (1991) [and Study 6 in this volume, pp. 132–7.]

Table 5.4 Electoral dismissals

Country	Elections 1989–2004	"Electoral dismissals"	Year(s) of dismissal(s)
Czech Republic	5	3	1990, 1992, 1998
Estonia	5	4	1990, 1995, 1999, 2003
Hungary	4	4	1990, 1994, 1998, 2002
Latvia	5	4	1990, 1995, 1998, 2002
Lithuania	5	4	1990, 1993, 1996, 2000
Poland	4	4	1991, 1993, 1997, 2001
Slovakia	5	4	1990, 1992, 1994, 1998
Slovenia	5	3	1990, 1993, 2004
CEE–8	*38*	*30*	

Notes: "Change of power" is not confined here to cases where a party or coalition in power hitherto has been replaced by a quite different party or coalition. The concept extends also to cases where (i) the government coalition changes to a significant extent after general elections, including (ii) where there is a change of leadership, and (iii) there is substantive change in certain priorities of government. For a full explanation, see Zdenek Kudrna's website: <*ies.fsv.cuni.cz/~kudrna/ Memo-Table4.pdf*>.
Source: Economist Intelligence Unit: *Country Reports*.

tem does not automatically guarantee the emergence of a democracy; there have been countries whose economic system is capitalist, but whose political structure does not fulfill the minimum requirements for a democracy. Indeed, a capitalist economic system can be compatible with partly, or even wholly dictatorial political regimes. But this independence does not hold in the other direction: democracy can only become a permanent form of political governance where the economy operates within a capitalist system. There is no democracy without capitalism.[9]

This leads to recognition of the following value-free historical fact: the new political structure of the Central Eastern European region fits into the main direction of historical progress. The question of whether this is laudable, and if so why, is returned to later.

---

[9] Several sharply conflicting views have developed over time about the connection between democracy and capitalism. The most convincing argument for me is that capitalism is a necessary, but not a sufficient condition for democracy. Of the classical writers on the topic, Hayek (1944) concurred, while Schumpeter ([1942] 1976) thought that democracy could evolve without capitalism. See also Rueschemeyer, Stephens, and Stephens (1992); and Usher (1981) on this relationship.

The idea that large-scale political and economic changes have certain main directions is acknowledged by some schools of history and other social sciences and denied by others. It is certainly neither a trivial nor an obvious thought. I distance myself from rigid and one-sided versions of this idea; I see no evidence that some kind of simple, linear, and at all times unidirectional movement takes place. I have tried to apply a carefully selected language when explicitly stating that in both the economic and the political spheres, there may be stagnation and backward movement, as well as permanent coexistence of various forms.[10] But these acknowledgements do not undercut one of the main ideas of this study: that it is possible to observe the main direction of the changes in the worlds of both economic and political institutions. The transformation that took place after the collapse of the Soviet and the Eastern European regimes has provided a new and important supplement to the debate about such main directions.

Six Characteristics

As a starting point for further analysis, let me summarize the six most important characteristics of the transformation that has taken place in the Central Eastern European region in the last 15 years.

1. and 2. The changes followed the *main directions* of development of Western civilization: in the economic sphere in the direction of the *capitalist economic system*, and in the political structure in the direction of *democracy*.

3. There has been a *complete* transformation, *parallel in all spheres*: in the economy, in the political structure, in the realm of political ideology, in the legal system, and in the stratification of society.

4. The transformation has been *non-violent*. Transformation has not been accompanied by bloody events, armed street fights, murders, or the sacrifice of human lives.

5. The process of transformation has taken place under *peaceful* circumstances. It was not preceded by war. The changes were not forced upon society as a result of foreign intervention.

---

[10] I want to reiterate that my ideas about the main directions are restricted to "Western civilization." I make no attempt to apply this concept mechanically to other civilizations. Such comparative analysis lies beyond the scope of this study.

6. The transformation has taken place at *incredible speed*, within a time frame of 10–15 years.

This has not been the first "great transformation" in world history, to borrow an expression from Karl Polányi.[11] He also emphasized the fact already known from study of world history that other "great transformations" have taken place at different times and in different regions of the world, sweeping transformations from one type of formation into another. Of the six characteristics just listed, three or four are discernible in other transformation processes as well. But the presence of all six characteristics together is unique in world history.

Allow me to present this conclusion in advance for now, before supporting it with historical comparisons.

Historical Comparisons

What follows is a comparison of five kinds of typical "great transformation" with what has happened in Central Eastern Europe. This obviously does not exhaust all possibilities for comparison; a number of interesting and important cases have been left out. (For example, the changes in Russia in the last 15 years, the transformation of the South European dictatorships into democracies, or a brand-new example: the changes in Iraq since the fall of the regime of Saddam Hussein.) Nonetheless, the five transformation cases scrutinized present some substantial lessons. It is not easy to follow the rhythm of these comparisons. To facilitate an understanding of this, *Table 5.5* presents a comparative overview of the logical structure.

A. First, let us compare the transformation currently being evaluated with the preceding movement in the opposite direction: destruction of the capitalist system and creation of a socialist system. For brevity's sake, this will be restricted to Soviet history. There is a similarity in characteristic no. 3: there too parallel changes transformed all spheres of society. The similarity is staggering in characteristic 6, the speed at which the changes took place. The Communist party grabbed power in 1917. The "great transformation" was completed by the end of 1932, when collectivization of agriculture basically eliminated private ownership of the means of production. Only 15 years

---

[11] This is the title of Polányi's best-known work, *The Great Transformation* ([1944] 1962).

Table 5.5 Comparison of characteristics

Characteristics	Central Eastern Europe	A. Transformation of the Soviet Union from capitalism into socialism	B. Hungary: Horthy restoration; Chile: Pinochet restoration	C. China: Transformation after Mao	D. West Germany: Transformation after WWII	E. The great historical transformation in Europe*
1. In the main direction of development of the economic system?	Yes	No	Yes	Yes	Yes	Yes
2. In the main direction of development of the political system?	Yes	No	No	No	Yes	Yes
3. Parallel in all spheres?	Yes	Yes	Yes	No	Yes	Yes (with time lags)
4. Without violence?	Yes	No	No	Yes	No	No
5. Without foreign military occupation?	Yes	Yes	Yes	Yes	No	No
6. Fast?	Yes	Yes	Yes	No	Yes	No (very long period)

*From the Middle Ages to Modernity, pre-capitalism to capitalism were required to put everything in place for the creation of what this book calls "classical socialism."[12]

The striking difference lies in characteristics 1, 2, and 4. At the end of World War I, Russia was about to embark on the road towards establishing a Western-type parliamentary democracy. Instead, the existing political authority was overthrown by a bloody revolution, the tsar and his family were executed, and the elite of the former regime were killed, exiled or sent to forced labor camps. The new political and social order was imposed on society with violence and terror. This is diametrically opposite to what occurred in the velvet revolution of 1989–90 and the non-violent nature of the current transformation.

The remainder of this discussion will be confined to transformations that share to some extent characteristic 1 with those taking place in Central Eastern Europe, in other words, where the changes in the economy point in the main direction of change in the economic sphere (or at least do not turn away from it).

B. Characteristic 4, the non-violent nature of the transformation, cannot be considered self-evident. It is worth illustrating this with two historical examples.

After World War I, communists under Béla Kun seized power in Hungary and proclaimed a Hungarian Soviet Republic. A few months later, Communist rule was ousted and capitalist order restored under the leadership of Admiral Miklós Horthy, who later became head of state. The Red Terror was replaced by the White Terror of the initial months. Lynching, hangings, and prison sentences were part and parcel of the transition, and it took several years before any sort of political consolidation was reached.

The second example is that of Chile. Here Allende and his government embarked on a path that presumably could have led to the formation of a socialist system. But before it developed fully, it was destroyed in 1973 by a coup headed by General Pinochet. The attempted restoration of the pre-Allende economic system was trademarked by a campaign of revenge, extra-judicial reprisals, political

---

[12] As for characteristic 5, the revolutionary transformation in the Soviet Union did not take place on the orders of foreign occupiers. It was dictated by the domestic political power structure. There was a different situation in Eastern Europe, where the will of the Soviet political leadership proved to be the final authority. Nobody could disobey their orders, due to the presence of Soviet military occupation forces.

murders, and torture. Democratic institutions could only re-emerge after much suffering and many years.

Let us compare these two historical episodes with what has just taken place in Central Eastern Europe. In the eight countries covered in this study, the politicians of the former regime were neither executed nor imprisoned, and there was no campaign of revenge against them. In a number of countries, the preparations for a new constitution included civilized discussions between the leaders of the former ruling party and the new opposition leaders readying themselves to take political power. The power shift took place without bloodshed or chaos at the highest levels of power. Whether the transformation occurred by violent means or non-violently seems at first glance a factual matter. Indeed it is, but how important the distinction is to people's judgment depends on their system of values. In line with the logic of my argument, an assessment will be offered in later sections.

C. Elimination of the socialist system continues to proceed in areas to the south and east of the eight countries under scrutiny. It would well fit into the logic of this analysis to take all the transformation processes one by one and make comparisons. Due to time constraints, however, I will compare the changes that have taken place in the Central Eastern European region with those of only one country: China. Of course, only the future will show how far the trend toward capitalist economic development in China will extend and how consistent it will be.

In terms of characteristic 1—and this has fundamental importance—the Chinese and Central Eastern European transformations are identical: both point in the main historical direction, toward the capitalist economic system.

The most important difference, however, comes in characteristic 2. In political structure, the development of the Central East European countries also points in the main direction of Western civilization: it has moved away from the previous system, towards democracy and respect for human rights. In China, the monopoly power of the Communist party has remained intact, resulting in repression and curtailment of human rights. While substantial changes continue in virtually every sphere of society, one cannot even begin to talk about the parallelism mentioned under characteristic 3.

Two things can be established about the fourth characteristic. On the one hand, the present transformation is "non-violent" in the sense that it is taking place without bloodshed, without armed battle. On the other hand, it would be far-fetched to call it a "velvet revolution."

Upon the death of the old tyrant Mao Zedong, the new leadership struck with an iron fist against those who had immediately surrounded him. When the demands of the students of Beijing exceeded the extent dictated by the rulers of the country, their protests were put down by military force. Those professing views displeasing to the party are put in jail.

With characteristic 5, there is no substantial difference: the changes in China, as in Central Eastern Europe, have not been forced by outside military intervention. Whatever change does take place has been carried out by internal forces.

However, the difference is very substantial in characteristic 6: the pace of institutional changes in China has been much slower than in Central Eastern Europe.

D. Let us consider the transformation of West Germany in the period after World War II, beginning with characteristics 1 and 2. The capitalist economic system had basically continued under the Nazis, but the political structure had deviated fatally from the main direction. With characteristic 3, there was no need for a complete transformation, only for a partial one. The most important differences are found in characteristics 4 and 5. This obviously could not be a transformation free of violence. First, the power of the Nazis had to be destroyed in a war that required grave sacrifices. That was followed by punishment of those guilty of war crimes and crimes against humanity. Then the Allied Powers kept the country under occupation for a long period. The creation of basic democratic institutions was imposed from the outside under the provisions of a peace treaty enforced by the Allied military presence. This became the starting point for reforms brought about by internal forces. With characteristic 6, the speed of democratization, measured on a historical scale, was very swift.

E. Having reached the end of the comparisons, it is time to return to the initial topic of our analysis: the centuries-long process that led to the original formation of the capitalist economic system and to democracy. In fact, several characteristics of these major transformations correspond to certain characteristics in the present (comparatively "small") transformation taking place in the Central Eastern

European region. By definition, characteristics 1 and 2 are the same, since the description of "main direction" has been distilled from the major historical transformations. With the totality of changes under characteristic 3, it is clear that the economic and political transformation has affected all spheres of social activity. But if these developments are considered in terms of a much shorter time frame than centuries, there is no longer the close parallelism observable in the Central Eastern European region in the last 10–15 years. In a sequence varying by country and with different time lags, events have accelerated either in the political sphere, or in the religious-intellectual-ideological realm, or in the economy. With characteristics 4 and 5, there are differences by country and period in how peaceful or devoid of violence the changes were, and when the changes were accelerated by bloody uprising, revolution, war and the conquest of foreign countries. Some historical schools maintain that the Modern Age began with the discovery (conquest) of America, while others date it to the outbreak of the French Revolution of 1789, which grew into a reign of terror.

The biggest difference can be discerned, of course, in characteristic 6, the speed of change. It took capitalism centuries to become the prevalent economic system of a whole country. Parliamentary democracy likewise resulted from processes that were centuries long. By contrast, both have now been completed with incredible speed in the Central Eastern European region.

From the perspective of large-scale historical comparisons, the transformation of the Central Eastern European region has indeed been extremely swift. But it is important to remember there were politicians and economic experts who urged even faster changes. Countries were encouraged to compete with each other. Odds were weighed as in a horse race: where would privatization be completed first? Would the Czechs, the Hungarians, or the Poles cross the finishing line at the end of the sixth or of the ninth year? The bizarre nature of such an approach to these events becomes apparent when they are analyzed in a historical perspective.

Some of the public also viewed the race approach with suspicion. In one international research project intended to measure the order of values of individuals, samples of citizens of a number of Central Eastern European countries were asked which they would prefer: radical reorganization of society through major revolutionary action, or gradual improvement of society through reforms. The latter was chosen by 75 percent of Czechs, 82 percent of Slovenes, and 67 percent of Lithuanians (Halman 2001, p. 170.)

Accelerating Factors in the Transformation Process

Comparative analysis of all six characteristics would deserve a separate study. Here I discuss only one—no. 6. Having seen that the gradual transformation of the past 10–15 years has been exceptionally speedy, it is time to ask what made that great speed possible.

1. As a first attempt, a simple answer can be offered: it is easier to do something for the second time than to create it in the first place. The well-known experiences of economic growth can be quoted. Rebuilding ruined economies has always been a faster process than constructing original ones.

But the "restoration" argument holds only in part.

Let us start with knowledge and experience. Even those who had gained some experience in the political or economic sphere in their youth, before the Communists came to power, were close to retirement age when the transformation began. Most of those who had been active in the pre-socialist era had passed away or retired. This type of knowledge is not genetically transmitted, and there were few families where accumulated economic, business or political knowledge of the pre-socialist period could be transmitted by parents to offspring. There was no such thing as "restoration" of old knowledge in the minds and thinking of individuals. It was a case of gaining new knowledge.

However, there are many exceptions. There were families during the socialist era who had preserved the old values and passed them on to younger generations. It is not unheard of for grandchildren in one way or another to carry on the trade of their grandparents. The socialist system had destroyed the political, economic, and social institutions of the previous era and they could not be instantaneously resurrected, but there were exceptions there as well.

Altogether, it can be stated that although the transformation was accelerated by the possibility at many points of returning to traditions, behavior patterns, and institutions developed earlier and utilizing them as starting points, such reversion was not the strongest accelerating force.

2. A significant proportion of individuals tend instinctively to take care of their own affairs and exhibit a spirit of enterprise. That spontaneous endeavor was curtailed in medieval society by a multitude of restrictions that were eliminated only gradually and slowly. The loosening and breaking down of such feudal restrictions and the expansion of private property and market coordination were intertwined processes. The constraints imposed by the socialist economic system were even more crippling than those of its predecessors; they virtually throttled any proclivity for initiative and entrepreneurship. The bureaucratic prohibitions set up by the centralized socialist economic administration were removed not slowly or gradually in the post-socialist period, they were broken down at breakneck speed. That meant the spirit of spontaneous enterprise, the unique driving force behind capitalism, burst upon the economic scene.

3. There was no strong resistance to the transformation. As capitalism and parliamentary democracy were developing, slowly and gradually, for the first time, there were various strata, groups and classes of society who fought against them. The new order won in a struggle against the beneficiaries of the *ancien régime*. After the victories of the new order, the adherents of the old order usually engaged in political, ideological, and in some cases, armed resistance against it.

This time it was different. Six years after Gorbachev started his reforms—by the time the Berlin Wall came down—the leaders of the Communist order in Central Eastern Europe had laid down their arms. There were no movements to incite people against the new order; its opponents did not resort to arms; there were no guerrilla fighters or terrorists. Most members of the former old guard had become disillusioned with their former ideals. The more resourceful ones changed sides and tried to become businessmen—many successfully—and even active players in the democratic political arena. Others wearily retired.

4. The most significant explanation for the speed of the transformation can be found in the effects of the outside world on the Central Eastern European countries. The "outside world" is used here in its widest possible sense, to refer to various outside influences and circumstances.

One of the effects has been the adoption of foreign examples. From the operational forms of corporate management and banking systems to political institutions, from media programs to advertising, from the organization of educational activities to the financing of the arts and sciences, there was hardly an area of social activity where foreign examples have not been followed.

There were numerous channels through which these examples found their way to the Central Eastern European population. People became acquainted with them on trips abroad, some made before 1990 and many more after the changes had begun. They read about them or watched them in movies. Teaching about foreign experience took place in schools, at universities, and at special seminars. Foreign consultants recommended their adoption.

I am not claiming that adaptation of foreign models is an easy matter. It is not enough to see how the British Parliament or a Zurich bank works and then expect everything to happen the same way in the Hungarian or Estonian Parliament, or a Czech or a Polish bank. It is easy enough to recognize the model, but it is much more troublesome and strenuous to learn how to use it, and adapt it to local conditions. If learning were not a difficult and ambiguous process, the bulk of the transformation would not have taken 15 years to complete, and there would be no need for further cumbersome work to apply the model more effectively.

Foreign investors also exerted an extraordinary influence. Not only did they bring in capital and technical know-how, they brought knowledge of how to run a company, and what kind of legal system and behavioral norms are required for a capitalist system to operate.

The eight countries being considered here joined important, Western-led international organizations, such as NATO, the OECD, and the WTO, and their relationships with the World Bank and the IMF became more active. The succession of admissions culminated in accession to the European Union. The process known as harmonization in Brussels parlance was not confined to the realm of legislation. Central Eastern Europe tried to assimilate Western examples in every respect. This accommodation was compelled and primarily driven by internal forces. However, there is no use denying that a certain level of external political pressure was also discernible. Characteristic 5 is relevant in that there was no foreign military occupation. No single foreign country, not even the great powers, "pushed" the small Central East European countries around. But "conditionality" did exist. The practice started with the Washington-based financial organizations and was gradually taken up by the European Union of tying the availability of funds for loans and grants, the expansion of existing relationships, and the guaranteeing of various additional rights, to satisfaction of certain preconditions. It is true, however, that these preconditions were generally formulated in such a way as to serve the long-term interests of the individual countries concerned. Still, many changes were forced upon them through external pressures, or at the very least, these pressures contributed to the speedier implementation of the changes.

The geographical proximity of the Western world must have contributed to the intensity of the external pressures. The quickest of the recent great transitions took place in the countries directly adjacent to developed European countries.

5. An important accelerating factor in the process was the availability of modern technology. This does not refer in this context to any special situation enjoyed by the Central Eastern European region. The pace of Central Eastern European transformation was faster in part because nowadays *everything* changes at a faster pace. Consider, for example, the speed of transportation and communication at the end of the Middle Ages and at the beginning of the Modern Age, and compare them with the possibilities available today. Computers, the Internet, e-mail, and mobile phones—to mention only four—exponentially accelerate the arrival of information for those desiring to emulate outside examples. This new technology also contributed to the accelerated pace of publication and dissemination of new regulations and norms.

Though there had been a great lag in the dispersion of high technology in the region before the transition, such development significantly accelerated. It is true that the spread of computers and use of the Internet are still relatively low,[13] but information certainly reaches decision-makers and opinion-makers swiftly, and the media is able to disseminate it rapidly to millions of people.

A First Assessment: Unparalleled Success

I am convinced that what has taken place in Central Eastern Europe in the last decade and a half is a success story unparalleled in history. I believe this even though I am fully aware of the grief and disap-

---

[13] TV and cell phones are exceptions in wide use.

pointment associated with it, an issue I address in the second half of the study. So to be a bit more precise, my assessment is as follows. Despite serious problems and anomalies, assessment of the situation from the perspective of great historical changes shows that what took place in this part of the world is a success story.

My conviction rests on a particular ordering of values. There may be disagreement from others, whose judgments rest on a different order of priority.

On my scale of values, I accord pride of place to democracy and human rights. Perhaps because, like many of my contemporaries in Central Eastern Europe, I have lived through various forms of tyranny, involving total deprivation of civil rights or humiliating curtailment of human rights, in which we were subjected to brutal discrimination applied according to various criteria. This is why I feel strong aversion to arguments that compare China's performance with that of the Central Eastern European region by placing biased and one-sided emphasis on China's much higher economic growth. The growth rate in the Central Eastern European region certainly is much lower than in China, although it is still respectable, and as I pointed out earlier, it is already faster than it was during the last decade of the previous regime. I am ready to resign myself to a lower rate of growth, rather than the leaps and bounds produced by the Chinese, so long as it is coupled with respect for democracy and human rights! I acknowledge there are those who do not see the world in this way and believe it may be worth foregoing or postponing democracy for an indefinite period in order to achieve more rapid economic growth.

At many times, the political institutions of democracy uncomfortably impede the concentration of the state's capacities on the promotion of growth, as well as on the forceful completion of reforms associated with greater convulsions. In my eyes, these drawbacks are far outweighed by the advantages of the greater rights and freedoms provided by democracy. For Central Eastern Europeans, the creation of democracy has been facilitated by integration with the European Union, which acts as a stabilizing force in the political sphere and in the economy.

I consider the transformation of the Central Eastern European region a success story because it has established a capitalist economic system within a historically brief timeframe, thereby restoring our nations to a course of development aligned with the main direction of history. It is not that I "love" capitalism. It is not a very likeable system. But I hold those of its characteristics dear that are indispensable to realizing the values I profess. In the long run, the economic advantages of capitalism will also become manifest in the Central Eastern European region: a sustainably higher growth rate of production, productivity, and consumption than the one experienced under the socialist system, technical innovation, an entrepreneurial spirit, and together with the above, an increasing level of prosperity for society as a whole. I also consider as primary values the economic growth and increase in the standard of living it brings (although not with the finality and one-sidedness of those willing to sacrifice democracy for it). Beyond the argument for the increase of material goods, there is another that has been mentioned earlier: the very existence of a capitalist system is an indispensable precondition for a functioning democracy. These are the benefits that according to my ordering of values overshadow the disadvantages of capitalism. I acknowledge that there are others who subscribe to a different system for weighing the advantages and disadvantages.

Finally, I consider the transformation of the Central Eastern European region a success story because it took place in a peaceful manner, devoid of violence. The formative impression behind my views on this must have been provided by my own life experience. I survived a world war, bloody persecutions, hard and soft dictatorships, vindictive campaigns, and the execution and incarceration of friends. It was enough! For me, the fact that there was no bloodshed this time, that no one was killed or imprisoned, was an exceptionally beneficial development. I admit there are those who view these changes differently. They believe that changes could have happened earlier had the former regime been overthrown sooner, even by force of arms. There are those who condemn the way the guilty have been left unpunished and find the dispensing of justice wanting.

The fact that external influences played a major role among the driving forces behind these changes does not change my favorable opinion. Foreign influences, such as knowledge, experience, culture, and capital, flowed into the Central Eastern European countries, enabling them to be better integrated into the European Union and into a globalized world. I am aware that some people feel offended by this, as they are concerned about the preservation of national traditions. They may also be disturbed by the fact that all this will undoubtedly place limits on the political sovereignty of individual states. I admit we are facing a difficult trade-off here.

I have tried openly and without circumlocution to disclose the ordering of values that underlies my own judgment. I do not do this for the sake of arguing for it. There is no place here for rational argumentation, something that we economists always attempt to engage in. There are meta-rational ideas, beliefs and desires concealed behind these valuations, and in this regard, there will inevitably be divergences of opinion between individuals professing different world views. Even if we should agree, from the perspective of the great events of world history, on what actually took place in the Central Eastern European region, we cannot count on arriving at a consensus in assessing the results.

From the Perspective of Everyday Life

Problems and Worries

Emotions of gain and loss, joy and pain mingle in the lives of everyone who participated or observed with empathy the transformation that has taken place in the Central Eastern European region. Far be it from me to engage in a cheap propaganda campaign for its success. We are not facing imaginary difficulties, nor are these problems encountered by only a small portion of the public. We are up against some very real and serious negative phenomena.

At the beginning of the new era, the real income of the majority of citizens living in the Central Eastern European region was significantly below the average for member-countries of the European Union, and a considerable proportion of them were at poverty level. Since that time—regardless of how much the world has changed around us—the real income of a significant proportion of the population has remained unchanged, and many among the impoverished have become mired at their earlier low standard of living. And there is a not negligible number of people whose standard of living has discernibly deteriorated. We cannot be certain that in every case, the degradation was attributable to the change in the political system, but it certainly took place during the period since 1990. These are individuals who see themselves as the clear victims of this period.

Table 5.6 Distribution of income: Gini coefficient

Country	Pre-transition 1987–9	Mid-transition 1996–7	Post-transition 2001–2	Percentage change from pre to post-transition
Czech Republic	19.8	23.9	23.4	18
Estonia	28.0	36.1	39.3	40
Hungary	22.5	25.4	26.7	19
Latvia	26.0	32.6	35.8	38
Lithuania	26.3	30.9	35.7	36
Poland	27.5	33.4	35.3	28
Slovakia	19.4	24.9	26.7	38
Slovenia	21.0	24.0	24.4	16
CEE–8	*23.8*	*28.9*	*30.9*	*29*
EU–15	*26.9*	*27.8*	*28.6*	*7*

Notes: The Gini coefficient is a measure of the degree of inequality in the distribution of income. It is equal to "0" in the case of total income equality (everyone receives the same income) and to "100" in the case of total inequality (one household receives all the income). In this table estimates are based on interpolated distributions from grouped data from various household budget surveys. Survey coverage may vary over time. Data refer to the distribution of individuals according to household per capita income. Five data points for the EU average are not available—Belgium (2), Spain (2), and Portugal (1).
Sources: CEE 8 data from various sources compiled for the UNICEF IRC (2004); EU 15 data: OECD (2005a) and World Bank (2005).

A dramatic restructuring has taken place in the distribution of income and consumption. Although critics of the socialist system rightfully complained that a system of material privileges indeed existed, the distribution of income and consumption generally lay within a fairly narrow range. The 10–15 years since have been long enough to effect a marked increase in the existing levels of inequality, as shown in *Tables 5.6* and *5.7*.[14] On the one side, a hitherto unknown level of conspicuous wealth has become readily apparent, while on the other, poverty that had been less obviously manifest has became deeply entrenched and much more visible. This is appalling to the sense of social justice of many individuals who have otherwise not been victims of the restructuring.

---

[14] Some Hungarian analyses show larger inequalities than those identified in *Table 5.6* (e.g. Tóth 2004).

Table 5.7 Consumption inequality

Country	Survey year	Share of income or consumption (percent)				Richest 10% to poorest 10%	Richest 20% to poorest 10%
		Poorest 10%	Poorest 20%	Richest 20%	Richest 10%		
Czech Republic	1996	4.3	10.3	35.9	22.4	5.2	3.5
Estonia	2000	1.9	6.1	44	28.5	14.9	7.2
Hungary	1999	2.6	7.7	37.5	22.8	8.9	4.9
Latvia	1998	2.9	7.6	40.3	25.9	8.9	5.3
Lithuania	2000	3.2	7.9	40	24.9	7.9	5.1
Poland	1999	2.9	7.3	42.5	27.4	9.3	5.8
Slovakia	1996	3.1	8.8	34.8	20.9	6.7	4.0
Slovenia	1998/99	3.6	9.1	35.7	21.4	5.9	3.9
CEE-8	1996-2000	3.1	8.1	39.5	24.9	8.2	5.0
EU-15	1994-2000	2.7	7.4	40.2	25.1	9.6	5.6

Source: UN 2004 database.

The serious problems just enumerated are connected to issues of employment. Open unemployment was unknown in the socialist economy; the employment rate was very high and every worker could feel secure at his or her work place. Indeed an inverse disequilibrium prevailed. The socialist economy created chronic shortages, including a chronic labor shortage—at least in the more developed and industrialized Central Eastern European countries. Whatever effect that had on efficiency, the workers enjoyed job security. That has come to an end. The employment rate has significantly declined. (See *Table 5.8*.) The employment rate differs from country to country, but it is lower than the average rate of the EU-15 region. Unemployment descended suddenly on society as a virtual trauma, as *Table 5.9* shows.

Job security disappeared. This happened at a time when life itself had become less secure on countless fronts. In socialist societies, those who avoided risky political activity had been surrounded by relatively solid and predictable conditions of livelihood. Now all of a sudden, everything was in motion and nothing known in advance. Previously, a company had been something that would exist forever. Now they were being formed or going broke from one day to the next. Previously, consumer prices had been fixed for long periods of time. Now they were in a constant state of flux. The average citizen could not

Table 5.8 Total employment (1989 = 100)

Country	1990	1991	1992	1993	1996	1999	2002	2003
Czech Republic	99.1	93.6	91.2	89.8	93.5	88.2	88.0	87.4
Estonia	98.6	96.3	90.9	83.5	74.0	69.2	70.0	71.0
Hungary	96.7	86.7	78.1	73.1	69.8	72.9	74.1	75.1
Latvia	100.1	99.3	92.1	85.7	72.4	73.9	75.4	76.8
Lithuania	97.3	99.6	97.4	93.4	87.0	85.0	82.0	83.9
Poland	95.8	90.1	86.4	84.3	88.3	90.4	85.8	85.2
Slovakia	98.2	85.9	86.9	84.6	85.5	82.3	82.1	83.6
Slovenia	96.1	88.6	83.7	81.3	78.7	80.1	82.8	82.1
CEE–8	*96.9*	*90.9*	*87.0*	*84.2*	*85.5*	*85.8*	*83.5*	*83.4*
EU–15	*101.8*	*102.3*	*101.1*	*99.6*	*100.7*	*105.2*	*109.2*	*109.5*

Source: UNECE (2005, n. 1, 125).

Table 5.9 Unemployment rates (Percentage of labor force)

Country	1990	1992	1993	1996	1999	2002	2003
Czech Republic	0.7	2.6	3.5	3.5	9.4	9.8	10.3
Estonia	..	1.6	5.0	5.6	6.7	6.8	6.1
Hungary	1.7	12.3	12.1	10.5	9.6	8.0	8.4
Latvia	..	2.3	5.8	7.2	9.1	8.5	8.6
Lithuania	..	3.5	3.4	6.2	10.0	10.9	9.8
Poland	6.5	14.3	16.4	13.2	13.1	20.0	20.0
Slovakia	1.6	10.4	14.4	12.8	19.2	17.4	15.6
Slovenia	..	13.3	15.5	14.4	13.0	11.3	11.0
CEE–8	*4.4*	*10.6*	*12.4*	*10.6*	*12.1*	*15.4*	*15.3*
EU–15	*7.3*	*8.7*	*10.0*	*10.2*	*8.7*	*7.7*	*8.1*

Note: Figures for Estonia until 1999 include only job seekers.
Sources: Registered unemployment rates for the CEE 8 from the UNECE (2004, n. 2, 85), standardized unemployment rates for the EU–15 from UNECE (2005, n. 1, 126).

make sense of interest rates or even rates of exchange. Although it had been incredibly difficult to obtain housing, once possessed, as a tenant or sub-tenant, it was virtually impossible to lose it again through eviction. Now you could be evicted for not paying the rent. Furthermore, public security deteriorated as the police state was dismantled *(Table 5.10)*. Everything that had been stiffened to a point of rigidity by overbearing authority and bureaucracy became malleable, risky and insecure under the influence of market forces, competition, and civil rights that guaranteed more freedom of movement.

Table 5.10 Crime rates (1989 = 100)

Country	1990	1994	1998	2002
Czech Republic	180	309	355	313
Estonia	124	200	270	321
Hungary	153	175	272	193
Latvia	117	146	137	190
Lithuania	118	189	260	247
Poland	161	163	192	253
Slovakia	150	293	198	227
Slovenia	96	110	139	193
CEE–8	*156*	*194*	*228*	*249*

Note: Crime data cover reported and registered crime only. Crime rates are subject to varying national legislation.
Source: UNICEF IRC (2004), database.

Corruption had existed under the old regime, mostly in areas of mutual favors could be bestowed through political or personal contacts. Although there were even incidents of bribery, these were uncommon and generally took place at lower levels of the shortage economy, as a way of "greasing the wheels." The majority of corrupt activities remained unseen and behind the scenes. Now corruption became ubiquitous in a myriad of transactions in the political, economic, and cultural sphere, in private transactions large and small, and at the highest and lowest levels of the governmental and social hierarchy. Many corruption cases have become public knowledge. Everyone is angry, and often unwillingly, many people are soiled by corruption. It is almost impossible to avoid becoming involved where one or another of the parties engages in shady transactions, even if the client, the citizen, the seller or the buyer, would not otherwise have attempted a bribe or been involved in a phony tax-evasion scheme.

People are also upset about the disorders in the political arena. Many judge that the multi-party system has failed to create the preconditions for sober political rivalry, and instead brought unbridled struggles for power, lies, empty promises, and continual opposition ranting and raving against whoever happens to be in power. Much of the population does not place sufficient trust in Parliament. In this respect, the difference between the 15 old and the 8 new EU members is enormous, as *Table 5.11* shows. Politicians are suspected of being involved in corruption, sometimes because they have indeed violated the law, or at the least the unwritten code of ethics, and sometimes because they have been slandered by political rivals.

Just some of the most serious issues have been mentioned here. I could continue, but I think this much suffices to demonstrate that we are not talking here about trifling inconveniences, but about genuinely serious, even overwhelming problems.

Table 5.11 Confidence in Parliament and other institutions

Country	Parliament	Civil Service	Education system
	(Percentage of population whose confidence is enjoyed)		
Czech Republic	12.2	21.8	54.6
Estonia	27.0	40.4	73.9
Hungary	34.0	49.6	64.3
Latvia	27.5	49.2	73.7
Lithuania	10.6	20.6	66.6
Poland	32.8	32.6	81.2
Slovakia	42.8	38.7	76.3
Slovenia	25.3	25.3	80.3
CEE–8	*29.3*	*33.8*	*73.7*
Austria	40.7	42.4	86.2
Belgium	39.1	46.1	77.9
Denmark	48.6	54.9	75.0
Finland	43.7	40.9	88.8
France	40.6	45.9	68.4
Germany	35.7	38.7	72.6
Greece	29.0	20.2	37.0
Ireland	31.1	59.3	86.4
Italy	34.1	33.2	53.2
Luxembourg	62.7	59.5	67.8
Netherlands	55.3	37.5	73.1
Portugal	49.2	53.6	59.8
Spain	46.4	40.5	67.6
Sweden	51.1	48.8	67.8
UK	35.5	45.9	66.3
EU–15	*39.1*	*41.1*	*66.8*

Note: Respondents were asked, "Tell me, for each item listed, how much confidence you have in them; is it a great deal, quite a lot, not very much, or none at all?" Those answering "a great deal" or "quite a lot" were counted as having confidence.
Source: Halman (2001, 187, 192).

Table 5.12 Life satisfaction over time

Country	1990–3	1995–7	1999–2002
	(Average on a scale of 1 to 10)		
Czech Republic	6.37	..	7.06
Estonia	6.00	5.00	5.93
Hungary	6.03	..	5.80
Latvia	5.70	4.90	5.27
Lithuania	6.01	4.99	5.20
Poland	6.64	6.42	6.20
Slovakia	6.15	..	6.03
Slovenia	6.29	6.46	7.23
CEE–8	*6.40*	*6.20*	*6.20*
Austria	6.51	..	8.03
Belgium	7.60	7.93	7.43
Denmark	8.16	..	8.24
Finland	7.68	7.78	7.87
France	6.78	..	7.01
Germany	7.22	7.22	7.42
Greece	..	..	6.67
Ireland	7.88	..	8.20
Italy	7.30	..	7.17
Luxembourg	..	..	7.81
Netherlands	7.77	..	7.85
Portugal	7.07	..	7.04
Spain	7.15	6.61	7.03
Sweden	7.97	7.77	7.64
UK	7.49	7.46	7.40
EU–15	*7.26*	*7.24*	*7.30*

Notes: Respondents were asked to mark their answer on a scale from 1 (most dissatisfied) to 10 (most satisfied): "All things considered how satisfied are you with your life as a whole these days." The typical size of sample was about 1000 respondents per country.

Sources: *World Values Survey* and *European Values Survey*; Sanfey and Teksoz (2005) use these data to study life satisfaction in post-socialist countries. The table reporting the summary data for the EU–8 countries is on p. 17 of their paper. I am grateful to Peter Sanfey and Utku Teksoz (EBRD), who provided the complementary data for the EU–15 countries and the data for region averages in direct communication.

Social Disposition

There have been numerous surveys of the prevailing mood and social disposition of the public in the Central Eastern European countries.

Table 5.13 Life-time satisfaction: Distribution of responses

Country	% not at all satisfied	% not very satisfied	fairly satisfied	% very satisfied
		(Percentage of answers)		
Czech Republic	5	26	57	10
Estonia	11	35	47	6
Hungary	11	34	45	9
Latvia	8	35	49	6
Lithuania	10	32	51	5
Poland	9	28	50	11
Slovakia	13	33	48	6
Slovenia	2	12	65	20
CEE–8	9	29	50	10
EU–15	4	17	60	19

Note: The respondents were asked the following question: "On the whole, how are you satisfied with your life in general? Would you say you are...?"
Source: Eurobarometer (2003).

They point to the fact that opinions are divided. Many more respondents in the older EU member-states answered "yes" to the apparently simple question, "Are you satisfied with your life?" than did so in the eight new member-states considered here (*Table 5.12*). The proportion of negative answers differs from country to country, as seen in *Table 5.13*. It appears as an approximate average that every third person in the region is somewhat or very dissatisfied with life.[15]

Cognitive Problems

The relative intensity or bitterness of people's reactions to troubles is not merely a function of the real difficulties associated with the problem itself. When one experiences hardship or observes the troubled with empathy, a great deal depends on how one perceives the problem at hand and how one deals with it. Let us attempt to survey some of the most important *cognitive problems* associated with our topic.

---

[15] The data in *Tables 5.12* and *5.13* are from different sources, based on different surveys. It is worth noting that despite the two kinds of approach, the characteristic differences between the regions are quite close to each other.

1. Before something happens, certain hopes and expectations are sustained. After something happens, there is often disappointment.[16] As disillusionment over socialism began to take hold, expectations became more pronounced. The hope emerged that the change of the system would resolve all problems quickly, for everyone.

Rightful hopes were intermingled with misconceptions and illusions. Expressions like "the West," "the market," "competition," and "democracy" elicited mythical images of unrelieved light. There were few sober warnings to be heard, least of all from credible individuals. (People were not prepared to listen to criticism of capitalism from adherents of the old regime).

The initial great hopes were thoroughly dampened by the deep transformational recession of the 1990s. People barely had time to recover from that before new unrealistic expectations took shape, this time connected with EU membership, kindled by various phrases referring to "convergence" and ostensible promises of manifold EU assistance. Many looked forward to the manifest and imminent benefits of accession with naive impatience.

The problems are great, but for many people they are magnified further by *disillusionment*.

2. It is a well-known phenomenon in social psychology that the way somebody feels about something depends not only on the real circumstances, but on *whom the individual compares himself to*. During the period when the socialist system was loosening up, people living in the Western periphery of the Soviet empire comforted themselves by noting that they were still better off than those living in the Soviet Union. Especially in a place like Hungary, my home country, where experiments with market-economic reforms had been going on for some time, this self-encouragement even sounded credible. But as the borders of all countries in the Central Eastern European region opened, and still more as they became member-states of the European Union, the "reference

---

[16] Hirschman (1982) pointed out that disappointment was part of the human condition. He refers to Kant, who stated, "Even if you were to grant man everything he wishes, all the same, at that very moment he will feel that that *everything* is not *everything*." (See Karamzin [1789–1990] 2003, p. 40). A state of ubiquitous insatiability and disillusionment is experienced especially by the denizens of Western civilization. In our case, this general feeling was exacerbated by frustration over the unrealized special expectations that followed the transition from socialism.

Table 5.14 Attitudes to regime: Old, new, and future

Country	Old regime	Current	In 5 years
		(Percentage of positive answers)	
Czech Republic	32	69	82
Estonia	55	75	79
Hungary	58	64	81
Latvia	50	51	71
Lithuania	59	70	84
Poland	51	51	67
Slovakia	51	51	65
Slovenia	68	69	74
CEE–8	*50*	*57*	*72*

Note: The respondents were asked the following question: "Here is a scale for ranking how our system of government works. The top, plus 100, is the best; the bottom, minus 100, the worst. Where on this scale would you put the former communist regime/our current system of governing with free elections and many parties/our system of governing five years in the future?"
Source: Rose (2005, p. 17).

points" generally shifted. People started to compare their circumstances with those in Germany, France, or Scandinavia. Of course, the higher the standards of comparison, the greater the dissatisfaction with the place the person happens to live. This impatience is understandable: now we are members of the European Union, when are we going to catch up with our fellow member-states? But it also leads to hopeless aspirations. Those who cling to the West as their frame of reference are likely to remain permanently bitter, impatient and disillusioned.

3. People easily forget; collective and individual memories are highly unreliable. Decades ago, there were floods of complaints from individuals because certain consumer items were unavailable and they had to wait many years for a car or an apartment or a telephone line. Nowadays it seems that I, once the author of a book entitled *Economics of Shortage* (1980), will be the last person left in Eastern Europe who still remembers the shortage economy and feels genuine delight that it is over. Chronic shortages have been replaced by abundant supplies. Nowadays, people grumble that we are awash among an incredible number of products, that prices are prohibitively high, and that people are tormented by the "consumer society."

People's poor memories mean that fundamentally important achievements and material or non-material benefits (such as freedom of speech, association, and movement, the free competition of ideas, the right to protest, and so on) are being disparaged, even though they are clearly discernible in people's everyday lives. Instead, current problems are being accorded greater relative weight.

Respondents to a 2004 survey were asked to indicate on a scale ranging from -100 to 100 their evaluation of the current government, as compared with the regime before the change in the political system. The results appear in *Table 5.14* and interpretation of them in Rose (2005). Although the present system received higher scores in all countries, it is remarkable that the ratings for the regime under the previous system were not far behind. Grotesquely, this all leads to feelings of nostalgia. There were people who did not participate in active resistance against the communist regime, but at least grumbled and hoped for change. Now quite a few of them find themselves thinking the old regime was not that bad after all.[17]

4. Finally, I would like to mention the flaws of causal analysis emerging as a result of distorted thinking in the last phase of processing experiences.

Causal Analysis

There are many causes behind the problems and difficulties suffered by the people of Central Eastern Europe. I will only emphasize a few of them.

One is that the region's level of development lags behind the West. This is not a new phenomenon; it is the result of centuries-long processes. Things have been this way for centuries. As *Table 5.15* shows, this relative gap widened further in the socialist period. There is a good chance that the relative backlog will gradually diminish, but it is highly unlikely that anything can occur in the social, economic, and political field to fill the gap (which is more like an abyss!) in the immediate future, as

---

[17] [It is worth stressing that one of the most favorable assessments of the pre-1990 system is made in Hungary, according to *Table 5.14*. An excellent account appears in Vásárhelyi (2005) of how Hungarian public opinion divides in its judgment of the Kádár regime and the change of system. The figures Vásárhelyi quotes again show how widespread is the nostalgia for the Kádár period and disillusionment over the change.]

Table 5.16 makes clear. Many of the negative phenomena, as well as the poverty, the lag in technological development, and the scarcity of available resources for health care, education, and scientific research, can be explained primarily (but not exclusively) by the fact that the region is at a medium level of development, well behind the front runners.

Part of the trouble has been the fact of being in transition. The structure of production had to be reorganized: old production lines had ceased to exist, but they were not replaced by new ones immediately. A new vacuum, new loopholes, and an absence of regulation occurred during the institutional transformation. While the old guard was removed in many places, the new management was still inexpe-

Table 5.15 A historical comparison with Austria

Country	1870	1913	1937	1950	1980	1989	2000
	(Austria's GDP per capita = 100)						
Czechoslovakia	62	60	91	94	58	54	43
Hungary	59	61	81	67	46	42	36
Poland	51	50	61	66	42	35	36

Note: Czechoslovakia in 2000 is a weighted average of the Czech Republic and Slovakia.
Source: Calculated from the OECD database accompanying Maddison (2003).

Table 5.16 Convergence times to Western Europe

Country	To 100% of EU–14 level	To 80% of EU–14 level
	(Catch-up period in years)	
Czech Republic	38	21
Estonia	60	45
Hungary	46	31
Latvia	74	59
Lithuania	68	52
Poland	72	55
Slovakia	48	33
Slovenia	30	9
CEE–8	*55*	*38*

Note: EU–14 means all old members, excluding Luxembourg. The results are based on the assumption of a real per capita GDP growth rate of 1.74 percent in the EU–14.
Source: Wagner and Hlouskova (2005, 367).

rienced. The fact that these difficulties are of a transitional nature does not reassure everyone sufficiently, as it stretches people's patience to wait for them to pass.

Other problems cannot be eliminated, because they emanate from the very nature of the new system. The capitalist economy, competition, market is not the ideal dreamworld. Capitalism, like every system, has certain inborn, system-specific drawbacks. As long as capitalism is what it is, there will be unemployment, great income inequality, losers in the competition, excessive advertising, and so on. Wise, forward-looking and consistent governmental policies can mitigate some of these innate faults, but they cannot completely eliminate them, and there remains the permanent threat of their return. Serious, level-headed believers in the capitalist system accept these problems because they find the overall package more palatable than the socialist system, despite its shortcomings.

The same can be said of democracy. Great multitudes of Central Eastern Europeans are becoming as disenchanted with democracy as disillusioned lovers. They are irritated by the often barren verbal tirades in Parliament, by the mutual accusations of the various political parties, by the lying promises, and by the scandalous affairs being swept under the carpet. Yet these are anomalies associated with democracy! They are not restricted to relative newcomers; similar occurrences can often be seen in great democracies with a long history. The importance of the truth reflected in Churchill's words will not be diminished, although they have been quoted millions of times. Even given all its faults, democracy is still a better system than any form of tyranny, regardless of how wise, enlightened, or clean-handed a dictator might be. Unfortunately, in the Central Eastern European countries a far from negligible proportion of the population does not think that way. *Table 5.17* draws attention to the disturbing phenomena.

Wrong decisions made by politicians—governments, the ruling party or the opposition, or the leadership of various advocacy groups—may create troubles, or exacerbate pre-existing difficulties brought on by extraneous circumstances. Consider the following example. It can be stated with certainty that capitalism gives birth to inequality. But tax policies favoring the rich while afflicting the impoverished, or poorly distributed state subsidies, can make matters even worse.

I have identified five different causes for the current problems: medium level of development, problems brought on by the transition,

Table 5.17 Endorsement of undemocratic alternatives

Country	Communist	Army	Dictator
	(Percentage regarding as better)		
Czech Republic	18	1	13
Estonia	8	2	40
Hungary	17	2	17
Latvia	7	4	38
Lithuania	14	5	40
Poland	23	6	33
Slovakia	30	3	25
Slovenia	23	6	27
CEE–8	*21*	*4*	*29*

Note: Respondents were asked the following: "Our present system of government is not the only one that this country had. Some people say that we would be better off if the country was governed differently. What do you think? We should return to Communist rule. The army should govern the country. Best to have a strong leader who can quickly decide everything."
Source: Rose (2002, p. 10).

the system-specific problems of capitalism and of democracy, and wrong decisions made by politicians. Of course there are others. One reason for the existence of a feeling of general malaise in society is confusion of these various causes in people's minds. In cases of multicausal phenomena, objective, clear identification and separation of various causes poses a difficult task, even for professional analysts. Small wonder that errors creep into the explanation of causes in the minds of people not specialized in the subject.

Value Judgments Again

I have tried to refrain from making false generalizations. Let me reiterate, as I emphasized earlier, that public opinion is divided: attitudes range from satisfaction with minor reservations, through grumbling and complaining, all the way to angry dissatisfaction. Allow me to make a few comments on the mood of those whose judgments tends towards the negative.

Those who make such judgments often employ an unfortunate mixture of half-true and half-erroneous establishment of the facts, half-substantiated and half-mistaken causal analysis, and an order of values that places the values of everyday life to the fore. Those who judge from this angle are not thinking in a historical perspective of centuries. They do not care what results the capitalist economic system and the democratic political order will produce in the distant future. They are experiencing the problems *today*, they are suffering from them now, or they are hurt by seeing others suffering now—and for that reason, their experience of the change that occurred in the system is as a failure, rather than a success.

No one has the right to disregard the negative judgments of disappointed individuals. No one has the right to accuse them of shortsightedness, or of turning a blind eye toward the comprehension of great historical interrelationships. We only have one life.[18] Someone of 50 or 60, say, and poor, perhaps also unemployed, will not be compensated by the promise of greater prosperity for subsequent generations, for he or she will not have a chance to enjoy it. It is hard even to bid the younger generation to have patience, for not even a lost moment today can be truly compensated for later by a better one.

Should I therefore retract the statement made in the first half of the study, that the great transformation of the Central Eastern European region can be characterized fundamentally as an unparalleled success? No, I do not want to retract it. I do not believe it to be possible, or for that matter permissible, to compile some kind of balance sheet on which to base a summary, comprehensive value judgment. That approach would imply there are successes (with a positive sign), and there are failures (with a negative sign), and if the balance is positive, the outcome should be declared a success, while if it is negative, it must be looked upon as a failure. I cannot accept that simple balance-sheet approach of just totting up.

I keep two accounts, not one, and do not merge them. On one account, I gladly acknowledge great success on a level of world history: the system created is superior to the old and has arisen without bloodshed, at incredible speed. On the other account, I have the list of good and bad experiences in everyday life: much joy and much pain. I consider it sensible and defensible to say that the events in this region can be considered simultaneously as a success in terms of

---

[18] The vicissitudes in people's lives and the way careers were broken by history are presented in a dramatic way in a new book by Ágnes Losonczi, eloquently entitled *Sorsba fordult történelem* (History as destiny—Losonczi 2005).

global historical significance and at the same time in many important aspects a process associated with trouble and suffering because it is a cause of pain, bitterness and disappointment to so many people.

The Tasks of the Economists' Profession

I have no intention of blaming the man in the street for not having processed his experiences flawlessly or perhaps for reaching mistaken conclusions about these problems. But I would not grant the same dispensation to us, who do research in the field of economics. I am not addressing this only to those who happen to live in Central Eastern Europe, but to all concerned with this region or similar issues, wherever they live.

Perhaps we have gone too far in accepting the famous comment of Keynes: "In the long run, we are all dead." The type of real long-term analysis I attempted in the first half of the study is quite rare. Nowadays many PhD programs do not require economists to study any history. One reason for the overly negative judgment of the current great transformation that is prevalent among the Central East European public is that social scientists have neglected to analyze and evaluate their results within the requisite historical framework.

The various social sciences are divorced not only from historical studies, but from each other. While I was preparing for this study, I encountered again the unfortunate fact that the political science literature on the transformation from dictatorship to democracy makes almost no reference to studies by economists, while economists virtually ignore the work of political scientists. Yet it is impossible to understand or evaluate the great transformations without taking an interdisciplinary approach.[19]

Mainstream economics relinquishes the task of profound criticism of the capitalist economy to those professing radical views. Even when it accepts that there may be problems, it lulls itself into believing these can be reassuringly resolved by appropriate measures. It denies that the system may have inborn, insurmountable genetic defects.

Careful, conscientious separation of the establishment of facts and evaluation of them is quite rare in our profession. It is not customary to point out frankly the order of values concealed behind the decla-

---

[19] [The problem of the interdisciplinary approach and where it stands is also considered in Study 8 of this volume, pp. 205–7.]

ration an economist makes. We consider it self-evident that we all share implicit values accepted axiomatically by our trade: efficiency, productivity, competitiveness, growth, perhaps the principle of fair distribution of income. Very few pay heed to any values beyond those.

There are academic economists happy to address a wider audience or reading public. Even those who do not aspire to do so, exert indirect influence. The leading politicians, statesmen, business people, journalists, and analysts who shape public opinion pay heed to them. Not only can the great transformations be accomplished more successful by making correct economic policy recommendations, our profession can also contribute to better-informed, better-balanced processing of experiences and to helping people to make the right evaluation of changes.

The great transformation in Central Eastern Europe is over. More than once, I have heard colleagues comment ironically, "With that, so much for your weird science of 'transitology'." I do not believe so.[20] How is the transformation of China and Vietnam going to continue? What will happen in Cuba? Nor is it permissible to confine one's attention to countries where there is still a Communist party in power. How will the "great transformation" proceed in Iraq, under foreign military occupation? How will Iran be transformed? What transformation will take place in other Muslim countries?

Each transformation is different. Nevertheless, there are elements common to them all. And the unique properties of each country can be understood only by comparing it with those of other countries. So "transitology" is far from over. Work undertaken with a desirably thorough approach has not even begun. I hope this study will act as a spur to conscientious study of the accumulated body of knowledge on this subject.

---

[20] [Study 7 of this volume deals with the question of what lessons can be drawn from the East European post-socialist transformation for countries in which such a transformation has yet to occur.]

6
What Does "Change of System" Mean?*

Introduction

The inspiration to write this study came from some of the speeches held at demonstrations in Kossuth tér, in front of the Hungarian Parliament in Budapest, in the autumn of 2006. According to one speaker, the aim was to be "a new change of system, a fourth republic." Similar passionate, angry demands were made in other speeches as well.[1]

---

* [I would like to express thanks to my colleague Noémi Péter, who helped me to review and process the theoretical literature on systems and system changes, and the political statements being heard nowadays. I thank Zdenek Kudrna and Eszter Nagy for their cooperation in the research on which the study is based. I am also grateful to Péter Gedeon, Gábor Halmai, László Kontler, Imre Kovách, György Kövér, Timur Kuran, Aladár Madarász, and Ákos Róna-Tas for their advice.
    The subject of this study—clarification of the concepts of capitalism, socialism, democracy, and change of system—has concerned me for a long time. As mentioned in the Preface, I first expressed my thoughts on this ten years ago in my article (Kornai, 1998). The title of the article I then published ("What change of system does and does not mean") underlines that it was an intellectual parent of the similarly titled study that appears here. The experience of the next decade and research done in it have allowed me to present here my matured thoughts in a more substantial form. The article of ten years ago has not been included in this volume to avoid overlaps and repetition.]

[1] The source of the sentence: "158 éve nem volt ilyen árulás"/"There has not been such treachery in 158 years," *Magyar Nemzet Online*, October 7, 2006. Some other quotations: "Some of the speakers in Kossuth tér want a new constitution based on the doctrine of the Holy Crown, a constitutional national assembly, a new change of system." (Ibid., September 21, 2006.) "The crowning of the anniversary and the real freedom and change of system will be the constitutional national assembly." ("Kitartanak a Kossuth téri tüntetők"/"The Kossuth tér demonstrators stick it out," *Figyelő*, October 16, 2006.) "They are already calling for a change of system, for according to the speakers, nobody ever consulted the people's will about what form of state they wished to live under in Hungary." ("Rendszerváltást követeltek a Kossuth téren"/"Change of system called for in Kossuth tér," *Magyar Nemzet Online*, October 5, 2006.) "The two speakers emphasized that a new constitution, a new change of system, and a new penal code are required." ("Új alkotmány, új rendszerváltás kell"/"New constitution, new change of system needed," *Hírszerző* internet newspaper, November 14, 2006.)

These words cannot be dismissed offhand, for an important problem is involved. What does the expression "change of system" mean? Has that change occurred, or has it perhaps not even started yet? This study sets out to answer these questions, in a calm and objective way.

The intention is not to convince the demonstrators in Kossuth tér or their spiritual brother-in-arms. There is a lot of disagreement among researchers in the social sciences and among a broader sphere of intellectuals interested in political affairs. One reason for this is confusion, misunderstandings and lack of clarification of concepts. The intention is to contribute to setting the conceptual apparatus in order.

Readers should be warned not to expect from this study a causal analysis of the fall 2006 demonstrations and disturbances, or political advice on government tasks in the months to come. The intention is to preserve a distance from day-to-day events in rethinking some fundamental problems of the post-socialist transformation.

Positive Versus Normative Approach

Two approaches can be taken.

One is a *positive approach*. What observed and experienced social formations existing in history can be called a "system"? What observed and experienced changes occurring in history can be called a "change of system"?

The other is a *normative approach*. What changes are endorsed or condemned by those who take a position on this question? What changes delight or appall them?

Mention will be made of the normative judgments of others, but I will also present here my own position. There is much debate about whether this distinction can be made.[2] The positive approach is said

---

[2] Unfortunately a further conceptual misunderstanding can be expected, notably from those unaccustomed to the positive/normative pair of opposites in the philosophy of science. It is quite frequent for a favorable judgment to be described as a "positive" opinion, and an unfavorable one as a "negative" opinion. Any crusade against this other meaning of "positive," in the interests of clarification, seems doomed to failure. The author's only endeavor here is to confine his use of the word "positive" to meaning the opposite of "normative," while preferring such synonyms as "favorable" and "unfavorable" for value judgments. I recommend others, at least professional analysts, researchers, and advisers, to do likewise, although I do not hope that many people are like to follow the recommendation.

to be illusory because the researcher's choice of topic, the system of concepts he or she employs, and the emphases and omissions in that, are all based on value judgments. Let it suffice in this case to undertake to make the distinction as far as possible. How far it is possible to remain "value-free" in a positive approach is not the main issue here. The main issue is that the two approaches involve answering radically different questions.

A positive approach leads eventually to a positive statement—a conjecture, a hypothesis. The question to ask then is whether the statement is *true*. Can it be supported or confirmed? Is it in any case a statement that can be refuted, or can the criterion of true or untrue not be broached at all?

These questions cannot be put with a normative approach, which leads to a value judgment: do I consider that which I am judging to be *good*? The statement is value-dependent. It may rest on a conscious choice of values, or just on senses of prejudice, emotion, distrust, anger, or outrage, or conversely sympathy and trust. This leaves open a possibility of attempting, by scientific examination, to explore the unspoken, perhaps unconscious system of values on which the judgment rests.

The distinction between the two approaches is well known. Yet much of the debate about the change of system has been marked by confusion between them. That distinction plays a key role in the argument about the change of system to be expressed here.

A Positive Approach to the Change of System

What should be qualified as a "socialist system"? A normative response can be made. Some would say the name true "socialism" is not merited by the formation that came into being in the Soviet Union and then the other communist countries, that it was only an insult to the noble concept of socialism. It was incorrect to talk of existing socialism when what existed was not true socialism at all.

I have no quarrel with those who see the description "socialist system" as an honor to be won, for which the formations developed under Lenin, Stalin, Rákosi, or Ceausescu fail to qualify. The epithet was also treated as an honor in the official rhetoric of the socialist countries, and by contrast with the previous interpretation, it was concluded that "existing socialism" had done well in its examination.

In a positive approach, the definition cannot be arbitrary; its starting point must be observation and analysis of reality. Let us take an analogy from the natural sciences. There are a great many breeds of dog. It seems almost incredible and unacceptable that a tiny Pekinese and a giant St. Bernard, so different in build, gait, coat, look, and character, should both be classed as domestic dogs (*Canis familiaris*). But it does not depend on the tastes of dog lovers or dog haters what breeds can or cannot be classed as dogs. Zoologists can describe precisely what dogs have in common and what positive criteria decide whether or not an animal belongs to the domestic dog (*Canis familiaris*) species.[3] Not the sympathy or antipathy for dogs and cats, but the positive criteria are the deciding factor whether they belong to dog or to cat species.

I employed a positive definition in my book *The Socialist System* (Kornai 1992b). There were 26 countries in 1987 that officially styled themselves a "socialist country."[4] What characteristics did they have in common? I was not trying to find as many similar traits as possible. On the contrary, I was trying to make the circle of characteristics as narrow as possible—but sufficient to distinguish clearly the countries that were within the socialist system from those that were not. To use the language of logic, what were the *necessary and sufficient conditions* for it to be possible to say plainly of a certain country at a certain time that it operated under a socialist system?

This calls for three necessary and sufficient conditions to be present concurrently.

1. A dominant role in ownership relations for public ownership, with private ownership present in at most a subordinate, auxiliary role.

2. A dominant role in the coordination of socioeconomic activities for centrally directed bureaucratic coordination, with market coordination present at most in a subordinate, auxiliary role.

3. A monopoly of political power for a Marxist-Leninist Communist party, i.e. a party whose program it is to abolish capitalism based on private ownership and the market, in other words a party inimical to capitalism. The Communist party will demonstrate by its actions that it is determined to implement such a program. This third charac-

---

[3] The positive criterion is that individuals of the same species must be able to breed and produce fertile offspring.

[4] [The 26 socialist countries appear in a table in my comprehensive work *The Socialist System* (Kornai 1992b). This appears in an updated form at the end of Study 7 in this volume (180–2).]

teristic precedes the other two in the succession of historical events. The Communist party will carry out mass confiscation and large-scale elimination or containment of the market.

These three *primary*, absolutely necessary conditions will suffice for the system to develop numerous *secondary* traits in common—possibly after long delays. For instance, they will suffice for legislation conforming to the system to appear, for government and economic leaders to adopt a mode of behavior compatible with the system's requirements, for most citizens to undergo socialization in line with the system's demands, and so on.

The concept of a "socialist system" denotes a *family* of systems. The configuration of institutions in any country changes over time: Brezhnev's Soviet Union differed from Stalin's. Countries differed from each other in the same period: Honecker's German Democratic Republic differed from Pol Pot's Kampuchea. But what they shared—as was clearly demonstrable in practice—were the three characteristics mentioned before.

What necessary and sufficient conditions must apply before it can be said that the capitalist system applies in a specific historical formation? The answer is symmetrical with what has been said about the socialist system.

1. A dominant role in ownership relations for private ownership, with public ownership present in at most a subordinate, auxiliary role.

2. A dominant role in the coordination of socioeconomic activities for the market, with centrally directed, bureaucratic coordination present in at most a subordinate, auxiliary role.

3. No political power standing against capitalism, private ownership and the market. These institutions are either supported actively or, at least, treated in a benevolent, "friendly," neutral manner.

It should be noted that the necessary and sufficient conditions do not include democracy. The capitalist system can operate in a tyrannical political structure that suppresses political rights and freedoms and whose leaders are not chosen by a parliamentary election system. All that is necessary for capitalism to survive is that the political regime should not be anti-capitalist. The problem of democracy is returned to later in the study.

The three conditions above were not picked from a set of candidate conditions, based on some arbitrary definition of capitalism.

The road to a definition resembles the one taken with the socialist system. It starts from experience and from observation of the traits of real historical formations. Taking a largish group of countries widely agreed to be called capitalist countries, let us look at what they have in common. They are found to meet all three *primary* conditions just given, while they may differ in their *secondary* features, such as the legal system, the economic activity and redistributive role of the state, the religious affiliations of their peoples, and so on.

The concept of the "capitalist system" (as with the "socialist system" discussed before) denotes a *family* of systems. Again, the configuration of institutions in each country changes over history: it differed in the Britain of the nineteenth century from what it is today, and at a given point in time, the Sweden and Norway of today differ from the United States or New Zealand. But all showed the three mentioned characteristics of a capitalist country.

The dichotomy of "socialism *versus* capitalism" is not precluded by the variance within the system families. It is also compatible with the fact that there have existed and will exist specific formations that cannot be easily included in either family. Here are some exceptions.

– Pre-capitalist and capitalist forms may coexist for a long time in less developed countries.

– Unusual forms of ownership are found in countries where the influence of Islam is strong or even theocratic political and ideological rule has appeared. These forms cannot be called either public or private ownership. Furthermore, there are coordination mechanisms in which Islamic law and/or tradition durably constrains the customary operation of the market (Kuran 2004). So the actual system in these countries does not fit into the capitalist family of systems and certainly cannot be called socialist either.

There is nothing here to unsettle analysts. It is possible to use classifications that prescribe strict delineating criteria, but acknowledge the existence of exceptional, ambivalent or vague cases that cannot be classified. For instance, the male/female dichotomy is workable despite the existence of hermaphrodites.

In contrasting *two* great systems I join an intellectual tradition pioneered by Marx, who brought forward the concept of *capitalism*. The capitalism/socialism pair is also used readily by others, including non-

Marxists—Károly Polányi, Max Weber, Ludwig von Mises, and Joseph Schumpeter, for instance.[5]

This is not the only possible approach to clarifying the concept of the system. Some analysts reject this sharp opposition of *two* great systems and two families of models, emphasizing that all existing systems blend various elements. Public property and private, bureaucracy and market, democracy and dictatorship, and many other individual characteristics have been found in each country, but combined in proportions that differ between countries and periods. There exist a great many combinations, and various typologies can be introduced from many points of view (Pryor 2005 and 2006).

I would not rigidly exclude this approach. I gladly use it to distinguish specific historical realizations *within the same family of systems*. As noted before, Kampuchea differed from the German Democratic Republic, as do Sweden and Norway from the United States or New Zealand. Yet I still argue that this strong dichotomy has a powerful clarifying and explanatory power.[6]

We are now furnished with a conceptual apparatus for deciding when the change of system has been completed.

The change of system is over once the country analyzed no longer exhibits the three primary characteristics of a socialist system, and the three primary characteristics of the capitalist system prevail.

It can be stated, according to that positive approach, that the change of system has been completed in the ten new post-socialist member-states of the European Union, including Hungary. (That is not to say it has only been completed in those ten countries, but my argument here does not call for clarification of whether the change of system has been completed in other countries or not.)

That is a positive statement, to be confirmed or denied by experience. I do not want to burden this study with a lot of statistics. I will confine myself to two tables from reports of the European Bank of Reconstruction and Development (EBRD), drawing from them a few data on Hungary.

---

[5] Concise reviews of the intellectual tradition that uses the capitalism concept and opposes the two great systems are found in Berend (2001) and Heilbronner (1980) and (1991).

[6] Present-day social scientists differ in their use of these approaches. Clear examples are seen in two respected and widespread economics textbooks used in American higher education. Fischer and Dornbusch (1983) uses the capitalism/socialism pair of concepts, but Mankiw (2004) avoids it.

– The first of the primary conditions has been met *(Table 6.1)*. Eighty per cent of Hungary's GDP derived from the private sector in 2004.

– The second of the primary conditions has been met *(Table 6.2)*. The EBRD gives expert "transition indicator scores" to countries, for how far they have advanced in the post-socialist transition in terms of various characteristic features of the market economy. The best score is 4+, which Hungary received in the two indicators to do with coordination mechanisms: liberalization of trade and of foreign-exchange transactions. That reflects the market mechanism already has a dominant role in coordination.

– I will not support numerically the statement that the third condition has been fulfilled: Hungary's political system and legislation protect private property and market institutions. The truth of that assertion can be checked by the reader.

A positive statement devoid of any value judgment has been made. *The change of system has occurred.* It is possible to rejoice over that or resent it. But there can be no debate between the rejoicers and the resenters about whether the ten new EU member-states have entered the family of capitalist systems or not, because the main systemic traits in this respect are similar to those in the other capitalist countries.

People have found it hard to take to the word "capitalism." Public thinking underwent deep indoctrination in the decades of Communist

Table 6.1 The share of the private sector in GDP, %

Country	1989	1990	1992	1994	1996	1998	2000	2002	2004
Bulgaria	10	10	25	40	55	65	70	70	75
Czech Republic	5	10	30	65	75	75	80	80	80
Estonia	10	10	25	55	70	70	75	80	80
Hungary	5	25	40	55	70	80	80	80	80
Latvia	10	10	25	40	60	65	65	70	70
Lithuania	10	10	20	60	70	70	70	75	75
Poland	30	30	45	55	60	65	70	75	75
Romania	15	15	25	40	55	60	60	65	70
Slovakia	5	10	30	55	70	75	80	80	80
Slovenia	10	15	30	45	55	60	65	65	65

Note: The calculations employed official (government) and unofficial sources. The proportion includes the official and unofficial activity of private firms. All firms in majority private ownership count as private.
Source: Based on EBRD (2006).

Table 6.2
Values for the EBRD index of transition to the market economy

Country	Trade	Price liberalization and foreign-exchange transactions
Bulgaria	4+	4+
Czech Republic	4+	4+
Estonia	4+	4+
Hungary	4+	4+
Latvia	4+	4+
Lithuania	4+	4+
Poland	4+	4+
Romania	4+	4+
Slovakia	4+	4+
Slovenia	4	4+

Note: The indicator score ranges from 1 to 4+. 1 = no or hardly any appreciable change since the period of central planning. 4+ = conditions equivalent to those of the industrial market economies.
Source: EBRD (2005, Table 1.1)

power, when newspapers, radio and television, schools, and universities, festive speeches and party seminars alike imbued people with the idea that capitalism was a hateful, reprehensible system. "Restoring capitalism" was not a goal even those put off by the existing socialist system. Nor did the radical opponents of socialism declare that they wanted a "capitalist system"—even in otherwise quite daring and forthright samizdat writings. Another reason why they did not do so was because they had not thought the matter through, or if they did support the restoration of capitalism, because they did not want to underline the fact for fear of alienating in their readers. Revealingly, politicians, political commentators, and social scientists continued to avoid the expression even after censorship and self-censorship had ceased.[7] It is not found in the first manifestos of the parties founded after 1989, which preferred such euphemistic expressions as "market economy," as more acceptable to a public attuned to anti-capitalism.

[7] My colleagues and I searched the issues of the periodicals *HVG*, *Magyar Narancs*, and *Hitel*, and only began to find the word "capitalism" appearing in articles in 1992–3. Not long ago, Péter György recalled his own prudish avoidance of it: "1989 denoted and promised a multi-party system, and hardly anybody spoke of capitalism. Government followed government, and each justifiably avoided acquainting the public with the reality of capitalism" (György 2006).

STUDY 6

A Positive Approach to Changing the Political Structure

Not only the ten new East European members of the European Union have fulfilled the minimum condition of ending monopoly power of the Communist party, with its anti-capitalist, Marxist-Leninist ideology, so opening the way to joining the capitalist family of systems. Far more than that has occurred; the change has been much deeper. Dictatorship has given way to democracy, and political monopoly of the Communist party to competition among several parties.

As underlined earlier, this political change is not a *necessary* condition for the change of system. Capitalism might equally have replaced socialism while one type of political tyranny was simply replacing another. Think of 1919 and the subsequent initial period in which red terror was replaced by white. Or recall the Pinochet coup. It was a stroke of historical luck that the two transformations—political and economic—coincided. It did not depend only on external conditions. Contributions came also from the movements and organizations of democratic opposition to the communist system, the process of intellectual enlightenment, and the ideological and moral commotion in the leadership of the Communist party, that is, *internal* forces. The role of internal forces was greater in some countries—perhaps Hungary and Poland most of all—and weaker in others, but it can hardly be denied that these internal forces were not decisively responsible for the collapse of the communist tyranny. Ultimately this was made possible by outside circumstances: changes in international power relations. The Soviet Union had managed to prevent Hungary in 1956, Czechoslovakia in 1968, and Poland in 1981 from leaving the socialist system, but it could no longer do so in 1989–90.

The word democracy has been used so far without explanation, but it needs defining, as conceptual clarification is the study's main purpose. Let me employ the same methodology as with the definitions of *socialism* and *capitalism*, though it is by no means a self-evident or exclusively accepted one. A positive, not a normative approach will be taken again. There are countries that are called democracies. Overseas countries like the United States, Canada, Australia, and New Zealand can certainly be included here alongside the older member-states of the European Union. What features do countries in this group have in common, and what distinguishes them from countries generally considered *not* to be democracies? As with the positively approached characterizations of socialism and capitalism, I am looking for the minimum set of characteristics, the necessary and sufficient conditions, the primary distinguishing criteria.[8]

Following Schumpeter (1942), the marks that distinguish democracy from other forms of government appear in its *procedural* characteristics. Taking a positive approach, a country's form of government qualifies as a democracy only if its leaders are elected by a well-defined procedure, whose main components are rivalry among political parties and repeated elections based upon this, as well as legislative activity by the Parliament so elected. Those who have been governing need not (and may not) be removed by demonstrations, mass pressure, insurrection, sedition, armed force, assassination, or conspiracy. They *can be removed* in a civilized way, by voting procedures at the next due elections. If the incumbent leaders are not re-elected, they hand over to the winners of the elections without resistance. These procedural characteristics can be considered the *minimum conditions* necessary and sufficient for democracy to apply.

I would like to underline what this description does *not* include.

a) It includes no statement on how mature or developed the democracy of the system in question is. It can fulfill the minimum conditions even if it is quite rough and ready otherwise, if government is insufficiently transparent, and if direct civil participation in political decision-making is weak.

b) The minimum conditions include no stipulations on the quality of government. A democratically elected government may be competent or incompetent, thrifty or wasteful, honest or dishonest, so long as the rules of democracy are kept in appointing its leaders.

c) The minimum conditions are not expressed in the conceptual apparatus of constitutional law. A country's constitution may already include the minimum condition of regular procedures for parliamentary elections and appointment of governments. But the form of government may still meet the minimum conditions if its constitution is vague on this. Britain, the pioneer of constitutional government, still has no codified constitution.

---

[8] [Interpretation of the concept of democracy has already been addressed in Study 5 (pp. 88–92). There is some inevitable overlap between the two discussions, but this account raises some points not covered in Study 5.]

d) The minimum conditions say nothing about the *stability* of democracy. They allow a *test* of whether there is democracy in a country at a particular time. But they give no political advice on how to defend democracy. This is an important warning that I need to append to my earlier writings.

Hungary today has democracy, because the procedural rules for electing and dismissing leaders have been kept so far. Electoral losers have resigned power and handed it over to the winners in a civilized manner. For the first time last year, in 2006, a government coalition was reelected—and it happened according to the procedural rules.

Yet the fact that this has happened so far is no absolute guarantee that it will happen hereafter. Fulfillment of the minimum conditions *today* is not a sufficient condition for the survival of democracy *tomorrow*. The minimum conditions must be respected time and again, day after day. If you have won, exercise your right to govern. If you have lost, accept the political defeat. It is not too hard to accept victory, but accepting defeat is the litmus paper that shows whether democracy is operating or not. If significant political forces fail to meet that minimum condition, democracy is in danger.[9]

Let us return to the list of what the minimum conditions do not include.

e) It is important to the argument to emphasize that the positive definition presented includes no value judgments.[10] It is possible to like or reject the democratic form of government that fulfills the minimum conditions. The discussion here is confined to whether or not there is democracy in a country at a particular time.

By the criteria of a positive approach it can be confirmed that democracy applies in Hungary (and the other nine East European EU member-states).

---

[9] [It was emphasized in Study 3 (pp. 53–7) that communists and social democrats are distinguished primarily by how they relate to the procedures of democracy. Communists are prepared to do away with those procedures, take power by force, and having obtained it, refuse to resign it again. They see democracy as something "formal," an empty set of rules of a game. Social democrats, on the other hand, never place themselves above the procedural rules of democracy, seek to enter government by winning elections, and are prepared to resign power when electorally defeated.]

[10] [Insistence of the democratic form of government features high in my own order of values. My normative statement of my view appears in Study 5 (p. 103).]

The Reception of Capitalism and Democracy—
A Normative Approach

Let us turn to a normative approach to the problems, treating them in two stages. First let us consider the arguments of those who do not dispute the positive statements that capitalism has replaced socialism and democracy has superseded dictatorship. They do not deny these; they are simply dismayed or appalled by what has developed since the changes.

I am fully aware of the fact that such discontent is widespread, but it does not betray its presence primarily in noisy demonstrations. More importantly, the public may grumble privately, rather than air their complaints in the street, but the dissatisfaction appears in reliable surveys of public opinion and several painstaking, objective empirical studies (Ferge 1996; Vásárhelyi 2005; Sági 2006).

Although this study is not intended to analyze the manifestations or causes of public dissatisfaction, some remarks need to be made on certain views often expressed among intellectuals and in political discourse. This study sets out to discuss three groups of views.

The first group consists of expressions of support for *reforming* capitalism: the criticism is confined to some features of the system. I view this as useful and try to practice such criticism myself. It may go quite far and be quite sharp, for it is common to find agonizing, unjust, morally reprehensible features specific to the capitalist system. There are some well-known examples, such as offensively unfair inequalities of income, wealth, and knowledge, mass unemployment, and a low employment rate. These awkward or harmful features cannot be eliminated, but they can be substantially reduced.

Those who share this group of views are not advocating withdrawal from the family of capitalist systems. They recommend a different variant of the system from the present one. Their aim is not to overthrow capitalism, but to alter some of its institutions, legislation, and customs. It is fortunate that such criticism is quite widespread.

The second group of views consists in advocating some *third kind of system*. The *first system*, capitalism, in bad.[11] The *second*, which tries to replace it, socialism, is bad. So let there be a *third* system or *third*

---

[11] The general criticism of capitalism today is closely bound up with protest against globalization, in which there are many, sometimes contradictory views involved. They consider the exploitation of poor, backward countries by rich ones to be outrageous, or conversely,

way, as it is sometimes called. Advocates of such views include some (yet not all) neo-Marxists, but similar opinions are held by people who have nothing in common with Marxism. Such views are found in Hungary and elsewhere.

Let the world be better and *different*, but where should the difference lie? It certainly must not resemble the ghastly system of Lenin and Stalin. But ask the advocates of such views what specific lessons should be drawn from the fall of the socialist system and the response is unconvincing. The typical reply is that its failure *per se* does not lead to any revealing conclusions. Lenin, Stalin, and their followers did a bad job; it is now time for socialism to be done well. Asked how, they do not know or feel an obligation to pronounce on the matter. They feel intellectually and morally justified in rejecting an existing bad system even if they cannot outline a better one in a constructive fashion.

In my view, the type of response just outlined is irresponsible, despite its long history—it was the response made by Marx, who did not take the trouble to devise the rules of operation for a future socialist society, and even scornfully decried those who tried to do so: "Thus the Paris *Revue Positiviste* reproaches me in that, on the one hand, I treat economics metaphysically, and on the other hand—imagine!—confine myself to the mere critical analysis of actual facts, instead of writing receipts (Comtist ones?) for the cook-shops of the future" (Marx [1867–94] 1974, p. 26). Engels in his *Anti-Dühring* mocks a scholar who claims to have found "a new social order... constructed in his sovereign head, in his mind, pregnant with ultimate truths," branding him "the epigone of the utopians" (Engels 1962, p. 363). Marx and Engels are suggesting it is "unscientific" to devise meticulously in advance how the future society will operate. A hundred million people have paid the heaviest price for their irresponsible omission, as the experiments to decide what the future society should be were done live, on them.

Capitalism has many repellent features indeed. I do not expect "the man in the street" or even writers presenting the dark side of the capitalist system in their works to recommend a better replacement.

---

they see danger in the competition less-developed countries bring to world trade, fearing for jobs at home. It would go beyond the scope of this study to examine these influential political and intellectual trends.

Nor do I expect constructive proposals from the rest of the intelligentsia unless research into social developments is their profession. But I think there are other requirements of economists, sociologists, political philosophers, or contemporary historians whose profession and vocation it is to study the processes of social transformation. Professional responsibility and intellectual honesty require them, having urged people to reject capitalism and carefully studied the historical lessons, to say what system to put in capitalism's place. Let them come forward constructively with alternative plans for society, and examine conscientiously the feasibility of the system recommended. Have they accounted realistically for human nature? Have they reckoned with the present state of technology? If they wish to have a democratic system of government, have supporters of their plan any chance of winning free elections? Or are they proposing another form of government? If there were such plans, we could think about them and debate them. There is no worthwhile way to debate about empty slogans and utopias.

Finally, I place in a separate third group the views of those who preach *ambivalent populism*. Here are some of the typical expressions their rhetoric include: "hawkish capitalism," "luxury profit," "banker government," etc. and many more. What kind of economic system would people who stir up feelings in that way like to see? What kind of rules could be used to turn their sloganized criticism into practical language? Would trading licenses be granted only to dovelike capitalists and withheld from those with hawkish characters? Should there be profit, but not luxury profit? Should there be a capitalist economy operating, but no banks, as banks cannot expect the state's rule of law to protect their property any more or enforce their contracts?

Such rhetoric displays a lack of courage to reject capitalism and a want of intellectual power to advance feasible, useful ways of reforming it.

"Replacing the Elite" and "Dispensing Justice"— A Normative Approach

That concludes the first stage of analysis of the normative approach, covering the views of those who acknowledge the fact of the change of system, but do not like its consequences.

STUDY 6

The second stage is to examine the views of those who doubt whether there has been a change of system at all. This mixes up the positive criteria with the normative. (Of course I am not saying the holders of these views have recognized the *positive/normative* distinction or thought out the basis of their position at all. That is immaterial to what I have to say. In analyzing these points of view, any view can be categorized irrespective of that.)

Views that confuse the positive and normative approaches share the same structure. The argument begins with a formula: "I see the change of system as incomplete (or possibly, as a process that has not yet really begun), because I only count a change as a 'change of system' if it meets the following condition or conditions." Then follow the normative condition or perhaps an ensemble of conditions.

A great many normative conditions were advanced earlier and still do so in the fuming political climate of the summer and fall of 2006. Some of the speeches made in Kossuth tér were quoted at the beginning of the study. These and similar contributions have been the source of several normative demands, of which six examples follow.

Example 1. We cannot talk of a change of system because the cadres of the old communist system still hold leading positions. A complete change of guard is essential to a change of system, that is, in the language of social science, there must be complete or almost complete replacement of the earlier elite by a new one.

Example 2. We cannot talk of a change of system while those responsible for the crimes of the old system remain unpunished. Dispensing justice is essential to a change of system.

Example 3. We cannot talk of a change of system while the present constitution remains in force. This constitution is unacceptable and its faults cannot be patched and darned with little amendments. We need a new constitution and in order to elaborate and accept it, a constituent national assembly is needed.

Example 4. We cannot talk of a change of system when the people have not been asked what system they want. We need a referendum to render the new system legitimate.

Example 5. We cannot talk of a change of system because real change has to tie closely to satisfaction of national demands. These demands range widely over revision of Trianon and restoration of the country's pre-1919 borders, or even introduction of racist regulations to counteract a perceived dominance by *non-Hungarians* or *not full Hungarians* or Jews.

Example 6. We cannot talk of a change of system while the present form of government remains. This resembles the form of republic customary in surrounding countries, whereas Hungary needs a very special form of state based on the doctrine of the Holy Crown. It is sometimes said that the country should not be a republic at all, but a kingdom.

All six views involve denying that a change of system has occurred, not for want of minimum conditions (the need for which is typically denied), but because normative conditions set by the speaker are not met.

This study is confined to the first two examples.

Replacement of the elite. Hungary and Eastern Europe changed from a socialist to a capitalist system at enormous speed. It is worth looking at some historical experiences in this respect. Mention can be made of the several hundred years that passed in England, the foremost country in the transition to capitalism, before pre-capitalist ownership was gradually superseded by capitalist. The power of monarchy gradually weakened, early signs of self-government and parliamentarianism appeared, then the weight of the electoral process and Parliament gradually increased until parliamentary monarchy and finally—in the latter half of the 19th century, the recent past in historical terms—democracy was in place. The change of economic and political system occurred in several stages over a long time. There were lengthy transitional periods with occasional standstills and temporary reversals or intervals of accelerated change. While the importance of the aristocracy in the elite gradually declined over the centuries, we cannot pick out any short period in the transformation process of this era when radical replacement in politics or in economics took place. (The one exception was a brief period in the mid-17th century followed by a rapid restoration.) The men of the old and the new systems lived side by side competing for power and wealth. There existed rivalry, struggle, and at the same time collaboration and cooperation among them in varying proportions (Kontler 1993; Rubinstein 1986; Stone and Stone 1984).

Hungarian history, after great delay (measured on historical scale), showed similar developments in the composition of the elite and the interactions within it in the second half of the 19th and first half of the 20th centuries. The composition of the political elite changed suddenly after the 1849 defeat in the war of independence, but the trend of continuity was resumed strongly again after the 1867 *Ausgleich.* The elite consisting of the various groups of the aristocracy, the great landowners, the gentry, the middle classes of civil service, and the business world coexisted. Its composition had changed, but there was certainly no radical change of guard. The earlier elite—the aristocracy and great landowners—continued to hold important positions of political power and their influence extended into the business field. There was both rivalry and collaboration apparent among the various strata and groups within this heterogeneous elite (Kövér 2002; Lakatos 1942; Lengyel 1987 and 1989; Péter 1993).

The one type of "great transformation" to carry out a change of elite in a rapid and brutal way was the overthrow of the capitalist system and creation of the socialist system. It came first in Soviet Russia and then after Communist takeovers in other countries.

What happened in Hungary in the most recent change of system? There have been some notable empirical studies that offer quite a clear picture. A radical hypothesis was raised at the beginning of the post-socialist transition, whereby the old elite would survive almost intact and the composition of the elite would hardly change, because a "*nomenklatura* bourgeoisie" would develop (Hankiss 1990) and "political capitalism" emerge (Staniszkis 1991). Though still widely held, this view has proved to be a gross exaggeration. Empirical researches have shown it did not even apply in the early period of transition (Böröcz and Róna-Tas 1995; Szelényi, Szelényi, and Kovách 1995). In fact only a small proportion of the new political and economic elite held higher positions under the old regime *(Table 6.3).* Many advanced from lower levels of the old politico-bureaucratic strata, while many others were recruited from social groups outside the old elite. (See also Kostova, Lazic, and Lengyel 1996.)

The general statements are further supported by data in *Tables 6.4* and *6.5.* Analysis of both rests on the assumption that continuity prevailed in the careers of members of the post-socialist elite if they had been members of the old Hungarian Socialist Workers' Party. This is a simplification, as many members of the old political and still more of the old economic elite were not party members. However, there was certainly a strong correlation between elite membership and

Table 6.3
Employment features of the Hungarian elite after the change of system (1993), proportions already holding such positions in 1988, %

Position held in 1988	All new elites	New economic elite	New political elite	New cultural elite
Cultural decision-maker	2.9	0.2	3.1	12.8
Economic leader	20.8	30.9	3.7	4.5
Party official	3.3	2.2	3.1	7.5
State official	5.6	1.6	20.5	2.3
Aggregate proportion	32.6	34.9	30.4	27.1

Source: Szelényi, Szelényi, and Kovách (1995).

Table 6.4
The proportion of former Communist-party members among the economic elite, %

1988	1993	1997	2001
83.3	66.1	49.8	26.8

Note: The same question was put in each of the four years and calculations made according to the responses.
Source: Csite and Kovách (1998); and Csurgó, Himesi, and Kovách (2002).

Table 6.5
Proportions of former Communist-party members among the elites, %

	Cultural	Political	Economic
Never a member	71.2	64.3	72.2
Former member	25.9	32.9	26.8
No response	2.9	2.8	1.0
Total	100	100	100

Source: Csurgó, Himesi, and Kovách (2002, 322.)

party membership; the criterion is a good proxy for continuity between the old and new elites. *Table 6.4* shows clearly that—although there was no drastic change of guard—partial dismissal of the old elite soon began. The trend continued, so that little more than a fourth of the new economic elite in 2001 had been a Communist-party member (Csite and Kovách 1998; Csurgó, Himesi, and Kovách 2002). The second of the studies just cited is the source of *Table 6.5*, which gives 2001 data for the political and cultural elites, as well as the economic. The trends are similar in all three segments: a clear, steady reduction in the proportion of former Communist-party membership. Bearing in mind the findings of surveys conducted by different methods, it can be said that the proportion of the new elite consisting of members of the old elite is shrinking. (Other prominent contributions to the literature on the change in the Hungarian elite include Kolosi and Sági 1997; Kovách 2002 and 2006; Laki and Szalai 2004; Lengyel 1997; Kostova 1996; Spéder 1999; and Szalai 1996a and 1996b.)

I admit that it also annoys me to see in leading positions people whom I know from personal experience did much damage while holding high posts under the old regime. To translate that into the language of this study, I also take a normative approach and I am often enraged, but I try to control my feelings. To return to the positive approach, I maintain my earlier view that a change of elite is not a *necessary* condition for declaring a change of system is complete. The capitalist economy throws up its own leading stratum, adopting and absorbing people capable of playing the role, and soon sorting out those unfitted for it, even if they have started from an advantaged position. That strong selection mechanism is one of the secrets of the capitalist economy's success. So too does political democracy throw up its own leading stratum. There is selection among parties and movements, as there is in market competition. Those who prove unsuited are eliminated sooner or later. Nobody can say that the selection mechanisms in these two spheres work perfectly. Untalented or dishonest people may sometimes take control, while talented and honest people are squeezed out. But the selection on the whole is quite effective. As time passes, this selection process becomes increasingly reliable, even though faulty selections can still be expected.

Unfortunately, there is not full equality of opportunity. It can really be an advantage for a person or his or her family to have been high up under the old regime as well. (On the other hand, that can be a drawback initially, by giving rise to antipathy in one's surroundings.) But the advantage will wear out as time goes by. Certainly nobody will be guaranteed a job forever if incompetent to do it. The change of elite is driven by the system itself.

Dispensing justice. If this is taken to mean criminal proceedings guided by law and ending in a judicial verdict, there has hardly been anything of the kind. Even the one or two trials to do with volleys of fire on demonstrators in 1956 have ended in an equivocal way. The only other move has been to regulate against certain jobs being done by some groups of the old political elite.

There were sharp debates in the early 1990s about dispensing justice. Legislation to exact retribution for crimes committed under the old regime was submitted, but the bill was not approved by Parliament. Opinions were divided within the political parties of the time and among the participants of the public debate. There was no broad consensus on what legal action would be fair. Ultimately, no solution was found in Hungary or any neighboring country because society was deeply divided over the desire for justice in a historical sense, according to Kende (2000). The debate gradually died down and efforts to take action were impeded by decisions of the constitutional court. The embers of the debate glowed occasionally, but soon turned to ash again.[12]

Let me repeat that I too was indignant when suddenly, at a concert hall, I ran into a judge who had given my friends prison sentences after 1956. Petty thieves and pub rowdies are locked up, but those who actively and enthusiastically took part in the oppression go free. When the public were enraged about informers under the old regime, I sympathized with the grumblers: the focus was on people who were little cogwheels in the machinery of oppression; not a hair was touched on the heads of those who served as engines or large transmissions.

Yet I still hold the view I expressed in connection with a positive approach: punishing the criminals is not a *necessary* condition for stating that the change of system is complete. Let us examine strictly and accurately the attribute "necessary." The new economic and political system can still operate if the guilty go unpunished.

The new system must be viewed without illusions, even if a higher morality would require the guilty to be punished. Neither the capitalist economic system nor parliamentary democracy is a triumph of pure morality. In one of the birthplaces of democracy, the United States, the first country to formulate and adopt a democratic constitution,

---

[12] On the debates in Hungary and efforts to settle them, see Fogarassy (2001), Halmai (2006), and Rainer (2000). Some of the afore-mentioned writings also cover similar processes that have taken place in the other post-socialist countries.

there were at that historical juncture many million black people suffering slavery. Some of the founding fathers themselves kept slaves. With the change of system and the change in form of government that coincided with it in this country the *minimum* conditions came about for the capitalist system and democratic government. That in itself is a historic victory of huge historical importance. But nobody can consider it more than the minimum. It is the starting point, and it depends above all on the leaders and citizens of this country where we go from here.

Between these two demands (replacement of the elite and dispensing of justice) there is a link that is worth considering thoroughly.

The change of system that began in 1989 took place without bloodshed or violence. Not long ago, we marked the fiftieth anniversary of 1956, and it is timely to make a comparison with events at that time. Certainly the initial movements then did not proclaim a change of system to be their goal. But if outside forces had not crushed them, it would probably have led to one. And it would not have been a change of system of which anybody could have said later that it had gone through without violence. It began with an armed uprising, and initially, the leaders of the old regime sought to defeat the rebels by force of arms. Soviet tanks appeared and fired shots in the streets of Budapest. Thousands died on both sides of the barricades. The intention took seed in the minds of many that those in charge under the old order be punished. There were many who sought revenge, and passions rose to the point of lynching in some places.

On this occasion, in 1989 and after, there was no sign of anything of that kind.[13] It was a "velvet revolution," as the Czechs so expressively put it. The reason for the lack of bloodshed was not that human nature had changed over three decades and a half. This transformation began with agreement and compromise, around the negotiating table. The script for the transformation was discussed point by point, with bargaining between the old and new leaders. Those who had previously exercised total power made no attempt to reach for their guns. Instead, they cooperated in developing democratic procedures and a capitalist economy. They did it with sour faces, but they did it. One reason why they cooperated was because they would not

---

[13] The exception among the new EU countries was Romania, where Ceausescu and his wife were executed at the beginning of the change of system.

be excluded from political or economic activity—as long as they accepted the new rules of the game.[14]

"Would you have wanted a revolution?" That classic remark by József Antall, first prime minister of the new democracy, is often quoted when people pressed for a total change of guard and punishment of the guilty.

There are contradictory values juxtaposed here: on the one hand, the change of guard and dispensation of justice, and on the other, the demand for non-violence.[15] According to a normative approach under my system of values, it is more important for great social transformations to take place without bloodshed, loss of life, or acts of violence, than for the old faces to disappear and justice to be done.[16] But I know that not everyone subscribes to my system of values. Some people want the people of the old regime to be removed and punished, even if it means violence.

How the elite was changed and justice done is Hungary's internal affair. There was no outside imposition of what should happen and what should be left out of the transformation process, for we decided for ourselves. Yet it is worth noting the great international influence exerted by what has happened and continues to happen in Hungary and the other East European countries.

Here I would like to draw attention to only one international effect, and that is the influence on the great transformation of China.[17] There is a change of system taking place in that vast country of 1.3 billion people. Will there be an uprising, bloody clashes, or a civil war claiming millions of victims? Or will it occur peaceably? So far the latter seems likely, for one reason, because the Communist cadres do not oppose the spread of capitalism. On the contrary, they are seeking their share of the profits. Party secretaries appropriate some or all

---

[14] No formal agreement was reached at the round-table discussions that would exclude the possibility of criminal proceedings against those responsible. (See Rainer 2000.) But the way that such judicial proceedings were omitted from events in subsequent years shows that there had been implicit agreement to do so on both sides.

[15] [I return in Study 7 (pp. 157–9) to the problems of dispensing justice and freedom from violence, and the dilemma of choosing among the contradictory values associated with these.]

[16] According to Kende (2000), Hungary may have gone too far in this respect in the early 1990s. It might still have been possible then to find procedures for dispensing justice compatible with the non-violent nature of the transition. It remains questionable, of course, whether these could still be employed today, 15–18 years later.

[17] [China's great transformation is returned to in the Appendix to this study.]

of the factory assets. Municipal firms fall under the control of mayors. Sons and daughters of generals study at expensive business schools to prepare them for high positions in business. This is all rather repulsive, but it has the advantage that the Communist party becomes the quartermaster instead of the enemy of capitalism. It is an immoral process, but it disarms the resistance of the old lords to the new system, giving them an interest in its prosperity.

Chinese observers of Eastern Europe see it as though something of the kind occurred here as well. But what if they saw us stringing up from the lampposts old cadres thought responsible for the crimes of the old order, or if not lynching them, legally imprisoning them on a mass scale for old offences? What if those old cadres were excluded from business and political life? That could easily warn the Chinese Communists away from peaceful transition. Then, instead of surreptitious introduction of capitalism, they might prefer unbridled oppression and resistance to the change of system.

It is no naïve exaggeration to say that people in China are observing what happens in Eastern Europe. They observed closely the Hungarian reform of 1968, which had strong influence on China's own reform measures. On the opposite side, they followed closely the actions of Gorbachev, seeing them as warning, lest China disintegrate as the Soviet Union did. They still monitor events in Eastern Europe and draw conclusions from them in their own way. Similar lessons are being drawn by Vietnam and Cuba. Those of us who have not become irrevocably provincial would do well to keep an eye also on the indirect and distant effects of East European transformation.

Concluding Remarks

The main purpose of the study has been to suggest a *means and method of approach*. How can one approach a *positive definition* of a social structure? How can positive and negative approaches be *kept separate* in theoretical analysis? These are by no means easy problems and solving them by no means a trivial task. I have tried to give examples of these theoretical tasks.

As mentioned in the introduction to the study, I am not engaging in debate with the demonstrators in Kossuth tér, nor with the commentators on domestic events seen every day in the press and on television. But I still hope that the ideas I have put forward on a quite abstract plane may contribute to further cool consideration and so to dampening passions.

When absorbed in daily events and assessing them, we all tend to lose our sense of perspective. We cannot see the wood for the trees. Recalling the *fundamental* facts of the change of system—and how the capitalist economy and parliamentary democracy came about—may help to distinguish the lesser experiences of daily life from the truly great historical transformation.

It has almost become fashionable to dismiss the last 16 years. I object! We have to recall the basic changes and defend ourselves from such irresponsible attacks in order to formulate a more balanced way of thinking.

I would also like to encourage readers to consider the relative weights of the requirements and conditions for the transformation. If I have convinced people there are minimum conditions for a change of system and democracy, they must give highest priority to defending those conditions.

[Appendix

The Transformation of China

I was asked the following question several times after lectures I gave on interpreting the change of system that Central Eastern Europe had undergone: How could the transformation of China be fitted into the scheme described here? Had there not appeared in China a third system that was neither socialism nor capitalism?

Transformation in China has been far slower than it was in the post-socialist countries of Eastern Europe. But slow though it has been, it is not true to say it has arrived at a new system whose main features will remain unchanged for a long time. It is not permissible to confuse a slowly changing motion picture with one that has frozen into a still! China has undergone radical changes in the main characteristics of its system in the three decades since the death of Mao Zedong, and further changes are still occurring.

Table 6.6 shows how public ownership has dwindled and the share of private ownership has increased. The latter—according to the official

Chinese classification used in the table—had reached 60 percent by 2003. It can be added here that what is termed "collective property" in the Chinese statistics covers not only assets under the classic state ownership of old, but some unusual hybrid structures. Most city or village "collective" enterprises include an ownership role for the local mayor, party secretary or enterprise director. Although I do not have fresh national statistics to hand, it appears from the interim reports that the expansion of the private sector relative to the publicly owned sector has continued since 2003. The first characteristic of capitalism—a dominant role for the private sector—either applies or is near to applying.

The bureaucratic coordination mechanism of the command economy has long since gone or applies only within a narrow sphere. The market mechanism has become the dominant coordinator of economic activity. This appears clearly from *Table 6.7*. By 2003, 87–97 percent of production (depending on the type of product) was for sale at market prices, not prices fixed bureaucratically. The second characteristic of the capitalist system—predominance of market coordination—clearly applies.

As for the third condition, there is a difficulty here with discrepancies between word and deed, the loudly proclaimed rhetoric and the actual practice. There has been discussion of this in Study 3 (99. 57–60). While Marx, Engels, Lenin, and even Stalin have not been denied publicly by the Communist party in speeches or in ceremoniously adopted resolutions, and fidelity to the ideas of Mao is emphasized, the Communist party has long since rid itself of its anti-capitalism in governmental practice. At one time, it would have been inconceivable for a "capitalist" to be a member of a Bolshevik-type party, but now it is permissible under official party rules. There is increasing interpenetration of the leading stratum of the Communist party and the owning and managing elite of the capitalist economy. This takes a number of forms. Party cadres, high officials, and generals appointed by the Communist party, engage in business activity. Conversely, the leading people in the business world, including possessors of enormous fortunes, may be "elected" members of national or local assemblies (i.e., the party picks them for the task), placed on the committees of party organizations, or even chosen as the top person of a party organization. The process of interpenetration is widened through family contacts. If the part functionary himself does not become a "capitalist," his wife, sibling, or child may do so, while the relatives of "capitalists" are building themselves into the Communist-party machine. A new

Table 6.6
Proportions of private and state sectors in China
(% of value added, by form of ownership)

	1998	1999	2000	2001	2002	2003	Change
Non-farm business sector							
Private sector	43.0	45.3	47.7	51.8	54.6	57.1	+14.1
Public sector	57.0	54.7	52.3	48.2	45.4	42.9	−14.1
– state-controlled	40.5	40.1	39.6	37.1	35.2	34.1	−6.4
– collectively controlled	16.5	14.7	12.7	11.2	10.1	8.8	−7.7
Total (79% of GDP)	100.0	100.0	100.0	100.0	100.0	100.0	
Business sector							
Private sector	53.5	54.9	56.3	59.4	61.5	63.3	+9.8
Public sector	46.5	45.1	43.7	40.6	38.5	36.7	−9.8
– state-controlled	33.1	33.0	33.1	31.2	29.9	29.2	−3.9
– collectively controlled	13.4	12.1	10.6	9.4	8.6	7.5	−5.9
Total (94% of GDP)	100.0	100.0	100.0	100.0	100.0	100.0	
Economy-wide							
Private sector	50.4	51.5	52.8	55.5	57.4	59.2	+8.8
Public sector	49.6	48.5	47.2	44.5	42.6	40.8	−8.8
– state-controlled	36.9	37.1	37.3	35.7	34.6	33.7	−3.2
– collectively controlled	12.7	11.3	10.0	8.8	8.0	7.1	−5.6
Total (100% of GDP)	100.0	100.0	100.0	100.0	100.0	100.0	

Source: OECD, (2005b, p. 81).

Table 6.7
Proportions of transactions conducted at market prices in China
(% of transaction volume)

	1978	1985	1991	1995	1999	2003
Production goods						
Market prices	0	13	46	78	86	87.3
State guided	0	23	18	6	4	2.7
State fixed	100	64	36	16	10	10
Retail sales						
Market prices	3	34	69	89	95	96.1
State guided prices	0	19	10	2	1	1.3
State fixed	97	47	21	9	4	2.6
Farm commodities						
Market prices	6	40	58	79	83	96.5
State guided	2	23	20	4	7	1.6
State fixed	93	37	22	17	9	1.9

Source: OECD, (2005b, p. 29).

leading stratum of a special consistency is developing before our eyes—a stratum with a deep interest in spreading and maintaining the capitalist system (Qian 2003, *Economist* 2007).

To put it another way, the third, political characteristic of the capitalist system has been fulfilled. Or at least it can be said that China is advancing steadily in that direction.

It has been pointed out in several studies in this book, including this one, that democracy is not a necessary condition for the existence of a capitalist system. There are also capitalist economies operating under conditions of tyranny. Central Eastern Europe had the exceptional historical good fortune to have both transformations—from the socialist to the capitalist system and from dictatorship to democracy—coincide. China has not been so blessed. The minimum conditions for democracy do not apply in China. There is nothing like a multiparty system, with competition and free elections between rival ideological and political trends. The state uses its power to crush any independent organization or movement promoting principles different from the official ones. In that respect the old regime still prevails (*Economist* 2005, Human Rights Watch 2007). While the hypocritical references to Marxism-Leninism become rather embarrassing during the economic transformation, the ideology of "proletarian dictatorship" fits in better with the emphasis placed on hardline state power that tolerates no independent statements of opinion.

To sum up, the transformation of China is not an "exception" that refutes the theory put forward in the study. It can be fitted without difficulty into the analytical scheme outlined in this volume, notably in this study. Furthermore, a still bolder statement can be risked: the analytical scheme provides a useful tool for analyzing the Chinese transformation in depth.]

7
What Can Countries Embarking on Post-Socialist Transformation Learn from the Experiences So Far?*

Introduction

Table 1 in my book *The Socialist System* (Kornai 1992b) lists 26 countries where the "socialist system" was operating at the end of the 1980s.[1] The first two columns of the table at the end of this paper, *Table 7.1*, repeat the relevant data, listing the same 26 then-Communist countries. Columns 3 and 4 show an important difference, however. Three formerly unitary countries (Czechoslovakia, the Soviet Union, and Yugoslavia) have since been divided into a number of successor states.

Several other essential changes have also taken place in the Communist world. When I was writing the book just mentioned, I used a *political* criterion to decide whether a country had a Communist system. The term is applicable to a country for as long and only for as long as a monopoly of political power is retained there by a Communist party professing a Marxist-Leninist ideology. That was the case with the political structure of all 26 countries at that time (Column 7). The

---

* [Prepared for the Cuba Transition Project (CTP), Institute for Cuban and Cuban-American Studies, University of Miami. This publication was made possible through support provided by the Bureau for Latin America and the Caribbean, U.S. Agency for International Development, under the terms of Award No. EDG–A–00–02–00007–00. The opinions expressed herein are those of the author and do not necessarily reflect the views of the U.S. Agency for International Development. I am grateful to Brian McLean for the excellent translation, to Julia Parti and Kathleen Hamman for the careful editing of the text, and to János Varga for his devoted research assistance.]

[1] Kornai 1992b, pp. 6–7. The book treats the expressions "socialist system" and "communist system" as synonymous.

term "Communist" can be applied at this time to only five countries: China, Vietnam, Laos, North Korea, and Cuba.

With the exception of North Korea and Cuba, all the countries that formerly belonged to the Communist system have undergone radical transformations in their *economies*. While economic changes have occurred in many dimensions, let us confine ourselves for a moment to one: the reallocation of property rights. Column 8 of *Table 7.1* shows that the economy of the *whole* former Communist region, with the exception of North Korea and Cuba, has moved much closer to that of market economies dominated by private ownership.[2] This change has been very strong in China and Vietnam, even though both are still run by communist parties. It is doubtful whether the Communist parties of these two countries have remained real Marxist-Leninist parties at all, for they have hardly retained their old ideology except in their rhetoric. Looking at the actions of the governing party in China and Vietnam, it can be seen that they wear a Communist guise, but they are actually friendly toward capitalism and actively engaged in implanting it.[3] Although the political regimes in China and Vietnam remain dictatorial, the actual behavior of the political authorities seems likely to move toward pro-capitalism. So it is also correct to say that both countries have shifted away from socialism toward post-socialist transition.[4]

In a decade and a half, a transformation of importance in world-history terms has occurred in the former Communist world, affecting one-third of the world's population. Are there lessons and remarkable experiences to be drawn from that transformation of the former communist world for other countries? My reply is a decided yes. This study advances some ideas to support that affirmative answer.

My arguments are not based on theoretical speculation, for I have gained first-hand experience in my own country, Hungary. Hungary's

---

[2] Unfortunately, data on the share of the private sector in a subset of countries are missing. According to the impressions gained by experts, the role of the private sector became significantly larger in those countries as well.

[3] It is another matter that they still rule dictatorially and repress political freedoms, for in that they are not alone. There have been and remain elsewhere many pro-capitalist, anti-socialist parties that enjoy a political monopoly and seek to retain it at all cost. [On this, see the Appendix to Study 6, pp. 147–50.]

[4] "Post-socialist transformation" has been defined in several ways by different authors. A question to ask here concerns their view on what marks completion of the transformation. [I set out my view on this disputed question in Study 6, pp. 125–31]

history is especially noteworthy because it began to reform its socialist economy very early, back in 1968. In addition, I have gathered extensive information about the transformation in the other Eastern European countries, the successor states of the Soviet Union, China, and Vietnam. This research is based upon primary as well as secondary sources. I have visited the various countries of the region many times and spoken with many experts on the subject. Several of them have been former pupils of mine, willing to disclose their problems openly and honestly. Furthermore, there is a rich literature available. My observations in this paper are confined to the experiences of countries where I have such knowledge. For brevity's sake, I do not repeatedly say that the empirical background of my remarks consists of some post-socialist countries, not all of them. As I know too little about countries undergoing post-socialist transition in Asia, Africa, and Latin America, I will not attempt to make use of their experiences here.

Those who suggested I write this study asked me to think over the lessons applicable to Cuba. While I have tried largely to do that, the conclusions I reach are more general. My arguments make clear that I am most concerned with those of the myriad of relevant experiences worth considering in all countries, whether they are on the brink of a radical system change or have crossed that threshold. In other words, the experiences described here are worth thinking about not only in regard to Cuba and North Korea, but perhaps also in Iraq or in other countries that will one day be freed from a strict dictatorship that is combined with some socialist features, such as centralization and/or a large state-owned sector.

Starting Points

Here let me make three warning observations as a starting point for further analysis. In the first instance, I will express these ideas on an abstract plane, before adding some illustrations in later sections of this study.

No Universal Prescription

Although the experiences of several countries over a decade and a half are available, they do not add up to a universal prescription for a general strategy for post-socialist transformation, or for specific tasks and tactical measures. On the contrary, in pondering the experiences I have known and studied, I would warn those thinking of radical transformation in Cuba or elsewhere to view with suspicion and reservations all arguments that purport to derive clear, confident, specific proposals from East European, post-Soviet, Chinese, or Vietnamese experiences.

I would be doubly suspicious of studies that support a confident proposal based on any ostensibly "scientific" apparatus. For instance, people did regression analysis based on a sample of data gathered from 10–20 countries over 10–12 years, creating basis for statements such as, "The faster the reform, the faster the growth will be." An initial glance at the statistics seemed to support this conclusion "backed by econometric means," until one day, serious macroeconomic difficulties appeared and growth slowed down precisely in the countries that had been reforming fastest.

It should be acknowledged that too little time had elapsed and too small a sample was taken to draw clear, statistically convincing, well-founded conclusions from the experiences with the specific, practical tasks ahead. Furthermore, the sample was too heterogeneous in many other features that fell outside the phenomenon being studied.

Consider how the many countries undergoing post-socialist transformation have included one as small as Albania and such a giant as China. Among them is a country as poor as Mongolia and another as rich as the Czech Republic. Some are industrially very advanced, and some, at least at the beginning of the transition, are countries where agriculture has very great weight in the economy. In one country, most of the population is Catholic, while in a second it is Protestant, in a third Orthodox, and in a fourth Muslim. With such varied initial conditions, countries would clearly take different courses in their transition to a market economy.

There is no universal prescription. There are no specific, practical recommendations valid equally for each country. This sharp warning is in itself an important lesson. But having drawn it, would it not be better to end this paper without further ado? I will continue because I am convinced that there are many useful lessons of other kinds, although the *nature* of the conclusions that can rightly be drawn has to be clarified first.

Careful study of the transformation processes that have occurred so far reveals what kinds of phenomena and relations play an important part in them. What are the problems that have to be addressed in good time that cannot simply be passed by in the hope they will somehow resolve themselves in due course? The approach I recommend makes use of a *checklist* of problems calling for notable, serious study and action. Of course, history can always come up with the unexpected. Cuba, for instance, may face difficulties not encountered by any transforming country so far. Yet it is useful to prepare intellectually (and perhaps actively) for the foreseeable problems at least.

There is no telling from the experience so far exactly when some measure has to be taken during the transformation process or what measure it will be. But if it is not possible to give a clear recommendation, it is at least possible to say something, from studying experience so far with the post-socialist transition, about the consequences some measure or other may have. What will be the direct and indirect political, economic, social, and cultural gains and losses by each major step? There is no chance of compiling easily quantifiable trade-off equations from previous experience with transformation, but it will be possible to say, qualitatively at least, which are *the trade-off relations most worth noting*. If this contribution of mine helps to promote a cost-benefit approach of that kind, it will have done a useful service, for there is a danger that politicians directing the future transformations may have too much confidence in their prophetic abilities, seeing the policy they advocate as the one redeeming solution that can satisfy all.

The history of post-socialist transformation so far has included quite a few spectacular failures—alterations whose political, economic, and social consequences were gravely detrimental, so that the price paid certainly exceeded the value of the benefits. Thus it is worth considering carefully what mistakes should be avoided unfailingly.

No Such Thing as a "Non-political" Decision

Specialists involved in the post-socialist transition often complain that too little heed is paid to *expert considerations* when decisions are taken. Economists object that efficiency criteria are relegated, doctors that health factors are ignored, theatre managers and museum curators that cultural considerations are not respected, and so on. And they all object to that everything is being "overly politicized."

There is little point in wringing one's hands. The change of system is, above all, a political process, so that politicization of every decision is inescapable. Capitalism is an attractive and resilient system. Even if the state and the political sphere were to stand aside (which is hard to imagine even on a theoretical plane), capitalism would still spread, gaining footholds wherever it had not been allowed to operate before. It would be enough just to lift the bans—but in itself it is a political act. In real life, the spontaneous expansion and intensification of capitalism is strongly influenced by decisions of the state. State regulation can hamper or hasten naturalization of the market economy based on private ownership. At best, it will set out to promote the healthy features of the development, while curbing or excluding the harmful or even criminal side-effects. At its worst, it will allow healthy development in line with its outgrowths, ignoring or tolerating abuses.

The political sphere—even if it would like to—could not resign its responsibilities for the quality of the transformation. Not that it would want to, of course. Politicians are driven simultaneously by their political philosophy and world outlook, the interests of the groups or strata they represent, and their own interests in wielding power (and in some cases financial interests as well). They cannot look with indifference on any projected measure or action by the state. Regardless of whether they are in office or opposition, they try to intervene and influence the course of events.

This has to be accepted from the outset as a reality. Whatever change is being made, the experts putting forward a proposal have to consider carefully its political implications. Where can they expect to find support and resistance? I myself have sometimes failed to carry out this vital piece of analysis. I hoped my recommendations would be acceptable to everyone. They never were. Reactions were sharply divided, and in some cases, a proposal of mine drew no support from any major political force.

Ethical Implications

So "expert" considerations are not enough in themselves; there are always political implications to reckon with as well. But that is still not enough. It is necessary to delve a further layer deeper, to analyze the experiences of post-socialist transformation thoroughly and decide what has been to the good and what to the bad in the course of events so far. "Good" and "bad" are *ethical* judgments. When sizing up the factual aspects of events, it is possible to aim at positive, value-free observations and descriptions. Reliable statistics on the proportion of private ownership constitute value-free information. But to add that the present distribution of property rights was reached too slowly or too hastily is to exercise a value judgment.

Analysts seeking to go beyond mere registration of events in the past or listing feasible alternatives and their consequences in the future have an obligation to show their colors. Let them state what system of values they use to judge that a past event or process was good or bad and what system of values they use when supporting or opposing some future measure. Or if they are eschew the idea of employing a system of values, let them at least meet the minimum requirements of intellectual honesty by carefully presenting the ethical implications. Discover and explain comprehensibly how, if this has been done in the past or this is to be done in the future, it meets ethical postulate A, but fails to meet ethical postulate B. Alternatively, if not this, but something else has been done in the past or is to be done in the future, it fails to meet ethical postulate A, but meets ethical postulate B.

Without attempting to be comprehensive, here are a few of the ethical dilemmas that have to be faced during the post-socialist transition:[5]

1. Should concomitant v*iolence* and bloodshed be avoided at all costs? Is the non-violent nature of the transition to be a basic postulate, or is violence permissible? If the latter is the case, what measure of bloodshed can be contemplated? How many victims? A few? Thousands? Hundreds of thousands? This raises one of the basic issues of human history: the dreadful dilemma of reform or revolution; peaceful transformation or rebellion, uprising, and civil war. This question cannot be avoided by those considering the issues of post-socialist transition. The 1956 Hungarian Revolution was a bloody uprising crushed with tanks. More than 30 years later, Hungary changed peacefully from a socialist system to a capitalist system. Not a single person was killed. Nobody had to be locked up in jail for opposing the change.

Romania was the one East European country to place its Communist dictator, Nicolae Ceausescu, and his wife, Elena, before a summary court, condemn them to death, and execute them in December 1989.

---

[5] [Study 6 deals with the first and second dilemmas, the ethical questions concerning the non-violence of the change and punishment of the guilty (pp. 137–46). The ideas expounded here expand on those arguments.]

Those now considering how a change of system should be carried out in a place where it has not yet occurred have to take sides in this grave ethical dilemma.

Many who put forward proposals on a future post-socialist transformation have actually tried to evade the problem, for instance, by assuming that the measures they propose will only come up after the basic change has occurred *in some form.* They devise in advance, for example, a plan for reforming public administration. Yet the social context for the future will differ if people are being lynched from the lamp posts, summary courts are condemning people to death, and foreign occupation forces are patrolling the streets, or in contrast, if the political change takes place non-violently. If the reformers envision a non-violent scenario, let them say so, because this condition is not self-evident.

2. Although it ties in with the previous dilemma, there is a separate question of *dispensing justice* to decide (Barahona de Brito et al. 2001; Horne and Levi 2004; Huyse 1995). The system to be replaced committed crimes. Does blame attach only to the "system" or also to specific people who are still alive? Who can be deemed guilty and to what degree? Anyone who imagines that under totalitarianism, a pack of gangsters imposes a reign of terror and everyone else is innocent knows little about such systems. How wide or narrow a segment of the population should be declared criminal and punished accordingly? Should the guilty be allowed to go free or be condemned, at least morally?

Who should reach the verdicts? For the more complete the totalitarian nature of the dictatorship has been, the more illusory the independence and impartiality of the judiciary will be, especially initially.

It should not be imagined that the problem can be left to a few lawyers or political philosophers concerned with the ethics of dispensing justice. To continue the earlier example, as people begin to think of reforming the administration of state, the changes required are presumably not just organizational. Some people must be dismissed and replaced. This process of selection and replacement, one of the main factors in the change of system, will coincide in time and interpenetrate the process of dispensing (or sabotaging) justice. Or replacement may interweave with justice openly, if legislation is passed prescribing in a transparent fashion which individuals are to be restricted in the public role they may take, because of their activities under the old regime. With or without legislation, there will be a lack of transparency, unfair actions, and corruption. Some people will be dismissed from their jobs without due process or passed by for appointments because they were compromised under the old regime. Inevitably, others will be pushed forward by former comrades precisely because they belonged to the *nomenklatura*.

The demand for dispensing justice is one of the basic ethical postulates of humanity. What can be said against it? Worth mentioning above all is the difficulty of dispensing justice. For with the exception of a few martyrs, no one is entirely blameless. Mihály Babits, a great Hungarian poet, wrote in one of his verses at the time of the Nazi dictatorship: "Among criminals, the silent are accomplices." The sin of keeping silent was committed by many people who did not dare to speak out.

Dispensing justice is hard, because no impartial, independent, competent judiciary or judicial apparatus will have arisen as the post-socialist transition begins. Do we want to have revolutionary courts with powers over life and death? Is it tolerable for the morally charged issue of justice to become a vulgar device of political parties in their fight against one another (Gonzalez-Enriques 2001)?

Another consideration is that once the avalanche of dispensing justice has begun, there is a general atmosphere of fear. Everyone is afraid of being called to account. Those with even a little to hide are afraid, but so are the entirely innocent, for fear of being accused or even convicted without cause. Even a suspicion is enough; some of the mud will stick, even if innocence is later proved.

Once the wheels of justice have begun to turn, it becomes hard to ensure continuity in administration and business. Many of the specialists needed are soon removed or may simply resign, and there are not always competent people to replace them. In all walks of life, there arises a difficult trade-off between justice and continuity. The more radical and rapid the former, the more frequently the latter is broken.[6]

---

[6] [During the political transformation after the lightning Iraqi war, the American leadership running the country laid down that all members of the ruling party under the overthrown dictatorship had to be removed from the state administration, the police, and the army, in a "de-Baathification process" (Peter Galbraith 2006). This tough process of unselective cleansing led to the virtual collapse of the state administration and internal security. The strict initial selection process later had to be eased somewhat for the normal functions of the state to be restored. Several critical analyses on the subject have been published. The title of one (Anderson 2004) is particularly revealing: "The United States' de-Baathification program fuelled the insurgency." See also David (2006), Porch (2003), and Otterman (2005).]

STUDY 7

3. Mention was made under the last point of the *speed* of transition, but it is worth discussing separately. It is understandable that people are impatient after decades of dictatorship and penury and want to live under the new system immediately. Speed has intrinsic value in their eyes.[7]

But speed has its price. Haste and superficiality of thinking will mean that draft measures are laden with mistakes. No essential change can be carried out in isolation. The favorable effects of an essential change will appear only in company with other changes. Haste can mean the necessary comprehensiveness of a reform is lost, and the accompanying changes and auxiliary regulations are not planned and prepared adequately. Sometimes a reform taken too fast may go into reverse. It may not become clear until after a reform that postponing it would have been better than forcing the pace.

There is no convincing theory, model, or even rule of thumb for calculating an "optimum speed" of transition. For my part, I consider the studies on the subject to be pseudo-scientific bluff. It is like setting out to establish the optimum speed for urban traffic. In fact, drivers have to decide a speed for taking each corner, depending on the road, the traffic conditions, and what the traffic taking the corner and the pedestrians are likely to do.

But the uniqueness and complication of the decisions are not the only reason why there is no optimum speed. Another is the *choice of values* behind the decisions. Different decisions will be taken by drivers who are possessed by "speed-mania" even in dense urban traffic, who are determined to arrive at their destination at a given point of time at any cost, or who want to avoid an accident by all means. All three types were found during the post-socialist transition. Some politicians were speed-crazy and wanted to tell the world press and the Washington financial institutions already in 1995 or 1996 that their country had finished privatization first. Others wanted to proceed cautiously (or ultra-cautiously).

4. Now let us look at some *dynamic* ethical considerations more closely. One of the central problems in economics is the dilemma of "present versus future." The usual example given to students when the concepts of discounting and present value are explained is the

---

[7] [The question of a mania for speed has already been dealt with in Study 4 (pp. 79–80). The line of argument there is amplified here from further points of view.]

dynamics of consumer flows. Is it better to consume more today, or save and invest more for the sake of more future consumption?

The problem of discounting appears when a change of system is being planned. Those alive at the time of the change of system look back on a difficult past. Most of them have suffered oppression, poverty, and shortages of goods and services. They hope they can now live better at last. Should the required institutional and structural changes be arranged so that they cause as little inconvenience and financial burden to the public as possible? Should priority go to maintaining, or if possible, maximizing living standards, so that all of the people feel they are real winners by the change of system? This would certainly smooth the transition and help to avoid disruption.

Or is it more important to create firm institutional foundations for the new infrastructure and hire reliable, efficient staff members? Must this mean further sacrifices by the present generation on behalf of the future? Should people today suffer all the disorganization associated with a rapid transformation of the institutional system and all the losses consequent on a fall in production? All these things have to be done with a firm hand, to eliminate the slightest risk of reversal and create a market economy that operates well *in the long term*.

Some of the sharpest, mutually exclusive, "either-or"-type dilemmas have been presented here. Of course, there are intermediate strategies as well. The trade-off between present and future becomes complicated indeed if the choice variables are extended beyond the customary macroeconomic variables (production, consumption, savings, investment) to *institutional* variables as well. What I have sought to emphasize here is the idea that those taking a position on these questions have to realize that their decisions are ultimately ethical choices. They are also deciding how the population will divide between winners and losers and on the distribution of joy and suffering between present and future generations.

Some Lessons

In this section, I would like to draw attention to experiences so far in five aspects of the change of system. Even with the most impartially presented arguments, it is usually possible to tell what system of values an author espouses. Let me spare my readers the task of discovering this by making it plain for each point the value premises on which my line of argument rests.

Representative Democracy

Communist dictatorship may be followed by several kinds of political regime:

– A repressive, strongly anti-Communist regime (a military dictatorship or authoritarian rule by an extreme nationalist-conservative party or group, for instance). That was the case when the repressive regime of General Augusto Pinochet followed that of Prime Minister Salvador Allende, which had been taking Chile along the socialist road. Autocratic rule, in which the dictatorial features are covered by a fig leaf of some aspects of parliamentarism (elections, a powerless legislature). Such regimes can be said to have arisen in some Soviet successor states in Central Asia, in some cases with continuity with the previous communist regime, members of whose political elite managed to jettison their Marxist-Leninist ideology and gain power in conjunction with business circles.

– A semi-autocratic, semi-parliamentary system. A typical example was the regime of Boris Yeltsin in Russia, in the years after the disintegration of the Soviet Union.

– An expressly parliamentary system, with real competition among parties for the right to govern.

The order in which the regime types are given is not a random one. The list progresses from extreme dictatorship through intermediate grades to full institutional democracy. There are no sharp dividing lines among the alternatives listed, in fact. However, there is an acid test for distinguishing the last category, a full multi-party system, from the rest. The democratic rules can be said to apply if a governing party or politician that loses a general election duly withdraws, handing over power without demur to victorious opponents. Once this has occurred not once but twice, the test is a robust one. Hungary and Poland have both passed it.

In fortunate cases, the spread of political democracy and conversion of the economy into a market economy based on private ownership proceed hand in hand, reinforcing each other. But that is not always the case. Democracy involves painstaking and easily protracted processes. Groups involved have to be heard before each regulation is introduced. A parliamentary majority has to be convinced about the plans for reform. Resistance is often stronger from within the ruling party than from the opposition. There have been cases in Eastern Europe where a government of a social democratic complexion has introduced radical privatization rules, for instance, or reforms to make the labor market more flexible, thereby curtailing the rights of workers, which meant, of course, overcoming strong opposition from within a governing party.

How much easier a "reforming dictatorship" is in that respect! If the leading group of the Chinese Communist Party decides on a market-oriented measure, it takes it, and that is that. There is no bother with convincing people, taking it through parliamentary committees, or enlisting support from a free press and television that might otherwise turn the public against it. This makes an especially big difference if the reform calls for short-term financial sacrifices from some sections of society. If inflation has to be curbed, for instance, that involves righting the country's macroeconomic balance and eliminating the budget deficit. The tougher the political authorities are able to be, the simpler it is to push through such painful measures.

It cannot be verified that there is any universal, long-term conflict between introducing democracy and executing reforms designed to produce a balanced, stabilized market economy, but there is no asserting the opposite either.[8] Situations have sometimes arisen in which such conflict has appeared, so that trade-off relations subsist between the application of democratic procedures and the requirements of effective reform. Where that is the case, priorities have to be established.

For me, I can say that the requirements of democracy would take priority. I disagree with those who argue that "the conditions for democracy will ripen later" and "the important thing now is to push on with economic reform." That point of view has become especially widespread among business people and economic experts in poorer, economically less developed transition countries. I disagree, but if they say it directly, at least it becomes clear that *two systems of values* are opposed: one in which priority goes to human rights, freedoms, and democracy and one in which preference is given to financial prosperity and economic growth.

---

[8] See, for instance, Barro (1996) and (1999); and Tavares and Wacziarg (2001).

Confrontations between systems of values are part of a pluralist society. It is unacceptable, however, if double standards are applied. This can be found among Western advisers and observers dealing with less developed transition countries: "Of course, democracy is essential for *us*, as Westerners," they say, "but it is less important for *them*" (referring to the Chinese, Asians, or inhabitants of poorer countries). How do they know? While the repression lasts, there is no way of telling. Furthermore, those who have never had democracy cannot know what it tastes like. The appetite comes as you eat. People begin to feel that democracy is essential once it has become consolidated and institutionalized.

Citizens in places where the post-socialist transition has not yet begun should be ready for this dilemma to arise. People should prepare themselves mentally for daily encounters with this basic choice and its ramifications, as preparation and introduction of each reform proposal comes onto the agenda.

Creating a State of Law

This is a vast, comprehensive task. Rather than defining it, let me point to a few important, characteristic constituents of it. There have to be basic human rights and acceptance of a multiparty system, based on political competition, and a constitution embodying parliamentary institutions. Creating a state of law entails enacting modern, constitutional civil and penal codes to enforce private contracts. It calls for a range of special laws that regulate business activity in a market-compatible way, along with the provinces, rights, and obligations of various state authorities. Parallel with this legislative activity, an independent judiciary has to be established. There have to be guarantees that the police and law enforcement systems do not abuse their powers. Everyone must be held accountable. It cannot be tolerated that anyone or any institution—a party, an authority, or the state itself—be above the law (Sajó 1998 and 2002).

Simply listing these requirements is a warning that legal reform and the creation of the institutions and organizations for a state of law call for circumspection and precision, which in turn require quite a lot of time. It would only discredit the concept of a state of law if new, hastily drafted laws had to be repeatedly amended or if faulty reorganizations constantly had to be reorganized.

Every sphere of the transformation—the political process, the business world, or the arts and sciences—requires an adequate legal or legislative background. Lack of it will only lead to trouble and conflicts, a lesson learned from bitter experience in many places undergoing the transition to a market economy.

That is the lesson—I cannot and would not wish to draw a more specific or tangible conclusion. Western advisers in the early years of the East European transition frequently mentioned the "sequencing" problem and urged researchers to try to devise theories and models of "optimal sequencing." I do not think the problem is theoretically soluble. There are times when it is possible and even expedient to forge ahead a little with some measure, in the knowledge that the requisite legal environment will arrive somewhat later. But forging ahead like that can also become dangerous or even counterproductive, if it is premature or if the requisite legislative and judicial branches are late in catching up. It is hard to coordinate the paces of different processes. This paper simply seeks to warn reformers to consider this aspect. Whatever non-legal field they are working in, they should not forget to clarify the legislative and judicial branches of government and take account of their complexity when pacing the changes.

Strengthening the Private Sector

Even in countries where the power relations have altered completely in favor of the market economy, there remain some staunch anti-capitalists. However, if they have not been convinced by the worldwide historic turn of events that buried the socialist system, this short contribution will certainly not cause them to question or change their ideas. So I am not addressing them, but those who, enthusiastically or less than enthusiastically, expect socialism to turn into some type of capitalism. These people agree in expecting that the proportion of state and collective ownership has to decrease sharply so that private ownership can become the dominant ownership form.

So far, there is agreement, but this expectation leaves open a number of questions.

Political and professional debate and press attention in Eastern Europe and the Soviet successor states concentrated mainly on what was to happen to firms and other assets previously in state or other collective ownership. Should they be returned to their former owners?

Should they be sold to whoever was willing to buy them? Should they be given to some distinguished group of the public, designated as entitled to receive them, such as employees of state-owned enterprises or tenants of state-owned housing? Or should the entirety of the ownership rights be distributed evenly among all citizens?

Before I comment on these questions, let me make a preliminary remark. The prime consideration, in my view, is not what happens to the state-owned property, but something much more comprehensive. What can be done to bring about as healthy and strong a development of the country's private sector as possible? I will put forward my position on that first, and only then turn to analyzing privatization.[9]

Healthy development of the private sector calls, above all, for the dismantling of the barriers to free entry that the Communist regime erected. Those wanting to do business have to meet some minimum conditions, of course—fire regulations, work safety, registration for tax purposes, and so on—but apart from that, freedom of enterprise needs to be ensured as far as possible. The Communist system eliminated *small and medium-sized firms* or confined them within very narrow bounds. Now these barriers to free enterprise have to be lifted quickly to allow private initiative to flourish. That in itself will cause masses of small and medium-sized firms to appear. The development will accelerate further if the entrepreneurs receive tax breaks, preferential loans, or other supports. The small and medium-sized business sector has grown very quickly in the transformation countries.

The question of devising a strategy to assist growth of the private sector includes a tough problem. To what extent should the country be opened to *foreign capital?* This again is a difficulty with political implications, indeed one in which values ultimately clash. Is it a supreme postulate to protect national sovereignty, ward off foreign influences, and protect the producers in firms owned by national citizens from competition with those owned by foreigners? If so, the appearance of each multinational and other foreign-owned firm or the acquisition by any foreigner of agricultural land or other property is a national affront. According to this view, the act of warding off foreigners has in itself intrinsic value. Opposed to this is the view that economic

---

[9] I submitted my proposals at the very beginning of the post-socialist transition in Eastern Europe. (See Kornai 1990.) After the first decade of the transition, I returned to the issue and confirmed my original position (Kornai 2000a [see Study 4, pp. 64–75]).

growth and mounting prosperity are more important. Countries recently released from the restraints of the socialist planned economy are short of capital and have great need of investment. From that point of view, the appearance of foreign capital should be welcomed. Foreign direct investment (FDI), of course, is not an act of charity. Investors expect profits, and when the time comes, some of those profits will be reinvested in the host country, and some will be repatriated. But this is not a zero-sum game, in which investors win and host country loses. Both sides may win. The host country finds that FDI generates employment, brings tax earnings into the state's coffers, spreads foreign expertise, and implants the working practices and discipline of industrially more developed countries (Lizal and Svejnar 2002).

For my part, I would be less interested in what passports investors hold than in their specific intentions. What investment are they planning, and what advantages and costs will it bring to the host country? Where there are mutual advantages to the FDI, I would encourage it or even assist it with governmental instruments. This position reflects my system of values, and it is conditional. It depends on the specific investment intention and the extent to which it promises to be favorable and deserving of encouragement and support.

Even if the government of a post-socialist country decides in *favor* of encouraging and supporting the inflow of foreign capital, the intensity of the flow should still not be thought to depend exclusively on current economic conditions. Whether foreign investors can count on protection of their property, whether they can enforce fulfillment of the contracts they conclude, and whether they can turn with confidence to the courts and the police for assistance if their rights are infringed—all will also depend on how firm the state of law is. Of course, the public's political mood must be taken into account as well. There is no use in the finance minister or a mayor encouraging foreign business people to invest against a background of xenophobic comments in the press or even in Parliament. Political and economic phenomena are closely connected here as well.

Experience in the post-socialist region suggests that *new* business plays the main role in spreading private ownership (Konings, Lehmann, and Schaffer 1996; Konings 1997). New "greenfield" investment is what dominates the growing private sector, whether it is new small and medium-sized firms and big domestic and foreign-owned investment schemes. It is revealing that most foreign investors prefer not to bother with updating an old factory inherited from socialism and find starting a brand new one simpler and more economic.

Privatization

The previous discussion leads to the still unanswered question of what should happen to firms that were state owned or perhaps collectively owned under the socialist system.[10]

Again, I do not think any simple, universally applicable answer can be given. There are several factors worth weighing.

The first is the condition of the firm at the time the problem arises. If it is technically obsolete, with broken, worn-out equipment, it is usually wiser to close it. If it is heavily indebted, it is worth considering bankruptcy proceedings, from which the creditors will gain a sizeable proportion of the ownership rights. The company will be wound up as an organization and a legal entity, but its material assets can be sold. This is customarily referred to as privatization via bankruptcy.

Another factor that strongly affects the decision is the country's *macroeconomic position*. If unemployment is rife, there is much more reason to keep a factory going, at least for a time, even if it will never be viable in the long term. This may mean putting off or slowing down a privatization where the new owner would immediately dismiss much of the workforce. That frequent side effect of privatization is borne more easily by society if the economy is expanding, so that new firms can hire labor released by the old firms.

The decision calls for special attention, sincere human consideration, and circumspection in countries where much of the population lives in poverty. (Cuba certainly belongs to that category.) There has to be caution about closing down inefficient firms and restructuring them in ways that involve reducing the workforce. Such action should be carried out, if possible, at times when the economic growth to accommodate the laid-off workers can be expected in the foreseeable future and after a safety net of social provisions has been installed to ease transitional difficulties. However, these social considerations must not be a pretext for postponing moves to wind up inefficient production indefinitely. For long deferment will only hold back production

---

[10] The reports of the EBRD (2000 and 2001) and the World Bank (2002) are rich in information and in appraisals of private-sector development and privatization.

growth—the one truly effective, permanent way of eliminating poverty. Privatization serves first of all to enhance economic efficiency. But that has *political* and *ethical* implications, which may come into conflict with the efficiency criteria.

Mention has been made of dispensing justice, of trying crimes perpetrated under the old regime and punishing those who committed them. Another side of justice is the question of compensating those who suffered under the old system. Should they receive back the property taken from them by the Communist authorities, that is, should there be restitution? Some post-socialist countries restored such property and others did so in part. (For instance, peasants, under certain conditions, were given back their land and house-owners their houses.) But restitution runs up against practical difficulties, if the original assets have been altered or modernized, or had investment put into them under the socialist regime, so that in their present material condition they *differ* from the assets confiscated. In those cases, there remains the possibility of financial *indemnity*, of the state paying financial compensation for the loss caused by the confiscation.

This presents a serious set of complex problems based on value judgments. Justice dictates that those harmed by the old regime should be compensated by the new. But who should pay the compensation? The state? Certainly, but the state has no money of its own. It spends the money of today's taxpayers. Why should *today's* citizens, some of them poor, pay out of their slim earnings the price of grave injustices committed several decades ago? So there are strong ethical arguments against compensation as well.

I incline to the second ethical stance, but I would like to leave the question open, simply indicating these aspects of the problem.

Do those working in a firm have a special claim on its ownership? Should the firms hitherto in state ownership not be transferred to *employee ownership* instead? These questions introduce socialistic ideas into the new "capitalist environment." The idea is quite muddled even within a socialist-oriented line of argument. The change of political system has occurred, and now it is time for ownership reform. At this point, state-owned firm A is doing well and making good profits, while firm B is suffering serious losses. The high profits at A are not the employees' doing. They are lucky to have inherited up-to-date equipment and a product range that suits the new market conditions. The losses at B have not come about through the employees' negligence.

STUDY 7

The technical equipment is poor, and there is no demand for the products under the new market conditions. Ownership of firm A, therefore, constitutes a gift from the nation to the firm's employees, while the employees at B will be taking over serious burdens from the state, if they agree to accept them at all.[11] What is the justification for rewarding the employees of firm A and penalizing those of firm B in this way? It contradicts the most elementary requirements of justice.

Plans were drawn up in several post-socialist countries to distribute ownership rights equally among all citizens.[12] The proposal was heard first in Poland and applied first in the Czech Republic as "voucher privatization." Every citizen could apply for a certificate (voucher) granting ownership over specified state assets. The same form of privatization was later applied widely in Russia. The rules of the Czech and the Russian schemes were not identical, but they matched in basic economic, social, and ethical respects. Some other post-socialist countries applied the same scheme, but less comprehensively than the Czech Republic or Russia did.

The undoubted advantage of the voucher approach is that it produces very rapid privatization. The property simply has to be taken from the state and divided among the citizens, who may buy shares with their vouchers, deposit them in investment funds, or sell them. The voucher system was opposed by advocates of another strategy: selling off state-owned firms at a fair price, using special auction procedures, to those offering the best terms for them.

Several kinds of arguments were advanced (World Bank 2002).[13] Voucher-scheme advocates pointed mainly to political considerations (Boycko, Shleifer, and Vishny 1993, 1994, and 1996; Shleifer and Treisman 2000). State ownership had to be ended as soon as possible,

---

[11] I have underlined the ethical implications here. There also arise the incentive problems well known from the literature on "self-management" and "worker management." Can the workforce resist the temptation to raise its own wages? Can labor discipline be maintained? See Roland (2000); Filatotchev, Wright, and Bleaney (1999); and Frydman, Gray, and Rapaczynski (1996).

[12] [My arguments here on voucher privatization overlap with those put forward in Study 4 (pp. 64–75). However, I have kept these few paragraphs in because cutting them would have broken off the line of argument in this study and altered the requisite proportions between its parts.]

[13] [I myself took an active part in the debate. I first expressed my point of view in *The Road to a Free Economy* (Kornai 1990) and then in a study (Kornai 1991). I returned to the debate in the essay (Kornai 2000) that forms Study 4 of this volume.]

thereby taking from the old economic elite their most powerful weapon and preventing any restoration of the old order. This is a strong argument, so long as the danger of Communist restoration is a possibility. Discussing whether the argument really stood up in the Eastern Europe of the mid-1990s or the Soviet successor states might be interesting, but it is peripheral to this study, which concerns the strategies of future post-socialist countries. If privatization takes place in a political environment that presents a danger of communist restoration, then a cogent argument exists for eliminating state ownership rapidly, which should take priority over other requirements. However, if domestic power relations and factors beyond the country's borders are strong enough to withstand any attempt at restoration of a Communist regime, this otherwise weighty argument no longer applies.

I have already mentioned a "mania for speed." Some people press for state ownership to be dismantled urgently, regardless of whether there is a danger of restoration. They want to give priority to the requirement of establishing the bases of a capitalist market economy *as soon as possible*, with privatization as the most important factor. Since this concerns a choice of values, one set of values can be countered only by another. Critics of this line of argument, including me, have emphasized that speed is not the most important objective; far more important objectives are the durability and operative efficiency of the new system. The mechanism for choosing owners efficiently was discovered a very long time ago: the market for property rights. The property of the state has to be sold at a fair price. Those who buy it will be prepared to pay because they reckon they can operate it economically and will do all they can to ensure that they succeed (Murrell and Wang 1993; Poznanski 1993; Zinnes, Clifford, and Sachs 2001).[14]

Other ethical arguments have also arisen in these debates. The earlier ideological defense lawyers for state ownership would stress that the factory belonged to the people as a whole. Therefore, if it belongs to all of the people, every citizen is entitled to part of the state property when it is privatized. This egalitarian argument seems bizarre to me when a capitalist system is being created. If a state-owned firm is sold at a fair price and the proceeds are returned to the state's capital account, there

---

[14] Frydman, Gray, and Rapaczynski (1999) add a further important consideration: the distinction between insiders and outsiders as potential buyers of state-owned assets. Sale to outsiders has significant advantages from the point of view of the future efficiency of the firm.

has not actually been any change in the wealth of the state, simply a change of form. Let us assume that the privatization proceeds are used to reduce the state's foreign debt or for productive investment such as development of the infrastructure. In that case, the wealth of the state, far from being reduced, will hopefully continue in a more efficient form. Nothing has been "taken from the people." In fact, the more effective utilization of the wealth of the state is to their benefit.[15]

A requirement for success in reallocating property rights is creation of a workable state of law. The privatization process must be preceded by a minimum level of institutional reform. This observation is supported by many positive and negative experiences.

Transparency

Several mentions have been made of a *fair price*, if the strategy of selling off state property is chosen. To put it more precisely, the assets have to be sold under a proper contract on fair terms.[16]

Here, unfortunately, I have to report negative experiences. There seem to have been frequent cases of negligence, fraudulent accounting, and wasteful expenditures by organizations charged with effecting the sales of state assets, and the process usually became tinged with corruption. These situations then deteriorated, because discovery and prosecution of the corruption and negligence were rare, while each country resounded with rumors of further, unconfirmed abuses impossible to check. Perhaps some of the rumors were unfounded and the problems exaggerated. Certainly a great deal of mud, justified or unjustified, stuck to these historic changes in ownership processes.

---

[15] At this point, it may be useful to explain how privatization actually can be undertaken: (1) There are small firms, which can be sold easily. This is called "small-scale privatization." (2) Larger, state-owned firms should be converted into joint-stock companies. There is no need to sell the whole company to a single person. Shares can be sold in small tranches. (3) Credit and amortization schemes can be introduced. After a small down payment, there can be a repayment schedule extending over many years. (4) There is no need to hurry. In a few years, private wealth will accumulate in the hands of successful managers, small business people, and others, and they will be able to buy more shares. These four suggestions are not mutually exclusive; they can be applied side by side.

[16] The contract may set not only the price, but other conditions for the buyer, concerning employment, technical reconstruction, investment, and cessation of environmental damage, for instance. It is another matter that if such costs are placed on the new owner, this may justify reducing the price to be paid for the assets.

Everyone is uncertain at this point. Does mud-slinging inevitably accompany such a huge transfer of wealth? Or can countries undertaking ownership reform in the future keep the process clean or at least contain the corruption at a lower level?

The defensive techniques are well known. What is needed is a body of legal regulation, expressed clearly, with no loopholes for those intent on enriching themselves (while observing the letter of the law) by making off with state assets under the nose of the treasury. The procedures have to be as transparent as possible. If one state agency is to be responsible for the sales, there should be another, independent agency to monitor them as closely as possible. Let the monitoring agency have access to every detail, and ways to veto transactions before it is too late. Parliament and the press must also have access to the monitoring process.

Price Reform and Liberalization

One basic requirement for a smooth-running market economy is for prices to play their part in controlling supply and demand. Among the biggest problems with the socialist planned economies were the gravely distorted relative prices of transactions.

Almost all economists agree on the direction in which the price system has to go. The need is for relative prices that reflect relative scarcity, to produce equilibrium on the market. Additional debates have occurred on whether adjustments should be done in one stage or several and at what speed (EBRD 2000 and 2001).

Efficiency considerations alone suggest that a radical reform is most expedient. All prices have to be freed from controls and the market allowed to set equilibrium prices. One natural concomitant of radical price liberation is import liberalization. A free flow of foreign goods into the country will force down high prices caused by low levels of domestic production. And if the country has been dependent on imports of a particular product and hitherto kept the price of it artificially low, liberalization of prices and imports will open the way for a rise in the product's relative price. This will prompt users to be more frugal with the product.

Rational economic arguments suggest there should be rapid and consistent liberalization, and these considerations cannot be refuted within their own logic. Yet so far, there has not been one case of rapid and consistent liberalization. Social forces resist, so that the situation becomes thoroughly politicized. Meanwhile ideas and values can be cited in protest against it, thus value choices are involved as well.

If the prices of the most essential goods and services that feature large in the budgets of lower-income households rise, these people and their political representatives will protest, which may, in turn, dissuade the government from making the requisite price adjustments. The prices of various energy sources, for instance, were kept artificially low for such reasons in several East European countries, and in some they remain so.

The interests of some producer groups may, understandably, be biased. In Hungary, for instance, an economically justified rise in petrol prices elicited protests by taxi drivers that escalated into a blockade of the Danube bridges, splitting the capital in two and paralyzing it, and forcing the government to retreat. Competition from imports and prices deemed too low brought repeated protests from agricultural producers.

There is no clear rule for calculating an optimum speed for price reform. It depends on what decision-makers see as more important: to improve economic efficiency with a rational system of relative prices, or to maintain a peaceable society with no causes for dissatisfaction that might translate into anti-government votes at the next general election. The decision about the speed and sequencing of liberalization of prices and imports has to be taken in relation to prevailing political and economic conditions. My preliminary impression from the information available is that it would not be wise to set a rapid pace, because the social and political prices of doing so would be too great. But let me repeat this is only a preliminary impression, not a decisive, clear-cut recommendation. A responsible position on this could only be taken after thorough and up-to-date appraisal of a particular situation.

The clash here is between ultimate values, not just political forces. How much will we listen to our minds, which prescribe an adjustment of prices, and how much to our hearts, which empathize with those whose meager real incomes will shrink further as a result of the reform? These same people were the main economic victims of the old regime, and now their penury is to be prolonged by the grave upheavals of the transition.

Reform of the Welfare State

One prominent feature of the socialist system is comprehensive redistribution. Citizens receive medical care, education, and pensions by right, and child care from a network of state-financed institutions (such as kindergarten and after-school centers).

Most socialist countries in which welfare states develop are poor and backward. The quality of the services is usually low: poor health care, low pensions, and so on. But the law prescribes equal access. In an earlier work of mine, I christened this formation a "premature welfare state."

The effects of a premature welfare state are inconsistent because the power of central decision-makers is increased and the sovereignty of individuals decreased. The state centralizes much of the income, while those in charge of its plans decide how much is spent on education, health, and the care of children and the elderly. Central planning is not confined to the aggregate targets; it goes down to tiny details as well. Decisions about the services mentioned are taken not by individuals or families, but paternalistically, by the state. Such paternalism becomes customary, and most people adapt to it. The generations born into the socialist system cannot conceive of things being otherwise. They expect and demand that the state look after them. This gives them a sense of security. They feel that egalitarian principles are being strongly applied in this respect.[17]

Socialism's provision of basic security, deriving from guaranteed state care and the application of egalitarian principles are popular with much of the public. That is one reason why many people support the socialist system, despite its grave violations of human rights, brutal repression, and the wretched state of the economies. Many other citizens experience mixed feelings about a particular regime, despising and hating certain attributes, while respecting others which they want to retain.

How the antipathy compares with the sympathy and the hatred with the desire to retain elements of the system varies by country and period. Whatever the case, the welfare functions of the socialist state are the ones that leave the most appreciative collective memories after the change of system.

---

[17] They are not applied consistently, as the upper ranks of the *nomenklatura* have privileges: special health-care facilities, easy university admission for their children, and so on.

Even in countries that never abandoned a market economy, based on private ownership or a democratic political system, and never followed the detour of building and then dismantling a Communist system find that reforming the welfare state is a bitter struggle. Mature, rich welfare states, not just "premature" ones, can no longer bear the fiscal burdens of the accustomed, institutionalized services. The otherwise welcome increase in people's life spans is shifting the age distribution of the population toward the old at the expense of the young, which steadily increases the costs of the health and pension systems. It becomes imperative to place limits on future increases in such costs, but any move to do so meets with protest. Think of the enraged public opposition in France and Germany to reforms of the pension and health insurance systems and associated cuts in state-financed services. If these are the public reactions in rich countries, what can be expected in less developed countries, where the poorer strata are even more dependent on state assistance? If economic reformers put violent hands on paternalist facets of the socialist system, they increase the nostalgia for the old order. Reform of welfare-state activity needs handling with caution, if only out of political expediency and a desire for political stability and sympathy for the new system.

Many welfare activities in some countries were performed by state-owned enterprises, not central or local organizations of the state. The firm ran a kindergarten and a doctor's surgery, paid off the pensions of its former employees, and so on. In China, it was especially common, as state assets were shed, new ownership relations developed, and the profit motive strengthened, for firms simply to cease meeting such welfare obligations. For example, a company kindergarten would close, but the children would not be provided for in a village or town kindergarten instead. Concerns for human welfare and political stability alike require that privatization should be coordinated with the transfer of such welfare functions, partly to central and local government and partly to commercial, market-oriented organizations. No new gaps should arise in the provision of welfare services.

I cannot offer a universal prescription for reforming the welfare state inherited from the socialist system, not least because there are fundamental value choices behind the possible measures of reform, here perhaps more than anywhere (Kornai and Eggleston 2001; World Bank 1994; Culyer and Newhouse 2000). Let us agree to respect *individual freedom of choice*. Individuals or families should be free to decide what health and pension insurance they will subscribe to, and which kindergarten, school, or university they will send their children to. The more consistently (and exclusively) society seeks to apply the principle of individual sovereignty, the more favor should be given to decentralized, market solutions in all the sectors mentioned. At the same time, most people have a sense of *solidarity* with those in a disadvantageous position and not capable of paying out of their own pockets the costs they will incur if they are in trouble—adequate medical insurance or a pension scheme, or university fees for their children. The more consistently (and exclusively) society seeks to apply the principle of solidarity, the more favor should be given to state redistribution and the paternalist solution. Furthermore, economic theory confirms that the market is failing in many respects in several segments of the sectors mentioned. Damaging cases of asymmetric information and adverse selection appear, impeding the operation of the market. This also becomes an argument for state intervention and redistribution.

The contradictions between values and the differences of interest among groups, strata, and generations of the public explain why great difficulties might be expected in the reform of the welfare state. For my part, I believe in judicious compromise. Let there be egalitarian provision up to a certain level—basic health care and education for all, and a minimum pension guaranteed for all old people. Beyond that, people should pay for what they want and not expect the state to foot the bill. This line of thinking suggests there should be parallel systems operating and augmenting each other: state pensions and private pensions, state-financed basic medical care and private medical care, and so on.

A proposal that satisfies no one completely and requires concessions, insight, and tact from all may be ignored during vehement clashes between ideologies and interests. In all likelihood, the warring forces will block each other's efforts, and reform will come to a standstill. This can be seen in several post-socialist countries. (It can also be seen in the developed world, for example, in the breakdown or halting progress of health care reform in the United States.)

Concluding Remarks

In conclusion, I would like to touch briefly on two questions.

First, in devising a program of transition, what role is played by the fact that the country concerned is extremely backward economically and many of its inhabitants are very poor? This, of course, has to be considered fully when every single decision is taken. Many economic problems obviously present themselves differently in Cuba, for example, than they did during the post-Communist transformations of a relatively developed East Germany and Czechoslovakia. That was what I had in mind in drawing attention in this study primarily to issues *not* closely tied to level of economic development. Readers can convince themselves of this by leafing back. The peaceful or violent nature of the transition, the problem of justice, the forms of privatization, and so on are connected in the main with political and ethical positions. I have pointed repeatedly to the *trade-offs* of the transition, the dilemmas and complex problems that oppose effective introduction of some measure of reform, and the possible social and political consequences of introducing them. In weighing the latter, it has to be considered that the consequences are borne by people who have suffered much already, not only political oppression, but material poverty as well. Decision-makers have to think twice about the burdens they personally can bear today for the sake of a better tomorrow.

My second remark concerns the role of advisers. I had studied the position of Cuba earlier, and I tried to gain more information as I set about writing this piece. Yet I have intentionally refrained from pronouncing on Cuba's specific problems or giving practical advice on what Cuba should do if post-socialist transition comes on the agenda. What should then be done? Those things are up to the Cubans themselves. Only they have the knowledge required; they must take responsibility for their decisions and live with the consequences of them.

I saw and heard from "inside," as a citizen of a post-socialist country, what domestic experts thought of foreign advisers with superficial knowledge of conditions in the country, confidently stating what should be done, based on experience elsewhere. The repellent intellectual arrogance of such advisers means their advice is usually ignored.

I have visited many post-socialist countries, but I have refrained from "advising," even if asked to do so. I have confined myself to talking frankly of our experiences in Hungary, and above all, of the dilemmas, conflicting group interests, political considerations, and value choices encountered.

I have tried to do the same in this paper. I should like those devising a working plan for post-socialist transition in Cuba to take a hard look at certain problems and think them over in a profound way. I hope they will not be fooled by false prophets or advocates of extreme ideas. Let the designers of the transformation insist on confronting the arguments on each side and weighing the pros and cons. Let them evaluate thoroughly the social and political consequences of each new regulation or reform. And to add a hope that lies behind every section of this paper, let them face the ethical implications and ask: What values will be promoted or damaged by this regulation or measure of reform?

I would hope this paper has achieved this modest purpose. I do not want to suppress the bitter reflection that leaders of one nation's political life show little inclination to learn from other nations' experiences. They tend toward the same, avoidable mistakes that plagued others. I sincerely hope that will not happen in Cuba, for there is an ample stock of previous experience, well worth learning from.

Appendix

Table 7.1 Survey of countries that counted as "socialist countries" in 1987

(1)	(2)	(3)	(4)	(5)	(6)	(7)	(8)
Serial number[a] 1987	Country	Serial number 2002	Country	Population (million)[b]	Area, 2002 (1,000 sq. km)[b]	Political system classification, 2000[c]	Ownership reform (share of the private sector in GDP) % in 2001)[d]
1.	Soviet Union	1.1	Armenia	3.1	29.8	Partly Free (SCA)	Large
		1.2	Azerbaijan	8.1	86.6	Not Free (SCA)	Large
		1.3	Belarus	10.0	207.6	Not Free (CA)	Small
		1.4	Estonia	1.4	45.2	Free (CD)	Large
		1.5	Georgia	5.4	69.7	Partly Free (TG/HR)	Large
		1.6	Kazakhstan	14.8	2,717.3	Not Free (CA)	Large
		1.7	Kyrgyzstan	4.7	198.5	Party Free (SCA)	Large
		1.8	Latvia	2.4	64.6	Free (CD)	Large
		1.9	Lithuania	3.5	65.2	Free (CD)	Large
		1.10	Moldova	3.6	33.8	Partly Free (TG/HR)	Medium
		1.11	Russia	145.4	17,075.2	Not Free (SCA)	Large
		1.12	Tajikistan	7.3	143.1	Not Free (SCA)	–
		1.13	Turkmenistan	5.4	488.1	Not Free (CA)	Small
		1.14	Ukraine	49.3	603.7	Not Free (TG/HR)	Large
		1.15	Uzbekistan	25.0	447.4	Not Free (CA)	Medium
2.	Mongolia	2	Mongolia	2.7	1,565	Free	–
3.	Albania	3	Albania	3.4	29	Partly Free (SCD)	Large
4.	Yugoslavia	4.1	Bosnia and Herzegovina	4.3	51.1	Partly Free (TG/HR)	Medium
		4.2	Croatia	4.4	56.5	Free (SCD)	Large
		4.3	Montenegro	0.7	13.8	Free (SCD)	Medium
		4.4	Serbia	10.1	88.4	Free (SCD)	Medium
		4.5	FYR Macedonia	2.0	25.3	Partly Free (SCD)	Large
		4.6	Slovenia	2.0	20.3	Free (CD)	Large

(1)	(2)	(3)	(4)	(5)	(6)	(7)	(8)
Serial number[a]	Country	Serial number	Country	Population (million)[b]	Area, 2002 (1,000 sq. km)[b]	Political system classification, 2000[c]	Ownership reform (share of the private sector in GDP) % in 2001)[d]
	1987		2002				
5.	Bulgaria	5	Bulgaria	8.1	111	Free (CD)	Large
6.	Czechoslovakia	6.1	Czech Republic	10.3	78.7	Free (CD)	Large
		6.2	Slovakia	5.4	48.9	Free (CD)	Large
7.	Hungary	7	Hungary	10.2	93	Free (CD)	Large
8.	Poland	8	Poland	38.7	313	Free (CD)	Large
9.	Romania	9	Romania	22.4	238	Free (SCD)	Large
10.	North Korea	10	North Korea	22	121	Not Free	
11.	China	11	China	1,287	9,561	Not Free	Medium[e]
12.	East Germany	12	Germany[f]	15.1[g]	108	Free (CD)	Large
13.	Vietnam	13	Vietnam	81.6	330	Not Free	Medium[h]
14.	Cuba	14	Cuba	11.3	115	Not Free	—
15.	Congo	15	Congo	3.0	342	Not Free	—
16.	Somalia	16	Somalia	8.0	638	Not Free	—
17.	South Yemen	17	Yemen	2.2[i]	355	Partly Free[j]	Large[k]
18.	Benin	18	Benin	7.0	113	Free	—
19.	Ethiopia	19	Ethiopia	66.6	1,222	Partly Free	—
20.	Angola	20	Angola	10.8	1,247	Not Free	—
21.	Kampuchea	21	Cambodia	13	181	Not Free	—
22.	Laos	22	Laos	5.9	237	Not Free	—
23.	Mozambique	23	Mozambique	17.5	237	Partly Free	—
24.	Afghanistan	24	Afghanistan	28.7	648	Partly Free	—
25.	Nicaragua	25	Nicaragua	5.1	130	Partly Free	—
26.	Zimbabwe	26	Zimbabwe	12.6	391	Not Free	—
1–26.	All countries counted as "socialist" in 1987 as a percentage of world total			32	31		

[a] In Kornai (1992b), the order of the countries followed the date of their shift away from capitalism (e.g., date of Communist takeover).
[b] Source: CIA (2002). Population data show the last official census in each country.
[c] Freedom House (2006a), (2006b).

Freedom House uses two types of rating, our table represents both. One of the ratings (see Freedom House 2006a) uses three categories: "Free," "Partly Free," "Not Free"; this is reported in the first place. The other rating (see Freedom House 2006b) applies five categories: "Consolidated Democracy" (CD), "Semi-Consolidated Democracy" (SCD), "Transitional Government or Hybrid Regime" (TG/HR), "Semi-Consolidated Authoritarian Regime" (SCA), and "Consolidated Authoritarian Regime" (CA). This can be seen in the brackets.

[d] Share of private sector in GDP (%): This classification is primarily based on the data in EBRD 2003. Notations:
Large = 60–100%
Medium = 30–59%
Small = less than 29%
– = Missing from the analysis, not classified
[e] 1998 data (37%). Source: Yang (1999).
[f] The former German Democratic Republic became part of the unified Federal Republic of Germany.
[g] 2000 data. Source: Federal Statistical Office of Germany (2003).
[h] 2000 data (35.7%). Source: Statistical Office of Vietnam (2002).
[i] Population in 1986. Source: Table 1 in Kornai (1992b).
[j] Since North and South Yemen united in 1990, this classification corresponds to the new united Yemen's political structure.
[k] Source: World Bank (2003).

8
The System Paradigm*

Introduction

This study applies the concept of a paradigm, as the title makes clear. The concept was introduced into the philosophy of science in a classic work by Kuhn ([1962] 1970). Kuhn did not offer a clear definition of the concept, which has itself been the subject of much debate.

As I was preparing for this study, I reread several works on the philosophy of science, and in particular on the methodology of economics. It was a remarkable reading experience, which warned me, if nothing else, to be cautious. For there is no trace of consensus among authors, even on how to interpret the basic concepts. There is an exasperated debate taking place. The alternative schools of thought on the philosophy and history of science disagree because of deep-rooted epistemological differences among their adherents. The result is a minefield that I would prefer to avoid.

However, it prompts me to start my line of argument by clarifying the concepts, to avoid eventual misunderstandings. I do not wish to contribute to the discussion of how far Popper, Kuhn, Lakatos, or others were right in their analysis of the history of science. It will suffice for a proper discussion if I say what sense I attach to the word "paradigm" in this paper. In the sense used here, scholars can be said to use

* [I delivered this paper as a lecture at the conference "Paradigms of Social Change" organized by the Berlin-Brandenburgische Akademie der Wissenschaften in Berlin on September 3–5, 1998. I would like to express thanks for the valuable comments made at the conference by Andreas Ryll and Helmut Wiesenthal, and those received from Ágnes Benedict, Bernard Chavance, Zsuzsa Dániel, and T.N. Srinivasan. I am grateful to Julianna Parti for her help in editing this paper.]

the same paradigm in their research and teaching if they show the following common attributes:

1. They work to solve the same or closely related puzzles. They view social reality from the same, or almost the same angle. They set out to illuminate the same, or almost the same range of phenomena, and are ready to abstract away the same or almost the same phenomena or leave them obscure. Those who work within a common paradigm have the same, or a closely related outlook, viewpoint and approach.

2. They use conceptual frameworks that are the same or closely akin. (Alternatively, it is relatively easy to compile a word list that translates the conceptual apparatus of one author into that of another.)

3. They use the same or a similar methodology for observing, processing experience and drawing conclusions; they support their statements by the same or similar methods.

I do not specify more common attributes than that. In other words, I do *not* expect "partners in paradigm" to start from the same axioms or arrive at the same main conclusions.[1] The most important community of attributes is the one summarized under point 1: I ascribe a common paradigm to those who are drawn to the same problem and seek to approach it in a similar way. To that extent they are working to a common research program.[2]

The concept of a paradigm described in the three points does not correspond accurately with the definition given by Kuhn, the author of the concept. However, it is quite close to what intellectuals less conversant with the philosophy of science mean by a paradigm today.

Many people doubt whether Kuhn's dynamic scheme (normal science within a paradigm, then a scientific revolution, then the triumph of a new paradigm) has general validity in the history of the natural sciences. The Kuhn scheme is certainly not characteristic of the history of the social sciences.[3]

---

[1] The "research program" concept devised by Lakatos (1971) is widespread, and according to many authors, richer, fuller, and more accurate than Kuhn's concept of a paradigm. The three points just made also appear in Lakatos's concept, although he stipulates other common attributes as well. All those who work within a "research program" in Lakatos's sense subscribe to the same "core theory" and are prepared to make the same auxiliary assumptions.

[2] Here I intentionally use the expression research program in its ordinary sense, not in the specific sense in which Lakatos defines it.

[3] This is convincingly shown in a study by Blaug (1986), in relation to the development of economics.

Using the expression paradigm in the less restricted sense I have given, it is obviously possible for alternative paradigms to live side by side in the social sciences, playing a constructive, progressive role.

I do not want to advocate a kind of unprincipled "peaceful coexistence" here. The history of the social sciences also contains instances where a paradigm has succumbed irrevocably to another, more viable approach. If the advocates of two, otherwise clearly distinguishable paradigms are concerned with similar puzzles, rivalry develops between them. Nonetheless, my main purpose is not to prove that the paradigm presented here is superior to some other paradigm, but to show that it is *different*, and that the difference is justified. It is different because it sets out to solve different puzzles, by partly similar and partly different methods from those of the other widespread coeval paradigms.

A System Paradigm, Not a Transformational Paradigm

The organizers of the Berlin conference asked me to speak on the "transformational paradigm." What is to be understood by this? Twenty-five countries that had communist regimes have set out on a path of transformation. The two words "transition" and "transformation" have been spoken and written countless times by politicians, journalists and scholars since 1989–90. Nonetheless, when I began to work on the paper, I saw increasingly clearly that the term "transformational paradigm" is misconceived.

It seems to be more expedient to talk of a "system paradigm." Rather than describing this concept in advance, I will leave it to reveal itself step by step. It will emerge that the transformation, along with the transition from one system to another, is one among several subjects that constantly occupy the advocates of the system paradigm. It would not be right to name a more comprehensive paradigm after one of its component topics.

Even if Kuhn's original concept of the monopoly of the prevailing paradigm is laid aside, there is no ignoring his view that a paradigm constitutes a *long-lasting* common way of thinking by a scientific community. Succeeding generations learn the previously developed paradigm in their textbooks. This is a criterion that the *system paradigm* meets. It looks back on a long history and it provides a certain community of researchers with the intellectual guidance that Kuhnian paradigms have usually provided.[4]

A Brief Intellectual History

There is only space here to outline the development of the system paradigm, without aiming at completeness. The system paradigm, unlike many other paradigms in the natural or social sciences, cannot be linked with a single great name, a great innovative figure who fomented a scientific revolution. It developed in a series of works, over a long period. Let me cite here the theories that display most expressively the specific attributes of the system paradigm that distinguish it from other paradigms.

The first name to mention must be Marx. There were certainly others before him who thought in terms of systems, but it was Marx whose work, above all *Capital* ([1867–94] 1974), made a lasting impression on people's way of thinking by creating the capitalist–socialist pair of concepts. He contrasted two formations: an existing one and a utopia that he considered desirable. He can be considered the pioneer of the system paradigm because he did not confine himself to examining a certain sphere of capitalism (the political sphere or the economic, or the social, or the ideological). He viewed all these spheres altogether and analyzed the interactions between them. Ever since, the influences that these spheres have upon each other, and the main directions of causality between them, have been among the main subjects pursued by researchers who think in terms of the system paradigm. Marx took a systemic view by not confining himself to examining some institution of capitalism or other, but looking at the sum of its institutions—not at one part or the other, but at the system as a whole.

Here I will leave open the question of whether Marx's answers to the questions he addressed were the right ones. According to the definition used in this paper, the questions to which answers are sought, the puzzles to be solved, form the main attribute of paradigm. Marx

---

[4] Even if "transformational paradigm" could be defined, it would still not meet the criterion of durability. For one thing, the period of transformation that began with the collapse of the communist system only started a few years ago.

asked many questions that researchers working within the system paradigm have sought to answer ever since. An outstanding example is *The Communist Manifesto* (Marx and Engels [1848] 1969), which posed the dramatic question of how the change of system, that is the transformation of society, took place during the transition from a pre-capitalist formation to a capitalist formation.

Some people may be surprised if the names that follow Marx in my brief account of intellectual theory are those of Mises (1981) and Hayek (1935a and 1944). The enraged opponent of capitalism and prophet of socialism is followed by two enthusiastic advocates of capitalism and committed antagonists of socialism. I am talking here not about physicists or chemists, but about social scientists, whose views of the world are based on values and political preferences. Although Marx on the one hand and Mises and Hayek on the other stand on opposite sides of the political spectrum, they share the common conviction that a comparison of capitalism and socialism is worth analysis and research. Their way of thinking bears common paradigmatic elements. They examine social relations and human interactions. They find the circumstances that induce certain groups of people to behave in a certain way important. In that and many other respects, they are among the creators of the system paradigm.

It is not forgetfulness on my part that I have yet to mention Hayek's opponent in debate, Oscar Lange. With due respect to Lange's theoretical achievements, I have to say that his famous study on socialism (Lange 1936–1937) is not among the works inspired by the system paradigm. It is a work of sterile economics. Lange disregards the question of what kind of political mechanism should be associated with the economic mechanism he describes. He does not deal with how the head of the public company he creates would behave, or what real social conditions would motivate people to act according to the "rules" that the Lange model prescribes on paper. Mises and Hayek do not sidestep the fundamentally important fact that politics and the economy are tightly connected. Incentives, communication, the collection and processing of information: questions such as these are in the foreground of their argumentation. The ideas of Mises and Hayek are outstanding representations of the system paradigm, while those of Lange's study are rather alien to it.

An important part in shaping the system paradigm was played by Karl Polányi. He takes us back to the left wing of the political stage, for although Polányi does not deny the merits of the market, he is strongly critical of it as a mechanism. His idea that the economy could be coordinated by various alternative mechanisms became an important element in the system paradigm. Besides the market, he pays special heed to coordination mechanisms controlled by the principles of reciprocity and redistribution. The title of one of his main works, *The Great Transformation* (Polányi [1944] 1962), implies that the changes after the collapse of the communist system were not the first such systemic changes. The market itself is a historical product subject to constant transformation.

Another great architect of the system paradigm was Schumpeter, especially his *Capitalism, Socialism, and Democracy* (Schumpeter [1942] 1976). Again the title itself is illuminating. Schumpeter wants to understand both systems in their entirety, including their political, sociological, economic, and ideological aspects. The book poses the characteristic puzzles of the system paradigm, enquiring, for instance, what provides the cohesiveness of a system, and what starts off the erosion of it.

Schumpeter underlined the need for synthesis of the various disciplines dealing with society, above all economics, sociology, political science, and history. He argued for efforts to be made to develop a universal social science.[5]

The main attributes of the system paradigm are clearly discernable in the work of Walter Eucken.[6] The concept of *Ordnung* (order) that he uses largely corresponds to what this study refers to as a "system"—principally the legal and institutional framework for economic activity. He distinguishes two main pure types—the centrally governed economy and the laissez-faire economy—and devotes special attention to middle-way solutions. Eucken is averse to the term "capitalism," which he sees as having been discredited by the Marxists. Like it or not, however, this does not exclude Eucken from the company of advocates of

---

[5] Shionoya (1995) gives an excellent summary of how this idea runs through all Schumpeter's writings, especially his works on theoretical history and methodology.

[6] Eucken's theory of "economic order" is summed up in Eucken (1940), and in its most mature form in Eucken ([1952] 1975). The former has been translated into English (Eucken [1940] 1950), but not the latter. Incidentally, it is unfortunate that the ideas of this very important European scholar should have gained little currency in the Anglo-Saxon social sciences.

Although I had studied Eucken's work earlier, I too forgot him when I was writing the first version of this study—influenced, perhaps by the selective quoting routine of the Anglo-Saxon literature. I am grateful to Professor Andreas Ryll for drawing my attention to this omission.

the system paradigm. His terminology can easily be translated into the different vocabulary used by his "paradigm partners."

Eucken was certainly inspired by direct experience of Hitler's Germany and post-war Germany and by outside study of the Communist world to recognize how transformation of the political sphere effects changes in the economic order.

I have talked so far about the great pioneers of the system paradigm. However, according to Kuhn, it is also part of a paradigm's function to permeate the everyday activity of the research community that believes in it, allowing the *normal science* of a discipline or sub-discipline to be built upon it. Kuhn sees the paradigm as a means of control, of applying intellectual discipline. So discussion of any paradigm has to involve not only the generals, but the officers, sergeants, and ordinary soldiers who observe the same intellectual discipline. Kuhn also points out how the paradigm of normal science manifests itself in daily university teaching and textbooks. It is a proof of the existence of the system paradigm that its spirit appears in many textbooks on *comparative* subjects—comparative economics, sociology, and political science.[7]

However, there is no course at any university and no textbook that might be called *comparative social science*, using this term according to the Schumpeterian interpretation. Lecturers or authors may possess a thorough, comprehensive knowledge and interest in neighboring disciplines to their own, but they have to make concessions to the departmentalization of the academic world. To that extent it is doubtful whether it is right to talk, in Kuhn's original sense, of normal science being pursued under the paradigm, since one of its characteristics—the interdisciplinary nature of the social sciences—has failed to gain full acceptance in academic education.

The situation is more promising if we look not at the state of education but at the academic interaction between researchers. Political scientists, economists and sociologists are working together more often as co-authors or as members of common research teams. They also hold joint conferences in certain topics.[8, 9]

---

[7] Let me mention as examples two textbooks on comparative economics published recently, which also cover problems of the post-socialist transition: Carson (1997) and Chavance (1994).

[8] A good example is presented by the conference organized by the French economist Bernard Chavance in Paris in 1998, designed to demonstrate that there is a broader group of scholars who work within the system paradigm. This was clearly expressed in the title of the conference: "Evolution and transformation of economic systems: socialism and capitalism compared."

[9] [To the issue of interdisciplinary connections I return in the Appendix of the present study.]

STUDY 8

Let me conclude this review of intellectual history by referring to my own work, which I summed up in *The Socialist System* (Kornai 1992b).[10] There I set myself the task of synthesizing the system paradigm. I did not try to present the paradigm itself in a "distilled" form, i.e. in the language of the philosophy of science. Instead I wrote in the spirit of the system paradigm about an existing, historical formation, the socialist system that had developed historically under the rule of the Communist parties. I described its birth, its mature form, and its erosion leading to self-destruction. If any readers of this paper would like to see in more detail what I mean by the system paradigm or its application, they can derive the idea from reading that book.[11]

The Main Attributes of the System Paradigm

After that review of intellectual history, let me try to sum up the main attributes of the system paradigm.

1. Researchers who think in terms of the system paradigm are concerned with the system as a whole, and with the relations between the whole and its parts. Narrow, partial analysis may be an important instrument of exploration, still it falls outside this angle of view.

2. The system paradigm cannot be confined within any traditional partial discipline (such as economics, sociology or political science). It has to be seen as a school of comprehensive, general social science. It pays particular attention to the interaction that takes place between the various spheres of the functioning of society (politics, the economy, culture, ideology).

Each of the scholars mentioned in the last section as pioneers had an original profession; they were exponents of one of the main disciplines. Polányi was an anthropologist; the others were economists. However, their work goes far beyond the boundaries of their original discipline. Each was an economist, a sociologist, a political scientist,

---

[10] I first attempted to apply the system paradigm in my book *Anti-Equilibrium* (Kornai 1971), but in a polemic manner and in many ways in a raw or half-mature form.

[11] [I would like here, near the end of the book, to add one more remark to what I have said so far: all *eight* studies have been written in the spirit of the system paradigm. As I underlined in the Introduction, that is precisely the strand that ties the studies in this volume together.]

a historian and a philosopher all at once. In other words they were social scientists. This comprehensiveness in their thinking was not a kind of incidental adventurism, or gained on flying visits to neighboring university departments. It was a decisive element in their way of thinking.

3. The attention of researchers guided by the system paradigm is not focused on economic, political or cultural events and processes as such, but on the more permanent institutions within which these events and processes occur, and which largely determine their course.[12] Special attention must be paid to the distinction between institutions which emerged historically, in the course of an evolutionary process, and other institutions which are *ad hoc* constructions of a bureaucratic decision. The concept of an *institution* has to be interpreted very broadly in this context. It includes, for instance, the prevailing legal order in the system concerned, its moral norms, the distribution of property rights and positions of power, the incentives working on the actors in society, and the information structure. The paradigm attaches special importance to whether attributes of the operation of a society are system-specific, or whether they are traceable to circumstances other than the system itself (e.g. the personality of the leading politician, the day-to-day political or economic situation, or the country's geographical location).

4. The system paradigm requires the understanding of the strong connection between an existing human organization and the historical process, which generated that organization. In other words, a researcher inspired by the paradigm must search for an explanatory theory in historical terms. A strong linkage is sought between various disciplines of social science and history.[13]

5. According to the system paradigm, individual preferences are largely products of the system itself. If the system changes, so do the preferences. Many of those whose work has been mentioned in the historical review are liberal in their political outlook, speaking out in defense of individual freedoms and advocating broad scope for individ-

---

[12] There is substantial overlapping and many points of contact between this attribute and the paradigm of "institutional economics" (see North 1990). However, I do not want to blur the distinction between the two, as the system paradigm and institutional economics differ strongly in other respects.

[13] Keeping in mind this linkage, perhaps it would be fair to include Max Weber in the list of great theorists who paved the way for the system paradigm.

ual choice. However, this is compatible with scientific examination of how far and in what way social circumstances influence individual preferences.

6. All paradigms dealing with society employ static models as one of their instruments, if only because of methodological difficulties. No scholar is unaware that everything in society is constantly changing. What distinguishes the thinking of those working within the system paradigm from that of their colleagues outside it is that their interest lies in the *big* changes, the great transformations. For instance, they enquire into what processes of decay are going on within a system, so that it will come to an end and give way to another system. They ask how there occurs a transition from one system to another system, or from one typical version of a great system to another.

7. Researchers guided by the system paradigm recognize that all systems have shortcomings or dysfunctions specific to them. Marx ascribes the various drawbacks of capitalism to the system, not to the cruelty of the mill owner. According to the interpretation of Mises and Hayek, it is not the brutality or paranoia of the socialist dictator, or the incompetence of planners, that causes the problems with socialism. Polányi argues that failures in the operation of the market derive from the nature of the market itself. Certainly Marx, Mises, Hayek, and Polányi find it easier to identify the problems in the system they are averse to than in the one they prefer. Schumpeter is the most impartial among these scholars, noticing what causes bureaucratic features to appear in capitalism, the system he prefers.

Whatever the motivation of researchers, they will find, if they think in terms of the system paradigm, that the challenge lies in studying the intrinsic dysfunctional features of the system considered. No system is perfect. Every system possesses harmful attributes that can only be alleviated, not eliminated, because the propensity for them to reproduce is deeply imbedded in the system.

8. Every paradigm has a method of approach, a methodology characteristic of it. One of the most obviously characteristic methods of the system paradigm is comparison. It explains an attribute of a system by comparing it with a corresponding attribute of another system, analyzing the similarities and differences between them. This comparison is mostly qualitative, although some attributes are easily measured, which offers a chance to make quantitative comparisons based on statistical observations.

It is not characteristic of the system paradigm for theoretical analysis to rely on mathematical models.[14] It would require a separate examination to say why not. There are certainly several factors, of which I would like to pick out the one that I find most important. Mathematical economics and other social-science researches that apply mathematical methods operate at a high level of abstraction. They are forced to analyze a narrow slice of reality, as that is the only way to construct a model suitable for mathematical analysis. One of the foundations of the system paradigm is to grasp reality, so far as possible, in its entirety, not just a thin slice of it. So it is prepared to make heavy concessions in rigor and exactitude. Its methodology is "softer" than that of a "semi-hard" (or ostensibly hard) economic paradigm. On the other hand, it is prepared to face puzzles the latter avoids. More will be said about this later.

Post-Socialist Transformation: The Great Challenge

The great transformation taking place before us at enormous speed provides an exceptional opportunity to test the system paradigm and develop it further. A series of countries has virtually jumped from one system to the other. Looking at the world as a whole, the transition from pre-capitalist formations to full-blown capitalism took centuries. Merciless violence was used by those directing the first manifestation of the socialist system, the classical Stalinist system, and even so, the transition lasted about 15 years. Now, on the way back to capitalism, less than a decade has gone by, and yet the most advanced of the East European countries—the Czech Republic, Hungary, and Poland—have largely undergone the transition, after "velvet" revolutions devoid of bloodshed or violence.

The actual process of historical change vindicates those who forecast that there would be a transition from the socialist system to the capitalist system. Although the transition has not been uniformly rapid,

---

[14] There are a few exceptions. For instance, the system paradigm inspired a study written by an outstanding representative of mathematical economics, the Nobel laureate Tjalling Koopmans, and a well-known figure in comparative economics, Michael Montias (Koopmans and Montias 1971).

STUDY 8

with standstills and reverses in a good many countries, few people now doubt that the direction of the transformation is towards a capitalist system.

Social scientists tend to envy their natural-scientist colleagues for being able to conduct laboratory experiments. In this case, history presented us with a veritable laboratory. It is too early to say whether we have made or are making good use of this opportunity. A paradigm has to pass examinations in several subjects to prove it is workable. There will be discussion in the final section of one of the basic subjects—its powers of prediction. Let us look here at two other, closely interrelated subjects. How has the system paradigm passed the test in explanatory power and in theoretical assistance to everyday practice?

The system paradigm has proved simply indispensable. Literally everybody, the researcher, the politician, and the journalist, thinks in terms of its concepts. Socialism and capitalism, the command economy and the market economy, bureaucracy and free enterprise, redistribution and consumer sovereignty: these and similar concepts have provided the framework for the analyses. Like Molière's *Bourgeois Gentilhomme*, unaware that he speaks prose until the Master of Philosophy enlightens him, many researchers into the post-socialist transition do not realize they are speaking the language of the system paradigm, not of their own discipline.

Typical puzzles to do with the system paradigm have become the centre of attention. What speed should the transformation go? Should there be a comprehensive package introduced all at once or should things be introduced in several stages? What is the right order to introduce the legal regulations required? What should come first and what afterwards? What are the political conditions required for the economic changes, and the economic conditions required for the political changes? How much can be left to spontaneous, evolutionary transformation, and how much needs to be done actively, by state intervention and promotion of changes? The answers vary, but the questions are the same. They are not confined to a few scholars. They are asked in the workshops preparing comprehensive World Bank and EBRD reports, and by the staffs of government think-tanks.

A convincing argument for the system paradigm can be grounded on observing the attitude shown by the "guest stars" of the post-socialist transformation.[15] After the dramatic changes of 1990, many Western academic economists, sociologists, political scientists, and legal scholars were keen not to be left out. They had to come and see for themselves, and if possible also give advice. The enthusiasm of most was temporary: they came, looked, won (or lost), and then left. That is why I call them guest stars. They were like performers leaving their company temporarily to appear with another.[16]

Let us distinguish two groups. As for the first, they were unable, even for the short time of the "guest performance," to step out of the paradigm that had defined their way of thinking hitherto. They usually did not exercise any real influence. Members of the second group, however, managed to shed, partly or wholly, their usual way of thinking, and consciously or instinctively, adopt the system paradigm. They sensed that this situation did not belong to a realm of "pure" economics or partial models. They could not follow the usual routine of an economist, simply assuming away the existence of anything that might threaten the susceptibility of the theorem to proof. It was not possible to tear certain parts of society and the economy out of context at will and focus the examination on them alone, looking there for "second best" solutions, because the consequences were influenced by the interaction between those parts and others that were being assumed away. The use of static models as an easy way of treating the problem is of no avail, as all the elements of the system are in very fast movement and transformation.

The latter group of "guests" was prepared, in most cases, to leave behind their rigorous models and argumentation and listen to their common sense, and indeed to their intuition. Their case shows that

---

[15] In writing somewhat ironically here about the part that the guests from abroad played, I do not wish to imply that the home-grown advisors performed better. There were those among the foreign and the home-grown experts who produced useful recommendations; there were others in each group whose advice proved less applicable or wholly mistaken. However, there was a perceptible difference between the foreigners and the domestic experts in the paradigmatic foundations on which their advice rested. Most of the academic economists educated at universities under the Communist regime were not influenced by the mainstream paradigm, in whose spirit the visiting economists from the West had been raised. Though they were much less educated in contemporary economics, the reform debates in the years before the collapse of Communism had trained their minds to think in terms of simultaneously changing the various components of the system.

[16] Portes (1994) uses another metaphor to describe the same phenomenon. They remind him of the carpetbaggers—the office-holders and political and economic entrepreneurs from the North who went to the South after the American War of Independence.

the reason the methodology of the system paradigm lacks models based on exact assumptions and theorems is not that its followers are insufficiently conversant with mathematics. Not even economists with the best of mathematical training have been able to construct models leading to really convincing conclusions about the exceedingly intricate problems of the transformation. So it is better to be intellectually honest. It has to be admitted that the system paradigm is one that only half-meets the criteria of the strict scientific method. On the one hand it requires of its exponents consistency of logic, with statements supported by argumentation and comparison with similar or contrasting cases. The stringency of the argumentation is increased by quantitative analysis, which has to be done wherever possible. On the other hand, those working within the system paradigm, or reviewing works written within it, may not require either strict mathematical proofs of propositions, or support for them from econometric analysis that has stood the trial of statistical tests.

It can safely be said that the system paradigm has been enriched by the post-socialist transition. The conceptual apparatus has become wider and more refined, the scope for comparison has grown, and econometric analysis applicable to international comparisons has become a more prominent part of the paradigm's methodology.[17]

Some Western researchers and advisors have certainly contributed to an understanding of the problems of transformation, and in some cases, even defined practical tasks in a useful and constructive fashion. This applies especially to those who have stayed longer or decided to specialize in this field. They have learnt in practice what their Western education omitted to teach them.

The minds of students at prestigious Western universities are conditioned to apply as routine the method of "assumption–theorem–proof" and the most up-to-date econometric techniques, but most of them are unfamiliar with the approach applied by the system paradigm. It has not become a conditioned reflex for them to say to themselves: "I must not simply ask what I am abstracting away. It is at least as important to ask what I *must not* abstract away. How does the partial problem I am examining relate to the whole?" Students are not encouraged to inquire how they can perceive the state of a country in all its complexity, or for instance, what they have to consider if they see that a

---

[17] For the latter development, see, for instance, De Melo et al. (1997) and Fisher et al. (1996).

country is in crisis. Students can receive a PhD in economics even if they have not increased at all the minimal knowledge of history, sociology, psychology, and philosophy they gained during their secondary and undergraduate studies. They can widen this knowledge of their own accord, of course, but there is no great appreciation or reward for doing so. On the contrary, it may arouse suspicions that they are *dilettanti* reaching out in to too many directions.

For about a quarter, or even a third of the world's population, the change of system has been a cathartic experience. We, who are living in the transforming parts of the world, cannot and will not continue to live as we did before. This sense of catharsis has not affected the social sciences as a whole. The "guest stars," with a few exceptions, have returned to their original troupe to continue with what they were engaged in before. They have left the unprecedented laboratory, if they really looked into it at all. The system paradigm has remained more or less detached and underappreciated, while the other paradigms, especially the neo-classical economic mainstream, have remained almost unaffected by it.

There has been no wide-eyed wonder and inner discontent with the state of arts in our discipline—the typical reactions of healthy intellects and open minds, found at times when something great happens. It is not a scientific revolution in Kuhn's sense that I miss. I am not calling for the mainstream paradigm to be superseded by another paradigm. All that is needed, after the great experience of the post-socialist transformation, is for mainstream normal science to recognize more clearly its limitations. It has to understand better what it is competent to do and what it is not. I may be wrong, but I have the impression there are very few people in the economic profession who accept this narrowed, more modest domain of validity for the mainstream paradigm. Indeed there are some who have drawn precisely the opposite conclusion from the change of the system in the 1990s. They mistake the victory of the actual capitalist system over the actual socialist system, for a victory of neo-classical mainstream economics over all other, alternative paradigms. In fact, actual capitalism triumphed for a variety of reasons, among others, some excellent properties, which have not been adequately analyzed or explained by the mainstream paradigm.

One important note must be added. There is also full justification for analyses that start from the capitalist system, and set out to study phenomena within it, provided that those who choose such an approach have clear notions about the limits of their research. Here let me refer to Section 1 of this study, where I say I do not demand a monopoly for the system paradigm. It is designed to supplement, not replace other paradigms that are applicable within their own bounds. At this point it would be tempting to discuss how far the competence of the mainstream paradigm reaches. What can it explain well, and what question does it fail to answer or answer badly? Conversely, where are the bounds of applicability of the system paradigm (and others)? However, I have to reserve my thoughts on this for another study.

Some Other Puzzles

The post-socialist transformation and transition into capitalism in Eastern Europe and the territory of the former Soviet Union will be over in the foreseeable future. The question of when it will end in each country can be left open at this point. It will take quite some time after transformation ends to digest the experiences from it scientifically. Will the system paradigm wither away, starved of scientific challenges, once we, our successors and our students have done this? The answer is definitely not. There are problems that look set to remain on the scientific agenda for very long periods of history and present a constant challenge to the system paradigm. These problems also challenge the complementary or rival paradigms. Let me explain this answer by listing four subjects that remain for subsequent research:

1. The Communist party retains a monopoly of power in China, which to that extent remains a Communist country. China's transformation, past and future, is one of the great puzzles to which conscientious researchers cannot delude themselves into thinking they have the key. The search for a solution certainly calls for participation by exponents of the system paradigm, even if it is not exclusively their concern. All the problems that have emerged during the East European transformation will crop up in China as well, but not in exactly the same way, of course. China's gigantic size and immense political, economic, and military potentials make it one of the most important research subjects of our time.

The transformation in three other countries, Vietnam, Cuba, and North Korea, where the political power of the Communist party still prevails, raises similar problems, although their weight in the world is of a different order of magnitude.[18]

2. The system paradigm can be of great assistance in analyzing alternatives *within* the capitalist system. This also is among the fields of research where there is a lot of overlap between the evolutionary paradigm and the system paradigm. Capitalism is not a rigid, uniform system. It exists in numerous mutant variants, among which history selects. Evolutionary changes take place within it. Studying and understanding the mutations and resulting variants could enrich the conceptual apparatus of the system paradigm, along with its problem-solving approach and methodology.

For instance, how do the Japanese, American, and German alternatives differ? The answer will not be satisfactory if it is sought only in the economy, the political system, or cultural traditions, or if the research is confined to one or two institutions, such as state intervention or labor relations. Greater understanding of the differences between alternative types of capitalism would have yielded a more convincing explanation of Japan's marvelous economic performance until recently, and of the causes, embedded in the system, of the serious problems that have arisen so rapidly. Such an understanding would also show more clearly how the American and German roads of modern capitalism differ and what they have in common.

Let us look briefly at the manifestations of normal science based on the system paradigm—the textbooks of comparative subjects. These concentrate mainly on comparing the two "great" systems, socialism and capitalism, and deal relatively little with the alternatives within capitalism. There is no consensus on the typology of these alternatives. Detailed descriptions of a prototype country (for instance Japan, Sweden, or the United States) serve as substitute for ideal types that rest on generalizations from real historical realizations and are suitable for theoretical analysis. The task of formulating such ideal types remains.

3. It is worth pondering the fact that in certain segments within the capitalist system, as in a kind of microcosm, certain problems of the macrocosms, the "big systems" are replicated. A good example of this

---

[18] [This issue is dealt with in other places in the book, in particular in Study 3 (pp. 49–60)] and Study 7 and also in the Appendix of Study 6. (pp. 147–50).]

STUDY 8

is provided by reform of the health system, which is on the agenda all over the world. The actual questions asked in the debate and the arguments of those making recommendations arouse feelings of *déjà vu* in someone like myself, who took part in the debates on reforming the socialist system. Why should public ownership be retained, or conversely, abolished in the health sector? Is it right or wrong for health-care activities to be coordinated by the market, or should it be left to the bureaucracy? How much scope is permissible or desirable to allow for consumer sovereignty? Who should set the prices of the provisions: the market, one particular actor in the market, or some state authority? What are the advantages and disadvantages of centralization and decentralization? If the health system were to operate according to some "market-socialist" pattern, in the spirit of some Lange-type economy, what behavior would be exhibited by the actors (the hospital manager, the doctor, the patient)? Not only the questions, but the phenomena are familiar. This is true especially in Europe, Western and Eastern, where health care is more or less free and the health sector forms an island of socialism (or at best market socialism) in a capitalist sea, with the familiar accompanying features: shortages, queuing, waiting lists, forced substitution, bureaucratic allocation, and rationing.

Naturally, those taking part in the debates on the health system in the West read and react to literature written by their Western colleagues, especially by exponents of the sub-discipline of health economics. It is depressing that the analogy with socialism has not occurred to anyone, even though debates of the same questions have been going on in that context for decades. Furthermore, many of the ideas have already been put into practice in the Communist countries, so that the results of them are discernible. It is, for instance, well-known that complete state centralization of an activity greatly decreases administrative costs in the first stage, and eliminates supplementary costs of competition such as advertising and influencing of buyers. That is so, but this high degree of centralization was accomplished on a grand scale, by the socialist system. So *ultimately*, has centralization proved fruitful? What does it imply in terms of citizens' sovereignty or defenselessness? What driving forces does it create or suppress in technical development?

It would be worth employing the approach, the conceptual apparatus and the methodology of the system paradigm, and the questions it poses, to supplement (but not replace) the present paradigm of health economics. It would be useful if the participants in these debates were to look through the literature on the debates on reforming socialism. It might emerge that there is no need to "rediscover" all the questions and answers. Such study would make valuable contributions to the debate on health reform, and draw attention to relations that have hitherto been ignored.

The health system is just one example of the many microcosms that could be viewed as systems and researched within the framework of the system paradigm.

4. I have left to last the most difficult question on my list: the global, historical transformation of the *great* capitalist system. There is a fairly wide consensus behind the view that it is justified to talk about two great systems in the 20th century: capitalism and socialism. It is also widely accepted that in the countries where the socialist system still prevails, wholly or partly, will eventually adopt the capitalist system. But to quote Fukuyama (1992), will history end there? Everyone knows that there are many significant changes taking place in production technology, interpersonal communication, the distribution of property rights and method of their enforcement, and the dissolution of national borders. Possibly, at the end of the 21st or 22nd century, a scholar—an advocate of the system paradigm—may dare say, "What we have now is another great system (or several other great systems), which differs from the capitalist system of the 20th century." I am not in favor of hastening such a statement, which would be unfounded as yet. What needs to be considered is how long today's capitalism will remain identical with itself. Putting forward this kind of question is one of the components common to the evolutionary paradigm and the system paradigm. I believe that the system paradigm provides unanimous criteria for drawing the line between socialism and capitalism. Possibly, but by no means certainly, the same criteria will apply when drawing a distinction between what has been known so far as capitalism and the system or systems, yet unnamed, that may replace it.

Failures of Prediction

The last problem I mentioned in the previous section leads to the subject with which I would like to conclude: the problems of future changes. What I have talked about so far is *not* the task of prognosis, but the narrower problem of deciding the moment at which the system so far called capitalism, by public consent, has changed to such an extent that it would probably be justified to consider it a different *great* system. There can be no avoiding the far more serious question of how the advocates of the system paradigm have fared in the test on a basic subject for all sciences, prediction.

The short answer (though excessively and unjustly short) is that they have failed. To be more precise, not all their predictions have been mistaken, but there have been some very important ones that history has belied.

Let us return to the names mentioned in the brief intellectual history, starting with Marx again. For several decades, it seemed as if the basic Marxian prediction would be validated, at least in part of the world: the capitalist system would give way to the socialist, private property to public, and the market to planning. Viewing the matter historically, such a development proved only transitional. The prediction was dramatically refuted by what happened in Eastern Europe and the Soviet Union.

Hayek predicted that if a capitalist country stepped out on the slippery path of centralization, state intervention, and planning, it would be unable to stop on the road to serfdom. That did not happen either. It is possible to stop after a quarter of that road has been covered. It is still possible to turn back halfway. The question is decided in the political sphere, by whether there are institutional guarantees to prevent tyranny.

Schumpeter's prediction was not actually far from Marx's, but he made it, not with the passion of a prophet, but with the resignation of an impartial scholar. It turned out that he greatly underestimated the vitality of the capitalist system and overestimated the long-lasting viability of socialism. He tried to understand the latter from the stilted models found in the theoretical works of Walrasian economists, instead of the bloody reality of the Soviet Union.

"Sovietology" has been roundly condemned for failing to predict the collapse of the Soviet Union and the associated Communist regimes. This criticism is partly justified. On the one hand, most representatives of comparative economics and political science considered it axiomatic that the capitalist system was superior to the socialist system, and produced many arguments to prove it. In that sense their works implied a general prediction (opposed to that of Marx or Schumpeter) that the socialist system would end eventually. On the other hand, "Sovietology" failed to make even a conditional prediction as to when or under what conditions the socialist system would succumb.

I am self-critical of my own work as well. On the one hand, I think that in one important aspect the predictive content of my works has been vindicated. While many of my colleagues in the East and the West thought that the reforms would prolong the life of socialism by eliminating some of its shortcomings, I was skeptical about them. I pointed out that although the reforms were improving people's quality of life, they were undermining the coherence of the system. Instead of perfecting the system, they were weakening its foundations, causing erosion, not stabilization.

What I did not foresee was the speed and acceleration of this erosion. However, it was not the system paradigm that prevented me foreseeing this. On the contrary, my problem was that I did not apply that approach and methodology with sufficient consistency and refinement. I did not study deeply enough. So I failed to perceive the interaction between various disintegration processes, for example mounting economic troubles, falling back in the arms race, disillusionment with communist ideology after some political freedom had been won, and mounting cynicism and corruption of the *nomenklatura*. To use Hegelian terms, the quantity was leaping into quality. I should have opened our eyes wide at the first signs of leaps and sudden changes.

It has to be confessed that though the exponents of the system paradigm do not deserve a fail mark, they did not do well in the prediction test. Rather than consoling ourselves with what I said earlier—that we got better grades in other subjects[19]—I think we should learn the lessons for our future work.

Although the utmost effort should go into improving the predictions, no wild hopes should be entertained either. The course of history is hard to foresee, and it is especially difficult to predict the date

---

[19] The Rabbi of Lublin had a reputation for being a great seer. One day he cried, in the presence of his disciples, "I see! I see!" "What do you see, wise Rabbi?" they asked. "I see Krasnik, the ghetto in Krasnik." "And what is happening in the ghetto in Krasnik?" "I see fire. There is fire coming to Krasnik!" The rabbi's disciples took buckets and hastened away to help their fellow Jews. However, when they arrived in Krasnik, they saw with their own eyes that there was no sign of a fire. The Jews of Krasnik began to make fun of them: "Well now, that famous rabbi of yours was quite mistaken." Whereupon the Lublin Jews replied, "True, there is no fire here, but it is a great thing that he was able to see as far as Krasnik."

of the sudden great changes. It can be declared on methodological grounds, and not as an excuse, that the scope for prediction is very limited in the sphere of investigation dealt with by the system paradigm. It is fair to expect reliable predictions of science in a sphere of frequently repeated phenomena. People regularly buy meat. Using a good model and reliable statistical data, it is possible to make a reliable prediction about the extent to which a one percent rise in the price of meat will reduce demand. The Soviet Union, on the other hand, came into being on one occasion and collapsed on one occasion. Since the latter event is unique and unrepeatable, one *cannot expect* a scientific prediction that goes into any detail about when it should occur, what events should precede it, or how it should occur. Now the system paradigm concentrates attention precisely on great, unique, unrepeatable social changes of this kind. Even if an adequate prediction was not made, there are a great many generalizable lessons to be drawn from subsequent careful analysis within the system paradigm.

The most important conclusion to draw from the failures of the predictions is the need to be very modest indeed. The system paradigm (and if justified, other paradigms) may be applied to explain both past and present, and to reason out practical recommendations, but great care should be taken when making predictions.

This paper has not covered the question of where the dividing line runs between educated opinion and scientific proposition in the study of society.[20] I mentioned in the introduction that I want to avoid, so far as I can, the minefield of the great debates on the philosophy of science. My caution in this respect leads me to refrain from analyzing the criterion of scientific activity at this point. I can only express the hope that we, the exponents of the system paradigm, will not be excluded from the world of science if we do not seek to measure the explanatory power of our message in terms of the ability (or a feigned self-confidence in ability) to predict.

---

[20] Rorty (1997) explored this question in an essay written on Kuhn's death. He credits Kuhn with having helped to demystify this dividing line. To remain within my own profession of economics, the same effort can be seen in the works of McCloskey, including his book McCloskey (1985), which caused a great storm. While I myself make great efforts time and again to support my assertions by the methods of argumentation and proof accepted in the discipline of economics, besides applying other supportive instruments, I share the view of Rorty and McCloskey. Such efforts should be viewed with a requisite measure of irony, and irony at one's own expense. I think that is suggested in the tone of this paper.

The more far-reaching and complex in its causes the phenomenon that is to be predicted, the more caution is required. The predictions made cannot be more than conditional. Intellectual honesty requires that we qualify even these cautious predictions by acknowledging that they are based on a fair degree of ignorance, partly on perceptions of a scientific nature, and partly on intuition.

[Appendix

*On the Segregation of the Social Sciences**

I traveled to China at the beginning of 2005. As I prepared the lectures I would deliver there, I tried to get to know the latest literature on the Chinese reform. Reading the writings of a succession of the best experts in economics, I found some remarks on the political aspects of the reform, but surprisingly, no references to articles in political-science journals. I was reading in parallel the studies by the best experts in political science, and there I found the opposite bias—frequent remarks on reform of the economy, but no references to journals of economics. There has been little or no intellectual dialogue between these two groups of China experts—or at least, that is my ad hoc impression.

These experiences prompted me to look at the ties between the various social-science disciplines nearer at hand. I had the assistance here of an economics student, Noémi Péter. We looked at four disciplines: economics, political science, sociology, and law. We chose five leading journals for each and studied a complete year: all the publications in 2004.

Various criteria were used to add up the number of references. (A description of how the journals were chosen, the quantification methods, and the grading principles, as well as the detailed numerical results appear in Kornai 2006.) We found altogether 316 economics articles where the numerical methodology we had devised was interpretable. They contained a total of 4885 references where it was possible to identify the discipline to which the source belonged.

---

* This appendix has been extracted from a longer study (Kornai 2006), which grew out of a lecture delivered at a conference on June 14–15, 2005, organized by the CEU and the World Bank.

STUDY 8

The main results of the survey are summarized in *Tables 8.1* and *8.2*. It was found, for instance, that 88.9 percent of the citations in economics journals referred to economics journals, 6.6 percent to interdisciplinary social-science journals, and 2.2 percent to political science journals on political science, 1.2 percent to journals of legal studies, and 1 percent to sociology journals. So the main source of information for members of the economics profession was work published in eco-

Table 8.1   The citation structure

Categories	Economics	Law	Political Science	Sociology	All
Economics (1)	4,344	256	341	625	5,566
Law (2)	60	3,428	70	190	3,748
Political Science (3)	109	84	1,379	286	1,858
Sociology (4)	50	15	110	3,077	3,252
Inter-disciplinary (5)	322	296	197	497	1,312
All closely tied to a specific discipline					
(6) = (1) + (2) + (3) + (4) + (5)	4,885	4,079	2,097	4,675	15,736
Other (7)	3,752	5,873	4,470	8,152	22,247
Total (8) = (6) + (7)	8,637	9,952	6,567	12,827	37,983

Table 8.2
Distribution of citations assignable to a specific discipline, percent

Type of publication in which reference was originally published	Type of journal in which reference appeared				
	Economics	Law	Political Science	Sociology	All
Economics	88.9	6.3	16.3	13.4	35.4
Law	1.2	84.0	3.3	4.0	23.8
Political Science	2.2	2.0	65.8	6.1	11.8
Sociology	1.0	0.4	5.3	65.8	20.7
Inter-disciplinary	6.6	7.3	9.4	10.6	8.3
All	100.0	100.0	100.0	100.0	100.0

Note: The figure of 100 percent in the last row refers to the set of all citations referring to the subset in line 6 of *Table 8.1*. For instance, of the citations of economics articles, the 100 percent consists of the 4885 *identified* citations in the column; 88.9 percent of these 4885 citations referred to economics journals.
Source: Author's calculations, with the help of Noémi Péter.

nomics journals by other members of the same profession. The profession is looking inward and hardly paying heed to the products of other social-science professions. The situation is similar with the other disciplines examined.

I would not like to attach excessive significance to the *numerical* findings from such a small body of data, but it is demonstrated clearly, even by this first approach, that the intellectual ties among the various branches of social science are weak.]

Previous Publications of the Studies in this Volume*

1. "The Coherence of the Classical System"
Extracts from the book *The Socialist System, The Political Economy of Communism*, Princeton: Princeton University Press, Oxford: Oxford University Press, 1992, pp. 19–21 and pp. 360–79.

Other publications: in Hungarian (1993), in German (1995), in French (1996), in Bulgarian (1996), in Russian (2000), and in Vietnamese (2002).

2. "The Inner Contradictions of Reform Socialism"
Journal of Economic Perspectives, Summer 1990, Vol. 4, No. 3, pp. 131–47.

Other publications: in Croatian (1989), in Hungarian (1990), in Spanish (1990), in Russian (1991), in English (1992), in Italian (1994), and in Chinese (2003).

3. "Market Socialism? Socialist Market Economy?"
"Socialism and the Market: Conceptual Clarification", Forthcoming in Kornai, J. and Y. Qian, eds., *Market and Socialism in the Light of the Experiences of China and Vietnam*, New York: Palgrave-Macmillan, 2008.

4. "The Speed of Transformation"
"Ten years after 'The Road to Free Economy': The Author's Self-evaluation", In B. Pleskovic and N. Stern, eds., *Annual Bank Conference*

---
* The permission of the publishers of the first publications to include the papers in this volume is gratefully acknowledged.

on *Development Economics 2000*, Washington D.C.: The World Bank, 2001, pp. 49–66.

Other publications: in Chinese (2000), in Hungarian (2000), in Russian (2000), in Bulgarian (2001), and in Vietnamese (2001).

5. "The Great Transformation of Central Eastern Europe: Success and Disappointment"

Economics of Transition, 2006, Vol. 14, No. 2, pp. 207–44.

Other publications: in German (2005), in Hungarian (2005), in Bulgarian (2006), in Croatian (2006), in Czech (2006), in French (2006), in Japanese (2006), in Russian (2006), in Rumanian (2006), and in Serbian (2006).

6 "What Does 'Change of System' Mean?"

Not yet published in English language. First publication in Hungarian: "Mit jelent a »rendszerváltás«? Kísérlet a fogalom tisztázására", *Közgazdasági Szemle*, 2005, Vol. 54, No. 4, pp. 303–21.

7. "What can Countries Embarking on Post-Socialist Transformation Learn from the Experiences So Far?"

Cuba Transition Project, Institute for Cuban and Cuban-American Studies, University of Miami, 2004.

Other publications: in Hungarian (2004), in Polish (2004), in Rumanian (2004), in Spanish (2004), in Croatian (2006), and in Greek (2006).

8. "The System Paradigm"

In *Paradigms of Social Change: Modernization, Development, Transformation, Evolution*, W. Schekle, W.-H. Krauth, M. Kohli, and G. Elwert, eds., Frankfurt/New York: Campus Verlag; New York: St. Martin's, 2000, pp. 111–33.

Other publications: in Hungarian (1999), in Russian (2002), and in Chinese (2003).

References

Afanas'ev, Iu. N., ed., *Inogo ne dano* (There is No Other Way), Moscow: Progress, 1988.
Alchian, A. A., "Uncertainty, Evolution and Economics Theory", *Journal of Political Economy*, Vol. 58, No. 3, pp. 211–21, 1950.
Anderson, J. L., "The United States' de-Baathification program fuelled the insurgency. Is it too late for Bush to change course?", *The New Yorker*, November 15, 2004.
Andreff, W., "French Privatization Techniques and Experience: A Model for Central-Eastern Europe?", in Targetti, F., ed.: *Privatization in Europe: West and East Experiences*, Aldershot: Dartmouth, 1992.
Antal, L., L. Bokros, I. Csillag, L. Lengyel, and Gy. Matolcsy, "Change and Reform", *Acta Oeconomica*, Vol. 38, No. 3–4, pp. 187–213, 1987.
Barahona de Brito, A., C. Gonzalez-Enriquez, and P. Aguilar, eds., *The Politics of Memory: Transitional Justice in Democratizing Societies*, Oxford: Oxford University Press, 2001.
Bardhan, Pranab K., and Roemer, J. E., eds., *Market Socialism: The Current Debate*, New York and Oxford: Oxford University Press, 1993.
Barone, E., "The Ministry of Production in the Collectivist State", in Hayek, F. A., ed., *Collectivist Economic Planning*, London: Routledge, pp. 245–90, [1908] 1935.
Barro, R. J., "Democracy and Growth", *Journal of Economic Growth*, Vol. 1, No. 1, pp. 1–27, 1996.
Barro, R. J., "Determinants of Democracy", *Journal of Political Economy*, Vol. 107, No. 6, pp. 158–83, 1999.
Berend, I. T., "Capitalism", in Baltes, P. B., and N. J. Smelser, eds., *International Encyclopedia of the Social & Behavioral Sciences III*, New York: Elsevier, pp. 1454–1459, 2001.
Black, B., R. Kraakman, R., and A. Tarasova, "Russian Privatization and Corporate Governance: What Went Wrong?" *Stanford Law Review*, Vol. 52, July, pp. 1731–808, 2000.
Blanchard, O., *The Economics of Post-Communist Transition*, Oxford: Clarendon Press, 1997.

Blasi, J. R., M. Kroumova, and D. Kruse, *Kremlin Capitalism: The Privatization of The Russian Economy*, Ithaca and London: Cornell University Press, 1997.

Blaug, M., *Economic History and the History of Economics*, Sussex: Wheatsheaf Books, 1986.

Bloch, M., *Feudal Society*, London: Routledge, [1939] 1989.

Bolton, P., and G. Roland, "Privatization in Central and Eastern Europe", *Economic Policy*, vol. 15, pp. 276–309, 1992.

Boycko, M., A. Shleifer, and R. W. Vishny, "Privatizing Russia", in Keasey, K.T. and M.S. Wright, eds., *Elgar Reference Collection. International Library of Critical Writings in Economics*, Vol. 106, pp. 578–631, Cheltenham, and Northampton, MA: Edward Elgar, 1993.

Boycko, M., A. Shleifer, and R. W. Vishny, "Voucher Privatization", *Journal of Financial Economics*, Vol. 35, pp. 249–66, 1994.

Boycko, M., A. Shleifer, and R. W. Vishny, "A Theory of Privatisation", in Parker D., *Elgar Reference...*, Vol. 123, pp. 180–90, 1996.

Böröcz, J., and Á. Róna-Tas, "Small Leap Forward: Emergence of New Economic Elites", *Theory and Society*, Vol. 24, No. 5, pp. 751–81, 1995.

Brabant, J. M. van, "Divestment of State Capital", in Poznanski, K. Z., ed., *Constructing Capitalism: The Reemergence of Civil Society and Liberal Economy in the Post-Communist World*, Boulder, San Francisco, and Oxford: Westview Press, pp. 117–140, 1992.

Braudel, F., *Les Jeux de l'échange*, Paris: Librairie Armand Colin, 1975. In English: *The Wheels of Commerce*, London: Fontana Press, Imprint of HarperCollins Publishers, 1985.

Braudel, F., *The Mediterranean and the Mediterranean World in the Age of Philip II*, New York: Harper and Row, [1949] 1972–1973.

Braudel, F., *Civilization and Capitalism, 15th–18th century. I–III; I. The Structures of Everyday Life; II. The Wheels of Commerce; III. The Perspective of the World*, Berkeley: University of California Press, [1969–1979] 1992.

Brenner, R., "Agrarian Class Structure and Economic Development in Pre-Industrial Europe", *Past and Present*, Vol. 70, pp. 30–75, 1976.

Broadman, H. G., "Reducing Structural Dominance and Early Barriers to Russian Industry", *The Review of Industrial Organization*, Vol. 17, No. 2, pp. 155–75, 2000.

Brus, W., *The Market in a Socialist Economy*, London: Routledge and Kegan, [1961] 1972.

Burke, P., *Interview Conducted by Karl Vocelka and Markus Reisenleitner*, http://www.univie.ac.at/Neuzeit/gburke.htm, 1990.

Burkett, J. P., "The Yugoslav Economy and Market Socialism", in Bornstein, M., ed., *Comparative Economic Systems: Models and Cases*, Homewood, IL, and Boston: Irwin, pp. 234–58, 1989.

Caballero, R. J., and M. L. Hammour, *Creative Destruction in Development: Institutions, Crises, and Restructuring*, Washington, DC: The World Bank, 2000.

Campbell, N. A., *Biology*, Menlo Park: Benjamin-Cummings Publishing Company, 1987.
Campos, N. F., and F. Coricelli, "Growth in transition: What we know, what we don't, and what we should", *Journal of Economic Literature*, Vol. 40, No. 3, pp. 793–836, 2002.
Carson, R. L., *Comparative Economic Systems*, Armonk, NY.: M.E. Sharpe, 1997.
Chavance, B., *The Transformation of Communist Systems. Economic Reform since the 1950's*, Boulder and Oxford: Westview Press, 1994.
CIA, *CIA World Fact Book*, CIA, http://www.odci.gov/cia/publications/factbook, 2002.
Coase, R. H., "The Problem of Social Cost", *Journal of Law and Economics*, Vol. 17, No. 2, pp. 357–76, 1960.
Coffee, J. C. Jr., "Institutional Investors in Transitional Economies: Lessons from the Czech Experience", in Frydman, R., C. Gray, and A. Rapaczynski, eds., *Corporate Governance in Central Europe and Russia*, Vol. 1, Budapest, London, and New York: Central European University Press, pp. 111–86, 1996.
Coffee, J. C. Jr., "Investing a Corporate Monitor for Transitional Economies: the Uncertain Lessons from the Czech and Polish Experiences", in K. J. Hopt, H. Kanda, M. J. Roe, E. Wymeersch, and S. Prigge, eds., *Comparative Corporate Governance*, Oxford: Clarendon Press, pp. 67–138, 1998.
Culyer, A. J., and J. P. Newhouse, eds., *Handbook of Health Economics*, Amsterdam, New York, and Oxford: Elsevier Science, North-Holland, 2000.
Csaba, L., *The New Political Economy of Emerging Europe*, Budapest: Akadémiai, 2005.
Csite, A., and I. Kovách, *Piacgazdaság és gazdasági elit 1993–1997* (Market economy and economic elite 1993–1997), Budapest: MTA Politikai Tudományok Intézete, 1997.
Csurgó, B., Zs. Himesi, and I. Kovách, „Elitek és politikai preferenciák" (Elites and political preferences), in Kurtán, S., P. Sándor, and L. Vass, eds., *Magyarország politikai évkönyve 2001-ről* (Political Yearbook of Hungary in 2001), Vol. 1, Budapest: Demokrácia Kutatások Magyar Központja Közhasznú Alapítvány, pp. 318–36, 2002.
Dabrowski, M., S. Gomulka, and J. Rostowski, *Whence Reform? A Critique of Stiglitz Perspective*, Warsaw: Centre for Social and Economic Research, 2000.
Dahl, R. A., *Polyarchy: Participation and Opposition*, New Haven: Yale University Press, 1971.
Dallago, B., "The Underground Economy in the West and East: A Comparative Approach", in Bornstein, M., ed., *Comparative Economic Systems: Models and Cases*, Homewood, IL, and Boston: Irwin, pp. 463–84, 1989.
David, R., "From Prague to Baghdad: Lustration Systems and their Political Effects", *Government and Opposition*, Vol. 41, No. 3, pp. 347–72, 2006.
Davis, C. M., "The Second Economy in Disequilibrium and Shortage Models of Centrally Planned Economies", *Berkeley-Duke Occasional Papers on the Second Economy in the USSR*, No. 12, July, 1988.
De Melo, M., C. Denizer, and A. Gelb, "From Plan to Market: Patterns of Transition," in Blejer, M. I., and M. Škreb, eds., *Macroeconomic Stabilization in Transition Economies*, Cambridge: Cambridge University Press, 1997.

REFERENCES

Desai, R. M., and I. Goldberg, "The Vicious Circles of Control: Regional Governments and Insiders in Privatized Russian Enterprises", *Policy Research Working Paper*, No. 2287, Washington, DC: The World Bank, 2000.

Djankov, S., and P. Murrell, "Enterprise Restructuring in Transition: A Quantitative Survey", *Journal of Economic Literature*, Vol. 40, No. 3, pp. 739–92, 2002.

Dyck, A., *Ownership Structure, Legal Protections, and Corporate Governance*, Annual World Bank Conference on Development Economics, 2000.

EBRD, *Transition Report 1999*, London: EBRD, 2000.

EBRD, *Transition Report 2000*, London: EBRD, 2001.

EBRD, *Transition Report 2001*, London: EBRD, 2002.

EBRD, *Transition Report 2002*, London: EBRD, 2003.

EBRD, *Transition Report 2004*, London: EBRD, 2005.

EBRD, Economic Statistics, 2006. http://www.ebrd.com/country/sector/econo/stats/sci.xls Date of access: January 20, 2006.

Economist, "The cauldron boils", *Economist*, September 29, 2005.

Economist, "Caught between right and left, town and country", *Economist*, March 8, 2007.

EIU, Country Data. http://www.eiu.com.

EIU, Country Reports. http://www.eiu.com.

Ellerman, D., "Voucher Privatization with Investment Funds. An Institutional Analysis", *Policy Research Working Paper*, No. 1924, Washington, DC: The World Bank, 1998.

Ellman, M., *Planning Problems in the USSR: The Contribution of Mathematical Economics to Their Solution 1960–1971*, Cambridge: Cambridge University Press, 1973.

Engels, F., "The Housing Question", In Marx, K., and E. Friedrich, *Collected Works*, Vol. 23, London: Lawrence and Wishart, pp. 317–91, [1872] 1976.

Engels, F., *Anti-Dühring. Herr Eugen Dühring's Revolution in Science*, 3rd ed., Moscow: Foreign Languages Publishing House, 1963.

Eucken, W., *Die Grundlagen der Nationalökonomie*, Berlin, Heidelberg, and New York: Springer, [1940] 1965. English translation: *The Foundations of Economics*, London: William Hodge, 1950.

Eucken, W., *Grundsatze der Wirtschaftspolitik*, Tübingen: Mohr, [1952] 1975.

Eurobarometer, *Public Opinion in the Candidate Countries*, survey conducted in October–November 2003; http://europe.eu.int./comm/public_opinion, 2003.

European Commission, *Comprehensive Monitoring Report of the European Commission of 5 November 2003 on the State of Preparedness for EU Membership of the Czech Republic, Estonia, Cyprus, Latvia, Lithuania, Hungary, Malta, Poland, Slovenia and Slovakia*, 675 final, Brussels: European Union, 2003.

European Values Survey: http://www.worldvaluessurvey.com.

Federal Statistical Office of Germany, http://www.destatis.de, 2003.

Ferge, Zs., „A rendszerváltás megítélése" (Assessment of the change of system), *Szociológiai Szemle*, vol. 1, pp. 51–74, 1996.

Filatotchev, I., M. Wright, and M. Bleaney, "Privatization, Insider Control and Managerial Entrenchment in Russia", *Economics of Transition*, Vol. 7, No. 2, pp. 481–504, 1999.

Fischer, S., R. Sahay, and C. A. Végh, "Stabilization and Growth in Transition Economies: The Early Experience", *Journal of Economic Perspectives*, Vol. 10, No. 2, pp. 275–78, 1996.

Fischer, S., and R. Dornbusch, *Economics*, New York: McGraw-Hill, 1983.

Fogarassy, E., „Visszamenőleges igazságtétel Közép-Kelet-Európában, a rendszerváltás után" (Retrospective justice in Central and Eastern Europe, after the change of system), *Jogtudományi Közlöny*, Vol. 56, No. 9, pp. 381–87, 2001.

Freedom House, *Democracy's Century: A Survey of Global Political Change in the 20th Century*, http://www.freedomhouse.org, 2002.

Freedom House, *Freedom in the World: 2006 edition*, http://www.freedomhouse.org, 2006a.

Freedom House, *Nations in Transit: 2006 edition*, www.freedomhouse.org, 2006b.

Frydman, R., C. Gray, and A. Rapaczynski, *Corporate Governance in Central Europe and Russia*, London: Central European University Press, 1996.

Frydman, R., C. Gray, and A. Rapaczynski, "When does Privatization Work? The Impact of Private Ownership on Corporate Performance in the Transition Economies", *Quarterly Journal of Economics*, Vol. 114, pp. No. 4, 1153–92, 1999.

Fukuyama, F., *The End of History and the Last Man*, London: Penguin Books, 1992.

Gábor, I. R., "The Major Domains of the Second Economy", in Galasi, P., and Gy. Sziráczky, eds., *Labor Market and Second Economy in Hungary*, Frankfurt and New York: Campus, pp. 133–78, 1985.

Galbraith, P., „The mess", *The New York Review of Books*, March 9, Vol. 53, No. 4, pp. 27–30, 2006.

Gerschenkron, A., *Economic backwardness in historical perspective: a book of essays*, Cambridge, MA: Belknap Press of Harvard University Press, 1962.

Giddens, A., *The Third Way and its Critics*, Cambridge: Polity Press, 2000.

Gonzalez-Enriquez, C., "De-Communization and Political Justice in Central and Eastern Europe", in Barahona de Brito, A., C. Gonzalez-Enriquez, and P. Aguilar, eds., *The Politics of Memory...*, pp. 218–47, Oxford: Oxford University Press, 2001.

Grossman, G., "The 'Second Economy' of the USSR", *Problems of Communism*, Vol. 26, No. 5, pp. 25–40, 1977.

György, P., „Kádár János – a forradalom évfordulóján" (János Kádár – on the anniversary of the revolution), *Élet és Irodalom*, Vol. 50, No. 45, p. 16, 2006.

Haggard, S., and R. R. Kaufman, *The Political Economy of Democratic Transitions*, Princeton, NJ: Princeton University Press, 2005.

Halmai, G., "Facing with the Legacy of Human Rights Violations. Post-Communist Approaches to Transitional Justice", in Gómez Isa, F., and K. de Feyter, eds., *International Protection of Human Rights: Achievements and Challenges*, Bilbao: University of Deusto, pp. 639–56, 2006.

REFERENCES

Halman, L., *The European Values Study: A Third Wave*, Tilburg: EVS, WORC, 2001.
Hankiss, E., *East European Alternatives*, Oxford: Clarendon Press, 1990.
Hayek, F. A., "The Nature and History of the Problem", in Hayek, F. A., ed., *Collectivist Economic Planning*, London: Routledge, 1935a.
Hayek, F. A., ed., *Collectivist Economic Planning*, Amsterdam: North-Holland, 1935b.
Hayek, F. A., *Road to Serfdom*, Chicago, IL: University of Chicago Press, 1944.
Hayek, F. A., *The Constitution of Liberty*, London: Routledge; and Chicago: Chicago University Press, 1960.
Hayek, F. A., *Order With or Without Design*, London: Centre for Research into Communist Economies, 1989.
Halman, L., *The European Values Study: A Third Wave*, Tilburg, Netherlands: EVS, WORC, 170, 2001.
Heilbronner, R. L., *The Worldly Philosophers*, New York: Simon and Schuster, 1980.
Heilbronner, R. L., "Capitalism", in Eatwell, J., M. Milgate, and P. Newman, eds., *The New Palgrave. A Dictionary of Economics*, Vol. 1, London: Macmillan, pp. 347–53, 1991.
Hewett, E. A., *Reforming the Soviet Economy: Equality versus Efficiency*, Washington, DC: The Brookings Institution, 1988.
Hirschman, A. O., *Shifting Involvements*, Princeton, NJ: Princeton University Press, 1982.
Hodge, C. C., "The Politics of Programmatic Renewal: Postwar Experiences in Britain and Germany", in Gillespie, R., W.E Paterson, eds., *Rethinking Social Democracy in Western Europe*, Portland: Frank Cass, 1993.
Horne, C., and M. Levi, "Does Lustration Promote Trustworthy Governance in Transitional Societies?", in Kornai, J., and S. Rose-Ackerman, eds., *Building a Trustworthy State in Post-Socialist Transition*, New York: Palgrave Macmillan, 2004.
Human Rights Watch, *China: Repression Spikes as People's Congress Closes*, http://hrw.org/english/docs/2007/03/14/china, 2007.
Huntington, S. P., *The Third Wave: Democratization in the Late Twentieth Century*, Norman, OK: University of Oklahoma Press, 1991.
Huyse, L., "Justice after Transition: On the Choices Successor Elites Make in Dealing with the Past", *Law and Social Inquiry*, vol. 20, pp. 51–78, 1995.
Illyés, Gyula (Smith, W. J., ed.), *What You Have Almost Forgotten*, Curbstone Press, 1999.
Karamzin, N. M., *Letters of a Russian Traveller*, Oxford: Voltaire Foundation, [1789–90] 2003.
Kende, P., „Igazságtétel" (Doing justice), *Beszélő*, 3rd series, Vol. 3, 86–90, 2000.
Kidric, B., *Sabrana Dela* (Collected works), Beograd: Izdavacki Centar Komunist, 1985.
Klaniczay, G., "The Middle Ages", in Smelser, N. J., and P. B. Baltes, eds., *International Encyclopaedia of the Social & Behavioral Sciences*, Amsterdam: Elsevier, 2001.

Klaus, V., *Renaissance: the Rebirth of Liberty in the Heart of Europe*, Washington, DC: Cato Institute, 1997.

Kolodko, G., *From Shock to Therapy: The Political Economy of Post-Socialist Transformation*, Oxford: Oxford University Press, 2000.

Kolosi T., and M. Sági, "Change of system–change of elite", in Zs. Spéder, ed., *Hungary in Flux*, Hamburg: Kramer, pp. 35–55, 1999.

Konings, J., "Firm Growth and Ownership in Transition Countries", *Economic Letters*, vol. 55, pp. 413–18, 1997.

Konings, J., H. Lehmann, and M. E. Schaffer, "Job Creation and Job Destruction in Transition Economy: Ownership, Firm Size and Gross Job Flows in Polish Manufacturing, 1988–91", *Labor Economics*, Vol. 3, No. 3, pp. 299–317, 1996.

Kontler, L., „Előszó" (Foreword), in Kontler, L. ed., *Túlélők. Elitek és társadalmi változás az újkori Európában* (Survivors. Elites and social change in modern Europe), Budapest: Atlantisz, pp. 7–9, 1993.

Koopmans, T. C., and J. M. Montias, "On the Description and Comparison of Economic Systems", in Eckstein, A., ed., *Comparison of Economic Systems: Theoretical and Methodological Approaches*, Berkeley: University of California Press, 1971.

Kornai, J., *Overcentralization in Economic Administration*, London: Oxford University Press, [1957] 1959.

Kornai, J., *Anti-Equilibrium. On Economic Systems Theory and the Tasks of Research.*, Amsterdam: North-Holland, 1971.

Kornai, J., *Economics of Shortage*, Amsterdam: North-Holland, 1980.

Kornai, J., "Bureaucratic and Market Coordination", *Osteuropa-Wirtschaft*, Vol. 29, No. 4, pp. 306–19, 1984.

Kornai, J., "The Hungarian Reform Process: Visions, Hopes and Reality", *Journal of Economic Literature*, Vol. 24., No. 4, 1687–737, 1986a.

Kornai, J., "The Soft Budget Constraint", *Kyklos*, Vol. 39, No. 1, pp. 3–30, 1986b.

Kornai, J., *The Road to a Free Economy. Shifting from a Socialist System: The Example of Hungary*, New York: W. W. Norton; and Budapest: HVG Kiadó, 1990. In Hungarian: *Indulatos röpirat a gazdasági átmenet ügyében* (A passionate pamphlet in the cause of hungarian economic transition), Budapest: HVG Kiadó, 1989.

Kornai, J., "The Principles of Privatization in Eastern Europe", *The Economist*, Vol. 140, No. 2, pp. 153–76, 1992a.

Kornai, J., *The Socialist System. The Political Economy of Communism*, Princeton: Princeton University Press; Oxford: Oxford University Press, 1992b.

Kornai, J., "Market Socialism Revisited", in Peterson, G. B., ed., *The Tanner Lectures on Human Values*, Vol. 14, Salt Lake City: University of Utah Press, pp. 3–41, 1993a.

Kornai, J., "The Evolution of Financial Discipline under the Postsocialist System", *Kyklos*, Vol. 46, No. 3, pp. 315–36, 1993b.

Kornai, J., "Transformational Recession: A General Phenomenon Examined through the Example of Hungary's Development", *Economie Appliquée*, Vol. 46, No. 2, pp. 181–227, 1993c.

REFERENCES

Kornai, J., *From Socialism to Capitalism: What Is Meant by the "Change of System"*, London: Social Market Foundation, Centre for Post-Collectivist Studies, 1998.

Kornai, J., "Ten Years After 'The Road to a Free Economy', The Author's Self-Evaluation", in Pleskovic, B., and N. Stern, eds., *Annual World Bank Conference on Development Economics 2000*, Washington, DC: World Bank, 2000a. [Study 4 of this volume.]

Kornai, J., "What the Change of the System Does and Does Not Mean", *Journal of Economic Perspectives*, Vol. 14, pp. 27–42, 2000b.

Kornai, J., "Disciplines of Social Sciences: Separation or Cooperation", in Bourguignon, F., Elkana, Y., and Pleskovic, B., eds., *Capacity Building in Economic Education and Research*, Washington, DC: The World Bank, pp. 13–28, 2007. In Hungarian: "A társadalomtudományok elkülönüléséről és együttműködéséről", *Közgazdasági Szemle*, Vol. 11, No. 53, pp. 949–60, 2006.

Kornai, J. and K. Eggleston, *Welfare, Choice and Solidarity in Transition: Reforming the Health Sector in Eastern Europe*, Cambridge: Cambridge University Press, 2001.

Kornai J., E. Maskin and G. Roland, "Understanding the Soft Budget Constraint", *Journal of Economic Literature*, Vol. 61, No. 4, pp. 1095–136, 2003.

Kostova, D., M. Lazic, and Gy. Lengyel, *The Transformation of the East European Economic Elites*, Budapest: Közszolgálati Tanulmányi Központ, BKE, 1996.

Kovách, I., ed., *Hatalom és társadalmi változás: A posztszocializmus vége* (Power and social change. The end of post-socialism), Budapest: Napvilág Kiadó, 2002.

Kövér, Gy., *A felhalmozás íve* (Curve of accumulation), Budapest: Új Mandátum Könykiadó, 2002.

Kuhn, T. S., *The Structure of Scientific Revolutions*, Chicago: The University of Chicago Press, [1962] 1970.

Kuran, T., "Why the Middle East is economically underdeveloped. Historical mechanisms of institutional stagnation", *Journal of Economic Perspectives*, Vol. 18, No. 3, pp. 71–90, 2004.

Lakatos, E., *A magyar politikai vezetőréteg 1848–1918* (The leading Hungarian political stratum), Budapest: Self-published, 1942.

Lakatos, I., "History of Science and Its Rational Reconstruction", in Cohen, R. S., and C. R. Buck, eds., *Boston Studies in Philosophy of Science*, VIII, 1971.

Laki, M., „Az ellenzéki pártok gazdasági elképzelései 1989-ben" (Economic ideas of the opposition parties in 1989), *Közgazdasági Szemle*, Vol. 47, No. 3, pp. 230–49, 2000.

Laki, M., and J. Szalai, *Vállalkozók vagy polgárok? A nagyvállalkozók gazdasági és társadalmi helyzetének ambivalenciái az ezredforduló Magyarországán* (Entrepreneurs or bourgeois? Ambivalences in the economic and social position of big business in turn-of-the-century Hungary), Budapest: Osiris Kiadó, 2004.

Lange, O., "On the Economic Theory of Socialism 1–2", *Review of Economic Studies*, Vol. 4, No. 1, October, pp. 53–71; Vol. 4, No. 2, February, pp. 123–42, 1936–1937.

Le Goff, J., *Time, Work, and Culture in the Middle Ages*, Chicago, IL: University of Chicago Press, [1977] 1982.

Lengyel, Gy., *The Hungarian Business Elite in Historical Perspective*, Institute on East-Central Europe, Columbia University, NY, 1987.
Lengyel, Gy., *Vállalkozók, bankárok, kereskedők: A magyar gazdasági elit a 19. században és a 20. század első felében* (Entrepreneurs, bankers, traders: the Hungarian economic elite in the first half of the 20th century), Budapest: Magvető Kiadó, 1989.
Lengyel, Gy., *A gazdasági elit átalakulása* (Transformation of the economic elite), Budapest: Közszolgálati Tanulmányi Központ, BKE, 1997.
Lenin, V. I., *State and Revolution*, Collected Works, Vol. 25, Moscow: Progress, pp. 381–492, [1917] 1964–1972a.
Lenin, V. I., *The Proletarian Revolution and the Renegade Kautsky*, Collected Works, Vol. 28, Moscow: Progress, pp. 227–325, [1918] 1964–1972b.
Lenin, V. I., *Left-wing Communism, an Infantile Disorder*, Collected Works, Vol. 31, Moscow: Progress, pp. 17–118, [1920] 1964–1972c.
Lerner, A. P., *The Economics of Control*, New York: MacMillan, 1946.
Lewandowski, J., and J. Szomburg, "Property Reform as a Basis for Social and Economic Reform", *Communist Economies*, Vol. 1, No. 3, pp. 257–68, 1989.
Liberman, E. G., "The Plan, Profits and Bonuses", in Nove, A. D., M. Nuti, eds., *Socialist Economies: Selected Readings*, Middlesex: Penguin Books, 309–18, [1962], 1972.
Lizal, L. and J. Svejnar, "Investment, Credit Rationing, and the Soft Budget Constraint: Evidence from Czech Panel Data", *Review of Economics & Statistics*, Vol. 84, pp. 353–70, 2002.
Losonczi, Á., *Sorsba fordult történelem* (History that has become destiny), Budapest: Holnap Kiadó, 2005.
Maddison, A., *The World Economy: Historical Statistics*, Paris: OECD, Development Centre Studies, 2003.
Mankiw, N. G., *Principles of Economics*, Manson, OH: Thomson–South-Western, 2004.
Mann, T., *Buddenbrooks. The Decline of a Family*, Penguin, Modern Classics, p. 586, 1971.
Marx, K., *Capital. Vol. I. A Critical Analysis of Capitalist Production*, London: Lawrence & Wishart; Moscow: Progress Publishers, [1867–94] 1974.
Marx, K., "Critique of the Gotha Programme", in *Marx/Engels Selected Works*, Volume Three, Moscow: Progress Publishers, pp. 13–30, [1875] 1970.
Marx, K., and F. Engels, "Communist Manifesto", in *Marx/Engels Selected Works*, Volume One, Moscow: Progress Publishers, pp. 98–137, [1848] 1969.
McCloskey, D., *The Rhetoric of Economics*, Madison: University of Madison Press, 1985.
McFaul, M., "The Fourth Wave of Democracy and Dictatorship", *World Politics*, Vol. 54, pp. 212–44, 2002.
McKinnon, R., *The Order of Economic Liberalization: Financial Control in the Transition to a Market Economy*, Baltimore: John Hopkins University Press, 1992.
Mises, L. von, *Socialism. An Economic and Sociological Analysis*, Indianapolis: Liberty, 1981.

REFERENCES

Murrell, P., "Conservative Political Philosophy and the Strategy of Economic Reform", *East European Politics and Societies*, Vol. 6, No. 1, pp. 3–16, 1992a.

Murrell, P., "Evolution in Economics and in the Economic Reform of Centrally Planned Economies", in Clague, Ch., and G. C. Rausser, eds., *The Emergence of Market Economies in Eastern Europe*, Oxford and Cambridge, MA: Blackwell, pp. 35–65, 1992b.

Murrell, P., "Evolutionary and Radical Approaches to Economic Reform", *Economics of Planning*, Vol. 25, No. 1, pp. 79–95, 1992c.

Murrell, P., and Y. Wang, "When Privatization Should Be Delayed: The Effect of Communist Legacies on Organizational and Institutional Reform", *Journal of Comparative Economics*, Vol. 17, No. 2, pp. 385–406, 1993.

Nellis, J., "Time to rethink Privatization in Transition Economies?", *Finance and Development*, Vol. 36, No. 2, pp. 16–9, 1999.

North, D. C., *Institutions, Institutional Change, and Economic Performance*, Cambridge: Cambridge University Press, 1990.

O'Donnell, G. A., P. C. Schmitter, and L. Whitehead, *Transitions from Authoritarian Rule: Comparative Perspectives*, Baltimore, MD: Johns Hopkins University Press, 1988.

OECD, *Economic Survey of the Czech Republic, 1998*, Paris: OECD, 1998.

OECD, *Economic Surveys: Czech Republic, 1999/2000*, Paris: OECD, 2000.

OECD, *Society at a Glance: OECD Social indicators, 2005*, Paris: OECD, 2005a.

OECD, *Economic Surveys: China, Vol. 13*, Paris: OECD, 2005b.

Offe, C., *Varieties of Transition: the East European and East German Experience*, Cambridge, MA: Polity Press, 1996.

Otterman, S., *IRAQ: Debaathification. Council of Foreign relations*, http://www.cfr.org/publication/7853/iraq.html, 2005.

Perkins, D. H., "Reforming China's Economic System", *Journal of Economic Literature*, Vol. 26, No. 2, pp. 601–45, 1988.

Péter, Gy., "Az egyszemélyi felelős vezetésről" (On management based on one-man responsibility), *Társadalmi Szemle*, Aug./Sept., Vol. 9, No. 8–9, pp. 109–24, 1954a.

Péter, Gy., „A gazdaságosság jelentőségéről és szerepéről a népgazdaság tervszerű irányításában" (On the importance and role of economic efficiency in the planned control of the national economy), *Közgazdasági Szemle*, Dec., Vol. 1, No. 3, pp. 300–24, 1954b.

Péter, Gy., „A gazdaságosság és a jövedelmezőség jelentősége a tervgazdaságban, I–II." (The importance of economic efficiency and profitability in planned economy I–II), *Közgazdasági Szemle*, June and July/Aug., Vol. 3, No. 6, pp. 695–711; and Vol. 3, No. 7–8, pp. 851–69, 1956.

Péter, L., „Az arisztokrácia, a dzsentri és a parlamentáris tradíció a XIX. századi Magyarországon" (Aristocracy, gentry, and parliamentary tradition in 19th century Hungary). in: Kontler, L., ed., *Túlélők...*, pp. 191–241, 1993.

Pinto, B., V. Derbentsov, and A. Morozov, *Dismantling Russia's Non-payments System:*

Creating Conditions for Growth, Washington, DC: The World Bank, Excerpts published in *Transition*, Vol. 10, No. 6, pp. 1–5, 1999.

Pirenne, H., *Economic and Social History of Medieval Europe*, New York: Harcourt, Brace, and World Inc., [1933] 1937.

Polányi, K., *The Great Transformation: The Political and Economic Origins of Our Time*, Boston, MA: Beacon Press, [1944] 1962.

Pomorski, S., "Privatization of the Soviet Economy under Gorbachev. I: Notes on the 1986 Law on Individual Enterprise", *Berkeley-Duke Occasional Papers on the Second Economy in the USSR*, October, 1988.

Popper, K., *The Logic of Scientific Discovery*, New York: Basic Books, 1959.

Porch, D., "Germany, Japan and the 'De-Baathification' of Iraq Strategic Insights," Vol. 2., No. 3. (March),
http://www.ccc.nps.navy.mil/rsepResources/si/mar03/middleEast3.asp, 2003.

Portes, R., "Transformation Traps", *The Economic Journal*, Vol. 104, No. 426, pp. 1178–89, 1994.

Poznanski, K. Z., "Poland's Transition to Capitalism: Shock without Therapy", in Poznanski, K.Z. ed., *Stabilization and Privatization in Poland*, Boston: Kluwer Academic Publishers, 1993.

Pryor, F. L., "Market economic systems", *Journal of Comparative Economics*, Vol. 13, No. 1, pp. 25–46, 2005.

Pryor, F. L., "Economic systems of developing nations", *Comparative Economic Studies*, Vol. 48, No. 1, pp. 77–99, 2006.

Przeworski, A., *Capitalism and Social Democracy*, Cambridge and Paris: Cambridge University Press and Editions de la Maison de l'Homme, 1985.

Przeworski, A., *Democracy and the Market*, Cambridge: Cambridge University Press, 1991.

Qian, Y., "How reform worked in China", in Rodrik, D., ed., *In Search of Prosperity: Analytic Narratives on Economic Growth*, Princeton: Princeton University Press, pp. 297–333, 2003.

Raeds, P., "When Were the Middle Ages?", in Sogner, S., ed., *Making Sense of Global History*, Oslo: The 19th International Congress of the Historical Sciences, Oslo, 2000, Commemorative Volume, pp. 292–307, 2001.

Rainer, J. M., „Az újratemetés felmutatta az ősbűnt" (The reburial showed the original sin), interviewed by L. Seres, *Élet és Irodalom*, Vol. 44, No. 42, 2000.

Roland, G., *Transition and Economics: Politics, Markets, and Firms*, Cambridge, MA: MIT Press, 2000.

Rorty, R., "Thomas Kuhn, Rocks, and the Laws of Physics", *Common Knowledge*, Vol. 6, No. 1, pp. 6–16, 1997.

Rose, R., *A Bottom-up Evaluation of Enlargement Countries: New Europe Barometer 1*, Glasgow: Centre for the Study of Public Policy, 2002.

Rose, R., *Insiders and Outsiders: New Europe Barometer 2004*, Glasgow: Centre for the Study of Public Policy, 2005.

Rose-Ackerman, S., *From Elections to Democracy*, Cambridge: Cambridge University Press, 2005.

Rubinstein, W. D., "Education and the Social Origins of British Elites 1880–1970", *Past and Present*, No. 112 (Aug.), pp. 163–207, 1986.

Rueschemeyer, D., E. H. Stephens, and J. D. Stephens, *Capitalist Development and Democracy*, Cambridge: Polity Press, 1992.

Sági, M., „A lakossági elégedettség alakulása" (Development of public satisfaction), in Szivós, P., and I. Gy. Tóth, *Feketén-fehéren, Tárki Monitor jelentések, 2005* (In black and white. Tárki Monitor reports 2005), Budapest: Tárki, pp. 149–62, 2006.

Sajó, A., "Corruption, Clientelism, and the Future of the Constitutional State in Eastern Europe", *East European Constitutional Review*, Vol. 7, No. 2, pp. 37–46, 1998.

Sajó, A., 2004. "Neutral Institutions: Implications for Government Trustworthiness in East European Democracies", in Kornai, J., and S. Rose-Ackerman, eds., *Building a Trustworthy State in Post-Socialist Transition*, New York: Palgrave Macmillan, 2004.

Samuelson, P. A., and W. D. Nordhaus, *Economics*, New York: McGraw Hill, 2004.

Sanfey, P., and U. Teksoz, "Does transition make you happy?", *EBRD Working Paper* No. 91, London: European Bank for Reconstruction and Development, 2005.

Schmitter, P. C., and Karl, T. L., "What Democracy Is ... and Is Not", *Journal of Democracy*, Vol. 2., No. 3, pp. 76–88, 1991.

Schroeder, G. E., "Anatomy of Gorbachev's Economic Reform", *Soviet Economy*, Vol. 3, No. 3, pp. 219–41, 1987.

Schumpeter, J. A., *The Theory of Economic Development. An Inquiry into Profits, Capital, Credit, Interest and Business Cycles*, Cambridge, MA: Harvard University Press, [1911] 1968.

Schumpeter, J. A., *Capitalism, Socialism, and Democracy*, New York: Harper and Row, [1942] 1976.

Shionoya, Y., *Schumpeter and the Idea of Social Science*, Cambridge: Cambridge University Press, 1995.

Shleifer, A., and D. Treisman, *Without a Map: Political Tactics and Economic Reform in Russia*, Cambridge, MA, and London: MIT Press, 2000.

Shmelev, N., "Avansy i Dolgi" (Credits and debts), *Novyi Mir*, June, Vol. 6, pp. 142–58, 1987.

Spéder, Zs., ed., *Hungary in Flux*, Hamburg: Kramer, 1999.

Staniszkis, J., "Political Capitalism in Poland", *East European Politics and Societies*, Vol. 5, No. 1, pp. 127–41, 1991.

Statistical Office of Vietnam, *Vietnam Statistical Yearbook 2001*, Hanoi: Statistical Publishing House, 2002.

Stiglitz, J., "Whither Reform? Ten Years of the Transition", *Paper presented at the Annual Bank Conference on Development Economics, 28–30 April 1999*, Washington, DC, 1999.

Stone, L., and Stone, J. C., *An Open Elite? England 1540–1880*, Oxford: Oxford University Press, Oxford, 1984.
Sun Yefang, *Some Theoretical Issues in Theoretical Issues*, originally published in the period 1958–1961. Edited and translated by K. K. Fung under title: *Social Needs versus Economic Efficiency in China*, Armonk: M. E. Sharpe, 1982.
Sutela, P., *Socialism, Planning and Optimality: A Study in Soviet Economic Thought*, Helsinki: The Finnish Society of Sciences and Letters, 1984.
Svejnar, J., "Transition Economies: Performance and Challenges", *The Journal of Economic Perspectives*, Vol. 16, No. 1, pp. 3–28, 2002.
Szalai, E., *Az elitek átváltozása* (Transubstantiation of the elites), Budapest: Cserépfalvi Kiadó, Budapest, 1996a.
Szalai, E., *The studies of transitions: Intellectuals and value change*, Budapest: Collegium Budapest, Institute for Advanced Studies, 1996b.
Szelényi, Sz., I. Szelényi, and I. Kovách, "The making of the Hungarian post-communist elite: circulation in politics, reproduction in the economy", *Theory and Society*, Vol. 24, No. 5, pp. 697–722, 1995.
Szűcs, J., *Vázlat Európa három történeti régiójáról* (Sketch of the three historical regions of Europe), Budapest: Magvető Kiadó, 1983.
Tamás, G. M., „A Kornai-bomba" (The Kornai Bomb), *Heti Világgazdaság*, November 11, Vol. 11, No. 45, p. 66, 1989.
Tavares, J., and R. Wacziarg, "How Democracy Affects Growth", *European Economic Review*, vol. 45, pp. 1341–78, 2001.
Tilly, C., *Big Structures, Large Processes, Huge Comparisons*, New York: Russell Sage Foundation, 1984.
Tóth, I. Gy., "Income composition and inequalities 1987–2003", in Kolosi, T., I. Gy. Tóth, and Gy. Vukovich, eds., *Social Report 2004*, Budapest, Hungary: TÁRKI, 2004.
UN, *Human Development Report 2004*, New York: United Nations, 2004.
UNECE, *Economic Survey of Europe 1999*, New York: United Nations Economic Commission for Europe, 1999.
UNECE, *Economic Survey of Europe 2001*, New York: United Nations Economic Commission for Europe, 2001.
UNECE, *Economic Survey of Europe 2004*, New York: United Nations Economic Commission for Europe, 2004.
UNECE, *Economic Survey of Europe 2005*, New York: United Nations Economic Commission for Europe, 2005.
UNICEF IRC, *TransMONEE 2004 Database*, UNICEF IRC, 2004.
Usher, D., *The Economic Prerequisite to Democracy*, Oxford: Basil Blackwell, 1981.
Vásárhelyi, M., *Csalódások kora. Rendszerváltás alulnézetben* (Age of disillusionments. Change of system from below), Budapest: MTA Társadalomkutató Központ, 2005.
Wagner, M., and J. Hlouskova, "CEEC Growth Projections: Certainly Necessary And Necessarily Uncertain", *Economics of Transition*, Vol. 13, No. 2, pp. 341–72, 2005.

Wallerstein, I., *The Capitalist World Economy*, Cambridge: Cambridge University Press, 1979.

Wallerstein, I., *The Modern World-System: Capitalist Agriculture and the Origins of the European World Economy in the Sixteenth Century*, New York: Academic Press. 1974.

Watson, J. D., *The double helix. a personal account of the discovery of the structure of DNA*, New York: New American, 1968.

World Bank, *Averting the Old Age Crisis: The World Bank Policy Research Report*, New York: Oxford University Press, 1994.

World Bank, *Transition: The First Ten Years: Analysis and Lessons for Eastern Europe and the Former Soviet Union*, Washington, DC: The World Bank, 2002.

World Bank, *Yemen, Comprehensive Development Review, Private Sector Development Building Block*, http://lnweb18.worldbank.org/mna/mena.nsf/0b0204cbcec37e6985256a9b00689867/7b49eaa789d09c5e85256b290071bc40/$FILE/BB-6.pdf, 2003.

World Bank, *World Development Indicators 2005*, Washington, DC: The World Bank, 2005.

World Values Survey, http://www.worldvaluessurvey.com.

Yang, Y., *The Size of China's Private Sector*, Asian Pacific School of Economics and Management, Australian National University, http://old.ccer.edu.cn/faculty/yyao/Size%20of%20PS.pdf, 1999.

Zinnes, C., Y. Eilat, and J. Sachs, "The Gains from Privatization in Transition Economies: Is 'Change of Ownership' Enough?", *IMF Staff Papers*, Washington, DC: IMF, No. 48, pp. 146–70, 2001.

Name Index

Afanas'ev, I. N., 27
Aguilar, P. N., 227
Alchian, A. A., 9
Allende, S., 95, 162
Anderson, J. L., 159
Andreff, W., 67
Antal, L. 27, 35
Antall, J., 145
Arrow, K. J., 52

Babits, M., 159
Balcerowicz, L., 76
Barahona De Brito, A., 158
Bardhan, P. K., 53
Barone, E., 51
Barro, R. J., 163
Berend, T. I., 129
Black, B. S., 69
Blanchard, O., 77
Blasi, J. R., 73
Blaug, M., 184
Bleaney, M., 69
Bloch, M., 84
Bokros, L., 211
Bolton, P., 67
Boycko, M., 170
Böröcz, J., 140

Brabant, J. M. van, 67
Braudel, F., 71, 83
Brenner, R. 83
Brezhnev, L. I., 127
Broadman, H. G., 69
Brus, W., 29
Burke, P., 84
Burkett, J. P., 27

Caballero, R. J., 71
Campbell, N. A., 11
Campos, N. F., 82
Carson, R. L., 189
Castro, F., 13
Ceausescu, N., 125, 144, 157
Chavance, B., 183, 189
Chubais, A., 79
Coase, R. H., 71, 72
Coffee, J. C. Jr., 69
Coricelli, F., 82
Culyer, A. J., 176

Csaba, L., 82
Csillag, I., 211
Csite, A., 141, 142
Csurgó, B., 141, 142

NAME INDEX

Dabrowski, M., 69
Dahl, R. A., 90
Dallago, B., 30
David, R., 159
Davis, C. M., 30
De Melo, M., 196
Debreu, G., 52
Denizer, C., 213
Derbentsov, V., 220
Desai, R. M., 69
Djankov, S., 74
Dornbusch, R., 129
Dyck, A., 67

Eggleston, K., 179
Eilat, Y., 224
Ellerman, D., 69
Ellman, M., 14
Engels, F., 7, 50, 136, 148, 187
Eucken, W., 188, 189

Ferge, Zs., 135
Filatotchev, I., 69, 170
Fischer, S., 129
Fogarassy, E., 143
Fourier, Ch., 40
Frydman, R., 170, 171
Fukuyama, F., 201

Gábor, R. I., 30
Gaidar, J., 78
Galbraith, P. W., 159
Gelb, A., 213
Gerschenkron, A., 17
Giddens, A., 57
Goldberg, I., 69
Gomulka, S., 61, 69
Gonzalez-Enriquez, C., 159
Gorbachev, M., 100, 146

Gray, C. W., 170, 171
Grossman, G., 30

György, P., 131

Haggard, S., 81, 89
Halmai, G., 123, 143
Halman, L., 99, 110
Hammour, M. L., 71
Hankiss, E., 140
Hayek, F. A., 9, 52, 70, 91, 187, 192, 202
Heilbronner, R. L., 129
Hewett, E. A., 27
Himesi, Zs., 141, 142
Hirschman, A. O., 113
Hlouskova, J., 116
Ho Chi Minh, 59
Hodge, C. C., 57
Honecker, E., 127
Horne, C. M., 158
Huntington, S. P., 89
Huyse, L., 158

Illyés, Gy., 12

Karamzin, N. M., 113
Karl, T. L., 91
Kaufman, R. R., 89
Kautsky, K., 57
Kende, P., 143, 145
Keynes, J. M., 120
Kidric, B., 29
Klaniczay, G., 84
Klaus, V., 69, 76
Kolodko, G. W., 82
Kolosi, T., 141
Konings, J., 74, 167
Kontler, L., 123, 139

Koopmans, T. C., 193
Kovách, I., 123, 141
Kövér, Gy., 123, 140
Kraakman, R., 69
Kroumova, M., 73
Kruse, D., 73
Kuhn, T. S., 183–6, 189, 197, 204
Kuran, T., 123, 128

Lakatos, E., 140
Lakatos, I., 183, 184
Laki, M., 61, 67, 141
Lange, O., 27, 51–3, 58, 187, 200
Le Goff, J., 84
Lehmann, H., 74, 167
Lengyel, Gy., 140, 141
Lengyel, L., 227
Lenin, V. I., 4, 11, 13, 16, 32, 50, 53, 54, 57, 136, 148
Lerner, A. P., 51
Levi, M., 158
Lewandowski, J., 69
Liberman, E. G., 29
Lizal, L., 167
Losonczi, Á., 119

Maddison, A., 86, 116
Mankiw, N. G., 48, 129
Mann, Th., 33
Mao Zedong, 13, 41, 59, 97, 147, 148
Marx, K., 4, 7, 11, 12, 28, 40, 49, 50–1, 57, 58, 71, 101, 128, 148, 186–7, 192, 202
Maskin, E., 37
Matolcsy, Gy., 211
McCloskey, D., 204
McFaul, M., 89
McKinnon, R. I., 67

Mises, L. von, 129, 187, 192
Moliere, 194
Montias, J. M., 193
Morozov, A., 220
Murrell, P., 61, 67, 74, 171

Nagy, T., 35
Nellis, J., 69
Newhouse, J. P., 176
Nordhaus, W. D., 48
North, D. C., 191

O'Donnel, G. A., 89
Offe, C., 89
Owen, R. 40, 49

Pareto, V., 51
Perkins, D. H., 27
Péter, Gy., 29
Péter, L., 140
Pinochet, A., 94, 95, 132, 162
Pinto, B., 70
Pirenne, H., 84
Pol Pot, 127
Polányi, K., 93, 129, 187, 190, 192
Pomorski, S., 30
Popper, K. R., 19, 183
Portes, R., 195
Poznanski, K. Z., 61, 67, 171
Proudhon, P.-J., 40
Pryor, F. L., 129
Przeworski, A., 57, 89

Qian, Y., 47, 150, 209

Raeds, P., 84
Rainer, M. J., 143, 145
Rákosi, M., 125

Rapaczynski, A., 170, 171
Roemer, J. E., 53
Roland, G., 37, 62, 67, 81, 170
Róna-Tas, Á., 123
Rorty, R., 204
Rose, R., 114, 115, 117
Rose-Ackerman, S., 90
Rostowski, J., 69
Rousseau, J.-J., 28
Rubinstein, W. D., 139
Rueschemeyer, D., 91
Ryll, A., 183, 188

Sachs, J., 171
Sági, M., 135, 141
Sahay, R., 215
Saint-Simon, C., 48
Sajó, A., 164
Sanfey, P., 111
Schaffer, M. E., 74, 167
Schmitter, P. C., 89, 90
Schroeder, G. E., 27
Schumpeter, J. A., XI, 9, 70, 71, 90, 91, 129, 133, 188, 189, 192, 202
Shionoya, Y., 188
Shleifer, A., 170
Shmelev, N., 27
Smith, A., 50
Spéder, Zs., 141
Stalin, J. V., 2, 13, 15, 16, 54, 79, 125, 127, 136, 148
Staniszkis, J., 140
Stephens, E. H., 91
Stephens, J. D., 91
Stiglitz, J. E., 82
Stone, L., 139
Sun Yefang, 29
Sutela, P., 14

Svejnar, J., 82, 167
Szabó, K., 35
Szalai, E., 141
Szalai, J., 141
Szelényi, I., 140, 141
Szelényi, Sz., 140, 141
Szomburg. J., 69
Szűcs, J., 17

Tamás, G. M., 45
Tarasova, A. S., 69
Tavares, J., 163
Teksoz, U., 111
Tilly, C., 83
Tóth, I. Gy., 81, 106
Treisman, D., 170

Usher, D., 91
Vásárhelyi, M., 115, 135
Végh, C. A., 215
Vishny, R. W., 170

Wacziarg, R., 163
Wagner, M., 116
Wallerstein, I., 83
Walras, L., 52
Wang, Y., 67, 171
Watson, J. D., 11
Weber, M., 129, 191
Whitehead, L., 89
Wright, M. S., 69, 170

Yang, Y., 182

Zinnes, C., 201

Subject Index

adviser, 18, 62, 68, 124, 164–5, 178, 195–6
affinity, 8–11, 18, 39, 53
affirmative action, 64
agriculture, 5, 10, 30, 93, 154
   private ownership in ~, 5
agricultural, 30–1, 166, 174
   ~ cooperative, 30
allocation, 8, 51, 72–3, 152, 200
   efficient ~, 72
apparatus, 5, 7, 9, 16, 18, 26, 29, 35, 37, 78, 124, 129, 199–200
   centrally controlled ~ of personnel management, 9
   hierarchical ~, 9, 35
associative coordination, 38, 40–1
autonomy, 5, 10, 29, 31, 37

banking system, 78, 100
Bolshevik-type party, 148
bourgeoisie, 4, 32, 50, 54, 75, 140
budget constraint, 3, 6, 8, 37–8, 53, 61, 65–71, 74, 78
   hardening the ~, 37, 61, 65–71
   soft ~, 3, 6, 8, 37, 53, 66, 70, 74

bureaucracy, 6, 12, 16, 25, 32–41, 71, 74, 108, 129, 194, 200
bureaucratic coordination, 3, 5–6, 12, 35, 38–40, 43–4, 48, 54, 58, 126–7, 148
   direct ~, 35
   indirect ~, 35

capital, 7, 10, 32–3, 50, 65, 68–9, 74, 101, 104, 166–7, 171, 174, 202
   ~ accumulation, 33
   inflow of foreign ~, 69, 167
   limitations on ~ accumulation, 33
capitalism, IX–XIV, 1, 7, 11, 17, 22–3, 32, 34, 49–51, 54–56, 59, 64, 66, 70–5, 79–80, 83–6, 91, 94, 98, 100, 104, 113, 117–8, 123, 126–40, 145–8, 152, 156, 165, 182, 186–9, 192–4, 197–202
   oligarchic ~, 73
   people's ~, 66
   reform of ~, 56
   remnant of ~, 11

SUBJECT INDEX

socialism versus ~, 128
capitalist, XI, 7–8, 11, 22, 31–4,
  37–8, 50, 56, 58–9, 72, 75, 80,
  83–5, 88, 90–7, 101–4,
  117–120, 127–157, 165, 169,
  171, 186–7, 193–4, 197–202
  anti-~, 34, 59, 127, 132, 165
  ~ country, 85, 128, 130, 202
  ~ economic system, 91–92,
  96–97, 103, 119, 143
  ~ economy, 31, 33, 37–8,
  83–5, 117, 120, 137, 141–2,
  144, 147–8, 150
  ~ production relations, 7
  ~ system, 11, 22, 50, 56, 58,
  75, 80, 85, 88, 91, 93, 101,
  104, 117, 127–131, 135–140,
  144, 148, 150, 157, 171, 193–4,
  197–202
  pre-~ forms, 84
causality, 2–3, 6–8, 18–9, 186
  main directions of ~, 2–3,
  6–8, 18–9, 186
censorship, 131
  self-~, 131
central planning, 7, 51, 54, 131,
  175
centralization, 5, 41, 48, 50, 153,
  200, 202
  ~ of information, 5
characteristic, XII, 2, 4, 7, 11,
  13, 16–7, 20, 26, 35, 47, 54,
  64, 66, 68, 75, 82–4, 92–101,
  104, 112, 126–30, 133, 147–8,
  150, 164, 184, 188–9, 192–3
Chile, 94–95, 162
China, 4, 13, 17, 21, 25, 27, 29,
  34–6, 45, 47–8, 57–9, 68, 94,
  96–7, 103, 121, 145–7,

149–54, 176, 181, 198, 205
  Cultural Revolution in ~, 36
classical socialist system, X, 2–5,
  11, 15, 19, 21, 35, 58
Coase-ism, 71–2
  vulgar ~, 71–2
cognitive problems, 112
collective, 31, 40, 79, 114, 148,
  165, 168, 175
  ~ memory, 114, 175
  ~ ownership, 79, 165, 168
  ~ property, 148
collectivization, 10, 31, 54, 79, 93
command economy, 13, 35, 54,
  148, 194
communication, 56, 102, 111,
  187, 201
communism, 49–50, 195
communist, 4, 7, 11, 13, 16–20,
  25–6, 49–50, 53–5, 57–9,
  74–5, 81–2, 85, 89, 93, 95–6,
  99–110, 114–7, 121, 125–34,
  138–48, 151–2, 157, 162–3,
  166, 169, 171, 176, 178, 182,
  185–190, 195, 198–203
  ~ country, 16, 125, 151, 198,
  200
  ~ party, 4, 11, 13, 16–20,
  25–6, 49, 53–5, 58–9, 75, 81,
  85, 89, 93, 96, 121, 126–7,
  132, 141–2, 146, 148, 151–2,
  163, 190, 198–9
  ~ system, 11, 49, 75, 82, 132,
  138, 151–2, 166, 176, 186,
  188
  undivided power of the ~
  party, 4, 19, 26
comparative social science, 189
competition, 5, 23, 37, 45, 55–8,

230

90, 108, 113, 115, 117, 132,
  136, 142, 150, 162, 164, 166,
  174, 200
  market ~, 142
  political ~, 55, 58, 90, 164
conceptual clarification, 47, 55,
  60, 132
conformism, 26
constitution, 96, 123, 133, 138,
  143, 164
  ~al national assembly, 123
consumer, 33, 40, 107, 114, 161,
  194, 200
  ~ prices, 107
  ~ society, 114
consumption, 87–8, 104, 106–7,
  161
contract, 31, 40, 64, 68, 74–5, 83,
  137, 164, 167, 172
  private ~, 31, 64, 68, 75, 164
control, 5, 7–11, 25, 33, 35–6,
  38–9, 41, 51, 54, 141–2, 146,
  173, 188–9
  administrative ~, 36
  central ~, 54
cooperative, 4, 30, 38, 40–1
  agricultural ~, 30
  ~ socialism, 40
  ~ ownership, 4, 40–1
coordination, 3, 5–7, 12, 17, 22,
  25–7, 35–6, 38–45, 48, 50–1,
  53–4, 56, 58, 64, 77, 100,
  126–8, 130, 148, 188
  associative ~, 38, 40–1
  bureaucratic ~, 3, 5–6, 12, 35,
  38–40, 43–4, 48, 54, 58,
  126–7, 148
  ~ mechanism, 5, 7, 17, 26–7,
  38–45, 48, 50–3, 128, 130,

148, 188
  market ~, 36, 38–45, 48, 54,
  64, 100, 126, 148
core owner, 65
correction, 75
corruption, 68, 109–10, 159,
  172–3, 203
creative destruction, 71, 77
crime, 97, 109, 138, 143, 146,
  158, 169
Cuba, 13, 21, 121, 146, 151–5,
  168, 178–9, 181, 199

debt, 68, 73, 172
decentralization, 29, 37, 41, 45,
  48, 53, 200
democracy, IX–XIV, 17, 41, 49,
  54–7, 59, 70, 74–5, 89–92,
  95–100, 103–4, 113, 117–8,
  120, 127, 129, 132–5, 139,
  142–7, 150, 162–4, 182, 188
  definition of ~, 133–4
  minimum conditions for ~,
  91, 133–4, 139, 144, 147, 150
  parliamentary ~, 17, 55, 59,
  89, 95, 98, 100, 143, 147
  procedural characteristics of
  ~, 133
  stability of ~, 134
democratic, 17, 22, 55, 57,
  59–60, 81–2, 90, 96–7, 100,
  119, 127, 129, 132, 134, 137,
  143–4, 162–3, 176, 182
  ~ minimum, 90
  ~ opposition, 132
democratization, 89, 97
development, 3, 7, 11, 13, 16–7,
  22, 44, 47, 56, 59, 61, 64,
  67–8, 70–1, 73, 79, 82, 92, 94,

231

96, 102–4, 115–8, 129, 151, 156, 166, 168, 172, 178, 184, 186, 196, 200, 202
  organic ~, 64, 67–8, 73, 79
  strategy of organic ~, 64, 67
dichotomy, 128–9
dictator, 12, 117–8, 157, 192
dictatorship, 12, 49–50, 54, 59, 81, 90, 93, 104, 120, 129, 132, 135, 150, 153, 158–63
  ~ of the proletariat, 49–50, 54, 150
disappointment, 45, 81, 113, 120
dismissal, 9, 91, 141
disturbances, 124
doctrine of the Holy Crown, 123, 139

Eastern Europe, 17, 29, 34, 52–3, 64, 68, 71, 74, 81, 83, 85–121, 139, 146–7, 150, 153, 163, 165–6, 171, 198, 202
economic growth, 99, 103, 104, 163, 168
economic policy, 26, 43, 45, 62, 68–9, 74, 121
efficiency, 22, 38, 44, 51, 56, 59, 73, 77, 107, 121, 155, 169, 171, 173–4
  economic ~, 38, 73, 169, 174
elections, 55, 59, 62–3, 74, 90–1, 114, 127, 133–4, 137, 141–2, 150, 158–2, 174, 177
  parliamentary ~, 90, 127, 133
electoral dismissal, 91
elite, 95, 137–45, 148, 162, 171
  change of ~, 140–2
  cultural ~, 141
  economic ~, 140–2, 171

new ~, 141
political ~, 140, 162
post-socialist ~, 140
replacement of the ~, 139, 144
employment, 107–8, 135, 141, 167, 172
  ~ rate, 107, 135
end of history, 85
enterprise, 5, 10, 30–2, 35–6, 45, 59, 66, 69, 74, 100, 148, 166, 176, 194
  free ~, 5, 69, 166, 194
  spirit of ~, 10, 74, 100
European Bank for Reconstruction and Development (EBRD), 82, 111, 129–31, 168, 173, 182, 194
European Union, 81–2, 87, 101–5, 113–4, 129, 132
expectations, 35, 44, 77, 82, 113, 165

fairness, 56, 73
forced growth, 6, 8, 14, 17
foreign trade, 6, 12, 36
  system-specific role of ~ 6
formation, 4, 9, 22, 93, 95, 97, 124–8, 175, 186–7, 190, 193
  social ~, 124
  historical ~, 127–8, 190
fourth republic, 123
freedom, 14, 28, 31, 89, 103, 108, 115, 123, 127, 145, 152, 163, 166, 176, 191, 203

GDP, 58, 67, 86–8, 116, 130, 149, 180–2

general equilibrium theory, 52
genetic program, 11–20
Germany, 13, 45, 55, 57, 86, 88, 94, 97, 110–1, 114, 176–8, 181–2, 189
  East ~, 13, 45, 178, 181
  West ~, 13, 55, 57, 94, 97
globalization, 57, 135
government, 10, 27–33, 35–7, 41, 56, 59, 62, 68, 69, 74, 76, 78, 90–1, 95, 109, 114–8, 124, 127, 130–4, 137, 139, 144, 148, 163, 165, 167, 174, 176, 194
  replacement of ~, 90
grey area of the economy, 53
growth, 6, 8, 12, 14, 17, 22, 30–3, 36, 41, 64, 66–7, 69, 74, 77–8, 80, 85–8, 99, 103–4, 116, 121, 154, 156, 163, 166–9
  forced ~, 6, 8, 14, 17
  economic ~, 99, 103, 104, 163, 168

historical comparison, 93, 98, 116
horizontal relation, 5
household plot, 30
Hungarian Socialist Workers' Party (MSZMP), 140

ideology, 3–8, 11–2, 15, 17, 19–20, 22, 27, 32, 47, 51–2, 54–5, 57–8, 60, 72, 92, 132, 150–2, 162, 190, 203
  official ~, 5–8, 11–2, 17, 19, 22, 55, 58
import, 6, 8, 173–4
  ~ hunger, 6, 8

~-permit system, 6
incentives, 8, 14, 29, 39, 48, 52–3, 170, 187, 191
  profit-based ~, 29
income, 8, 17, 30–1, 56, 59, 73, 105–7, 117, 121, 135, 174–5
  inequality in the distribution of ~, 106
inequality, 59, 106–7, 117–8
  ~ in the distribution of income, 106
information, XIV–XV, 5, 14, 41, 48, 52, 56, 67, 77, 102, 153, 157, 168, 174, 177–178, 187, 191, 206
  centralization of ~, 5
informers (of secret police), 18, 143
institution, 9–10, 16–18, 27, 31, 56, 64, 67, 70–72, 79–80, 83, 89, 92, 96–103, 110, 127–30, 135, 160, 164, 175, 186, 191, 199
  concept of an ~, 191
  political ~s, 10, 27, 92, 101, 103
institutional, 9, 33, 41, 50, 52, 73, 75, 77, 78, 84, 97, 116, 161–2, 164, 172, 176, 188, 191, 202
  ~ changes, 97
  ~ reforms, 78, 172
  ~ transformation, 84, 116
interdisciplinary approach (outlook), 13, 120
intimidation, 12, 18
investment, 8, 12, 14, 69, 74, 161, 167, 169–70, 172
  ~ hunger, 8, 14

invisible hand, 51
Islam, 128
justice, 56, 104, 106, 137–8,
   142–5, 158–9, 169–70, 178
   dispensing ~, 137–8, 142–5,
   158–9, 169

labor shortage, 3, 6, 8, 107
liberalization, 25, 65, 71, 130–1,
   173–4
liberty, 18, 22, 81
   civil ~s, 18
local government, 41, 176

market, 5, 7–8, 10, 12, 17, 25,
   31, 33–45, 47–59, 64–5, 70–7,
   81–3, 100, 108, 113, 117,
   126–31, 142, 148–9, 152, 154,
   156, 161–5, 169–77, 188, 192,
   194, 200, 202
   interpretation of the term ~,
   48
   ~ clearing price, 31
   ~ competition, 142
   ~ coordination, 36, 38–45, 48,
   54, 64, 100, 126, 148
   ~ economy, 5, 39, 47, 49–59,
   65, 70, 75, 130–1, 154, 156,
   161–5, 171, 173, 176, 194
   ~ socialism, 27, 39, 44–5,
   47–59, 64, 70, 200
   predominance of ~
   coordination, 48, 148
marketization, 37, 45
Marxism, 49, 51, 54, 57, 71, 136,
   150
   vulgar ~ 71
Marxist, 6–7, 50–51, 71, 83, 85,
   129, 136, 188

neo-~, 83, 136
Marxist-Leninist, 3–4, 55, 59,
   126, 132, 151–2, 162
   ~ party, 3–4, 126, 152
methodology, XI–XV, 83, 132,
   183–4, 188, 192–3, 196,
   199–200, 203, 205

nationalization, 4–5, 33, 54, 56–7
naturwüchsig (naturally grown),
   12, 28
nomenklatura, 140, 159, 175,
   203
non-violence, without violence,
   94, 144–5, 157
normative approach, XIII, 124–5,
   132, 135, 137–8, 141, 145
North Korea, 12–13, 21, 152–3,
   181, 199
nostalgia, 75, 115, 176

one-party system, 3–4
ownership, 3–10, 19, 27, 29, 34,
   38–44, 50–8, 63–75, 79, 93,
   126–30, 139, 147–9, 152,
   156–7, 162, 165–73, 176,
   180–1, 200
   change in ~, 74–5
   collective ~, 79, 165, 168
   concentration of ~, 73
   cooperative ~, 4, 40–1
   ~ form, 38–44, 53, 165
   ~ structure, 52–3, 58, 64–5,
   69
   ~ reform, 63–4, 66, 69–75,
   79, 169, 173
   ~ relations, 74–5, 126–7, 176
   preponderance of state ~,
   3–4, 6

private ~, 5, 10, 38–44, 53–8, 64–5, 93, 126–30, 147, 152, 156–57, 162, 165, 167, 176
private ~, in agriculture 5
public ~, 19, 50, 52, 54, 58, 126–7, 147, 200
small-scale peasant ~, 10
state ~, 3–8, 29, 34, 38, 41–4, 64, 66, 74, 148, 169–71

paradigm, XIII, 183–207
   system ~ XIII, 183–207
Parliament, 55–6, 63, 76, 89, 101, 109–10, 117, 123, 133, 139, 143, 167, 173
   trust in ~, 109–10
parliamentary, 17, 55, 59, 74, 89–90, 95, 98, 100, 127, 133, 139, 143, 147, 162–4
   ~ democracy, 17, 55, 59, 89, 95, 98, 100, 143, 147
   ~ elections, 90, 127, 133
party, 3–5, 9, 11, 13, 16–20, 25–8, 33, 35–6, 41, 44, 49, 53–9, 62, 67, 74–5, 81, 85, 89–93, 96–7, 109, 118, 121, 126–7, 131–2, 140–52, 159, 162–4, 180, 190, 198–9
   Bolshevik-type ~, 148
   Communist ~, 4, 11, 13, 16–20, 25–6, 49, 53–5, 58–9, 75, 81, 85, 89, 93, 96, 121, 126–7, 132, 141–2, 146, 148, 151–2, 163, 190, 198–99
   competition among ~s, 162
   Marxist-Leninist ~, 3–4, 126, 152
   multi~ system, 109, 131, 150, 162, 164

one-~ system, 3–4
   ~ membership, 141
   ~ organizations, 9, 36, 148
   ~-state, 58
   unshared (monopoly) power of the Communist ~, 4, 19, 26, 54, 96, 132
paternalism, 3, 37–8, 175
people's capitalism, 66
perestroika, 36
plan, planning, 3, 5–7, 9, 25, 28, 35, 51, 54, 56, 85, 131, 137, 158, 160–3, 167, 170, 173, 175, 178, 202
   central ~ing, 7, 51, 54, 131, 175
   ~s are made taut, 6
   ~ bargaining, 3, 6
   ~ed economy, 25, 28, 167, 173
politics, political
   ~ competition, 55, 58, 90, 164
   ~ economy, 6–7, 32
   ~ institutions, 10, 27, 92, 101, 103
   ~ monopoly, 54, 58, 132, 152
   ~ structure, 3–6, 17–21, 26–7, 49, 54–5, 58, 68, 82, 89–2, 96–7, 127, 132, 151
populism, 126
positive approach, 124–6, 129, 132–4, 141, 143
post-socialist, XI–XII, 61–2, 67, 72, 76, 79, 81, 86, 90, 111, 121, 124, 129, 130, 140, 143, 147, 151–60, 164–71, 177–8, 189, 193–4, 196–8
   ~ elite, 140
   ~ transition, 61–2, 72, 76,

SUBJECT INDEX

130, 140, 152–60, 164–6, 178, 189, 194, 196
~ transformation, XII, 79, 121, 151–8, 193, 197–8
~ EU member states, 129
power, 2–2, 25–7, 33–7, 48, 52–8, 71–4, 79, 85, 89–101, 109, 121, 126–34, 137–40, 144, 150–1, 156, 159, 162, 164–5, 171, 175, 191, 194, 198–9, 204
  central ~, 126
  monolithic structure of ~, 8
prediction, 2, 21, 35, 44, 76–7, 194, 201–5
price, prices, 3, 5–6, 15, 31, 34, 36, 39, 64–8, 73, 76, 107, 114, 131, 136, 148–9, 155, 160, 169–74, 200, 204
  administrative ~ setting, 126
  consumer ~s, 107
  market clearing ~s, 31
  weak responsiveness to ~s, 3, 6
primary conditions, 75, 127–30
private activity, 29–32
private ownership (private property), 5, 7, 10, 12, 30–1, 38–45, 52–8, 64–5, 83, 93, 100, 126–30, 147, 152, 156–7, 162, 165, 167, 176, 202
  security of ~, 64
  predominance of ~, 56
private sector, 8, 25–6, 29–39, 44–5, 58–9, 64–9, 79, 130, 148–9, 152, 165–8, 180–2
  development of the ~, 64, 67, 166
  imposing constraints on the

~'s ability to grow, 126
  strengthening the ~, 126
privatization, 61, 65–75, 79, 98, 160, 163, 166, 168–72, 176, 178
  forced rate of ~, 126
  insider ~, 126
  strategy of accelerated/rapid ~, 66, 126
  ~ through bankruptcy, 65, 126
  voucher ~, 69, 170
production, 3, 7–8, 11, 22, 32, 36, 38, 50–1, 54, 59, 65, 67, 85, 93, 104, 116, 148–9, 161, 168, 173, 201
  forces of ~, 126
  instruments of ~, 126
  restructuring of ~, 67
  small commodity ~, 32, 54
productive, 33, 50, 52, 54, 58, 71, 73, 85, 165, 172
  ~ assets, 50, 52, 54, 58
productivity, 67–8, 74, 85–8, 104, 121
  labor ~, 67–8, 85–8
proletarian dictatorship, 49–50, 54, 150
propaganda, 30, 34, 105
property, 4–7, 10, 12, 15, 21, 26, 30–1, 43, 45, 52, 54, 58, 65–6, 69, 72–3, 75, 83, 100, 129–30, 137, 148, 152, 157, 166–72, 191, 201–2
  collective ~, 148
  public ~, 54, 129
  private ~, 7, 12, 30–1, 43, 45, 52, 54, 58, 83, 100, 130, 202
  state ~, 30, 65, 73, 171–2
public, 14, 19, 22, 44, 50–63, 68, 73, 76, 79, 89, 98, 105, 108–11,

236

115, 118, 120–1, 126–31, 135, 143, 147, 149, 158–63, 166, 175–7, 187, 200, 202
~ ownership 19, 50, 52, 54, 58, 126–7, 147, 200
~ property 54, 129
~ sector 58, 149

quantity drive, 3, 6

redistribution, 17, 56–9, 175, 177, 188, 194
reference points, 113–4
references, XIV–XV, 1, 8, 49, 59, 61–3, 150, 205
referendum, 138
reform, X, 1, 20–3, 25–45, 48, 52, 56, 63–4, 66, 69–72, 75, 78, 79, 146, 153–4, 157, 160, 163–4, 169, 172–81, 195, 200–1, 205
ownership ~, 63–4, 66, 69–75, 79, 169, 173
plans for ~, 163
~ of the welfare state, 175, 177
~ socialism, 1, 25–45
~ socialist country, 25–6
repression, 10, 13–4, 18, 22, 30, 33, 49, 96, 164, 175
research program, 184
revolution, 7, 11, 16, 21, 23, 28, 36, 40–1, 50, 55, 57, 62, 80, 84, 90, 95–8, 144–5, 157, 184, 186, 193, 197
rhetoric, XII, 41, 48, 54, 60, 69, 125, 137, 148, 152

satisfaction, 102, 111–2, 118, 138
science, XI–XIII, 2, 19–20, 83–4, 92, 101, 120–1, 124, 126, 138, 165, 183–93, 197, 199, 202–6
comparative social ~, 189
philosophy of ~, XI–XII, 2, 124, 183–4, 190, 204
scientific, XIII, 21, 49, 116, 125, 154, 160, 184–4, 192, 196–8, 204–5
~ revolution, 184, 186, 197
~ socialism, 49
secondary traits, 127
secret police, 16, 18
selection, 9–10, 18, 34–5, 65, 68–71, 141–2, 158–9, 177
natural ~, 9–10, 18, 65, 68–71
~ mechanism, 141–2
shortage, 3, 6, 8, 13, 18, 31, 33–4, 37, 107, 109, 114, 161, 200
food ~, 13
labor ~, 3, 6, 8, 107
~ economy, 3, 6, 13, 18, 31, 34, 109, 114
small and medium-sized firms, 68, 166–7
small commodity production, 32, 54
social democrat, 55–60, 64, 134, 163
social disposition, mood, 82, 111, 118, 167
socialism, IX–XIV, 1–2, 5, 7–11, 14–23, 25–45, 47–60, 64, 68, 70–3, 79, 85–6, 94–5, 113, 123–5, 128, 131–6, 147, 152, 165, 168, 175, 187–94, 199–203
classical ~, 1–2, 5, 7, 10, 11,

SUBJECT INDEX

14–23, 25, 54, 95
concept of ~, 125
cooperative ~, 40
existing (or hitherto existing) ~, 85, 125
Leninist type of ~, 58
Marxist concept of ~, 49
market ~, 27, 39, 44–5, 47–59, 64, 70, 200
reform ~, 1, 25–45
scientific ~, 49
~ versus capitalism, 128
the notion "~", 58
theory of ~, 51
utopian ~, 1, 40
Walrasian concept (of ~), 51
socialist
classical ~ system, X, 2–5, 11, 15, 19, 21, 35, 58
~ countries, XI, 3–4, 9, 13–4, 18, 21, 25–37, 40, 45, 59, 67, 81, 85, 87, 111, 125–6, 143, 153, 167, 169–80
~ system, X–XI, XIV–XV, 1–5, 9, 11, 13, 15–23, 25–7, 34–5, 41–4, 48–51, 56, 58, 61, 67, 71, 77, 80, 84–6, 93–6, 99, 104, 106, 113, 117, 125–132, 136, 140, 151, 157, 165, 168, 175–6, 190, 193, 197, 200–3
soft budget constraint, 3, 6, 8, 37, 53, 66, 70, 74
solidarity, 22, 27, 177
sovereignty, 5, 105, 166, 175, 177, 194, 200
~ of individuals, 5, 175, 177
Soviet Union, 1, 7, 9–10, 13–21, 25–35, 40, 45, 53, 56, 81–2, 85, 94–5, 113, 125, 127, 132,

146, 151, 153, 162, 180, 198, 202, 204
sovietology, 202–3
speed, 61, 79–80, 84, 87, 93, 97–102, 119, 139, 160, 171–4, 193–4, 203
~ of transition, 160
spontaneous transformation, 10, 12, 28–32, 36, 39, 41, 48–9, 54, 84, 100, 156, 194
stabilization, X, XV, 63, 65, 69, 71, 75–8, 203
macro~, X, 63, 69, 75–8
Stalinism, 54, 79
standard of living, X, 85, 104–5
state, 3–9, 12, 20, 25–6, 29–45, 49–51, 56–9, 62, 64–8, 70, 73–4, 77–8, 82, 84, 86–7, 95, 99, 103, 105, 107–8, 112–4, 118–21, 123, 125, 128–39, 148–53, 156–9, 162, 164–77, 189, 194–202
dominance of the ~ sector, 20
form of ~, 123, 139
~ of law, 164, 167, 172
~-owned, 25, 29–39, 45, 58, 65–8, 153, 166–72
~ ownership, 3–8, 29, 34, 38, 41–4, 64, 66, 74, 148, 169–71
~ sector, 8, 20, 26, 35, 65–6, 149
~ property, 30, 65, 73, 171–172
preponderance of ~ ownership, 3–4, 6
party-~, 58
welfare ~, 56–9, 175–7
strategic investor, 65
strategy, 27–28, 48, 62–74, 79,

154, 166, 170, 172
~ of accelerated/rapid privatization, 66, 126
~ of organic development, 64, 67
superstructure, 7, 72
support, subsidy, 22, 32, 36–7, 56, 68, 118, 151, 166,
system
  capitalist economic ~, 91–2, 96–7, 103, 119, 143
  capitalist ~, 11, 22, 50, 56, 58, 75, 80, 85, 88, 91, 93, 101, 104, 117, 127–31, 135–40, 144, 148, 150, 157, 171, 193–4, 197–202
  change of ~, IX–XIV, 21, 26, 30, 35, 45, 75, 77, 115, 123–5, 129–32, 137–47, 155, 158, 161, 175, 187, 197
  classical ~, 1–5, 8, 10, 12–23
  communist ~, 11, 49, 75, 82, 132, 138, 151–2, 166, 176, 186, 188
  inner coherence of the ~, 10
  interactions among the elements of the ~, 8
  main characteristics of the ~, 11
  multiparty ~, 109, 131, 150, 162, 164
  prototype of the ~, 1–2, 11, 14–5, 18, 38, 199
  reform ~, 1
  revolutionary-transitional ~, 1
  socialist ~, X–XI, XIV–XV, 1–5, 9, 11, 13, 15–23, 25–7, 34–5, 41–4, 48–51, 56, 58, 61, 67, 71, 77, 80, 84–6, 93–6, 99,
104, 106, 113, 117, 125–32, 136, 140, 151, 157, 165, 168, 175–6, 190, 193, 197, 200–3
  ~ paradigm, XIII, 183–207
  ~ specific situation, 3
  welfare ~, 78

tax, taxation, 30, 33, 37, 56, 64, 78, 109, 118, 166–9
terror, 15, 31, 95, 98, 100, 132, 158
theocratic political and ideological rule, 128
Third, 40–3, 53, 57, 135, 147
  ~ forms, 40–3
  ~ system, 135, 147
  ~ way, 40, 53, 57
totalitarian power (dictatorship), 9–10, 58
totalitarianism, 5, 158
trade, 6, 12, 27, 36–7, 130–1, 136
  free ~, 37
transitology, 121
trust, 109–10, 125
  ~ in Parliament, 109–10
tyranny, 12, 55, 90, 103, 118, 132, 150, 202

unemployment, 3, 6, 56, 67, 107–8, 117, 135, 168
  ~ on the job, 3, 6, 67
  ~ rate, 108

value, 15, 22, 32, 35, 39, 43–4, 48, 57–60, 63, 65, 83–6, 91, 96, 98–9, 103–5, 111, 118–25, 130–1, 134, 145, 149, 155–7, 160–79, 187
  choice of ~s, 125, 160, 171
  ordering of ~s, 103–5

239

scale of ~s, 103
system of ~s, 44, 63, 83, 96, 125, 145, 157, 161, 167
~-free, 35, 86, 91, 125, 156–7
~ judgment, 22, 39, 43–4, 63, 83, 85, 118–9, 124–5, 130, 134, 157, 169
vertical relation, 5
Vietnam, 4, 10, 20, 47–8, 57–60, 121, 146, 152–4, 181–2, 199
voucher privatization, 69, 170
vulgar Coase-ism, 71–2

wage, 8, 70, 170
~ funds, 8
~-swindlers, 8
welfare state, 56–59, 175–7
reform of the ~, 175, 177
welfare systems, 78
western civilization, 83, 85, 88, 92, 96, 113
world view, XV, 10, 44, 105

Yugoslavia, 25, 27, 29, 35, 40–1, 45, 82, 151, 180

For Product Safety Concerns and Information please contact
our EU representative GPSR@taylorandfrancis.com Taylor & Francis
Verlag GmbH, Kaufingerstraße 24, 80331 München, Germany

T - #0020 - 200326 - C0 - 229/152/14 - PB - 9789633860014 - Matt Lamination